CLOUDS AND SUNSHINE

RUTH POLLOCK

Published in Australia by Sid Harta Books & Print Pty Ltd,
ABN: 34632585293
23 Stirling Crescent, Glen Waverley, Victoria 3150 Australia
Telephone: +61 3 9560 9920, Facsimile: +61 3 9545 1742
E-mail: author@sidharta.com.au

First published in Australia 2022
This edition published 2023
Copyright © Ruth Pollock 2022
Cover design, typesetting: WorkingType (www.workingtype.com.au)

The right of Ruth Pollock to be identified as the Author of the Work
has been asserted in accordance with the Copyright, Designs and Patents Act 1988.

This book is a work of fiction. Any similarities to that of people living
or dead are purely coincidental.

All rights reserved. No part of this publication may be reproduced,
stored in a retrieval system, or transmitted, in any form or by any means without the prior written
permission of the publisher, nor be otherwise circulated in any form of binding or cover other than
that in which it is published and without a similar condition being imposed on the subsequent
purchaser.

Ruth Pollock
Clouds and Sunshine
ISBN: 978-0-9578709-8-7 (pbk)
978-0-6456941-4-7 (ebook)
pp314

ABOUT THE AUTHOR

Ruth's paternal grandmother, Alida, passed away when she was two years old. Alida was a Swedish immigrant, who arrived in Australia in 1899 as a newlywed. She gave birth to her first child on the Western Australian goldfields in the summer of 1900. When Ruth realized she was the last one in the family in possession of the tales of her strong, gutsy grandmother, she believed the story should not go untold. This inspired her to write her first book, *Alida's Story* in which she shows how our lives are woven into the social history of the times.

Two years ago, Ruth and her husband, Don, who now live on the south east coast of NSW, moved from Victoria's High Country where they had worked their homestay holiday business for international students for over twenty years. Providing language tuition and local adventures for the young students from Asia and Europe had been a very satisfying experience but with the Covid 19 closure of international borders, the business had to close. It has been a dramatic lifestyle change for Ruth. So with much more free time at hand, she decided to develop her interest in writing. After following up her grandmother's story with her mother's and her own, Ruth then decided to write her first novel, *Clouds and Sunshine,* which touches on the aspirations she had as a young woman and develops as a story of intrigue and romance.

ACKNOWLEDGEMENTS

It has been a wonderful and absorbing experience writing this story. My appreciation and heartfelt thanks to all those friends and family members for their interest and assistance throughout the writing of this book. My friends in Gunnedah, contributed tirelessly to expanding my knowledge of the history and development of their wonderful rural district. Many thanks to Tony Edwards who told me of his parachuting experience at the MCG and who was always generous by answering my questions about parachuting. My gratitude extends to my dear daughter, whose understanding and support helped me overcome my limited medical knowledge, and to my neighbour Gary, whose knowledge and suggestions of police procedures was critical for me to get the correct perspective in certain scenarios. My husband, Don, has always been a willing, expert advisor for the big aviation and historical questions and the suggestions that make for interesting reading. I would also like to thank the members of our local Eurobodalla Writer's Group. Often, unknowingly, some knowledgeable discussions at our meetings influenced my writing. Finally, but importantly, I would also like to acknowledge Barbara, my editor, for her encouraging and time-consuming editing of the final draft.

These wonderful people, along with so many more who have helped with research, editing and encouragement, have made it possible for me to complete *Clouds and Sunshine*.

CHAPTER 1

While holding his hand and speaking in a low-key, sensual way, Fran gently but firmly led Jack to the bedroom. 'We've never had such an ideal time to try out the bed, Jack.'

She dropped Jack's hand and lifted her arm to twine around his neck. With her lips close to his ear, her soft whispering voice continued, 'We're alone Jack.'

She patted the bed as Jack watched her lithe body slip to the centre. Her arms were beckoning, and he had no time to think, so in one unstoppable action, he was on top of her, discovering the warmth and softness that he knew he had been promised. Fran was ready for his manly strength, there was no hesitation and at once he found her. The union of their bodies was the most natural and satisfying experience for them both. Something Fran had wanted years before when she had first realised the underlying passion she had for the handsome, hunky Jack Franklin. After the exhilaration and Fran's arms relaxed, Jack laid back, his mind racing with thoughts of how he had just betrayed Wally, his best mate. There was no further chatter between them for they both heard the door open and angry words followed in a loud slurred voice, 'What the hell is going on here?'

Fran pushed Jack away and screamed as she sat up and tried to pull her skirt down over her bare legs.

'You rotten bugger Jack, and you call yourself a friend.'

Jack scrambled from the bed struggling to pull on his trousers. He was still unsteady on his feet when a fist smashed into his face. With his unsteadiness as an additional force, he returned a strong punch to Wally's chest, which caused him to fall backwards over the end of the bed.

Fran screamed again. 'Wally, no more, no more. It's not Jack's fault.'

The room was silent. Jack moved across to check out Wally's collapsed body. He knelt down and called his name, 'Wally, Wally … C'mon mate, you okay?'

There was no reply from the crumpled body. In shock, with no words coming from his open mouth, Jack checked Wally's pulse as Fran clambered over the bed. 'Jack, oh Jack, he's dead!'

Jack was convinced Wally was showing no signs of life. He smelt of alcohol and was bleeding from a deep wound at the base of his head. Breathlessly, Jack spluttered, 'Christ, he's dead. Fran, he's hit his head really bad. There's an injury at the base of his skull, he must have hit the bedpost as he collapsed.'

A distraught Fran queried the implications, 'Jack what are we going to do? Wally told me he would be chopping down trees all morning. It is so unlike him to come home in the middle of a job.'

CHAPTER 1

'Fran, he smells of alcohol.'

'Jack, he has smelt of alcohol, every day for the past two years, ever since I threatened to leave him and take the kids to Ballarat.'

The stress of the situation stayed in Jack's voice as he asked, 'Fran, what are you telling me? You've been planning to leave Wally?'

Then with a broken voice, Jack continued, 'Fran, there's nothing we can do for him. You said he was up in the paddock clearing for a while, then maybe we should take him up to the clearing lot and that will be the cause of death that we report. He died from being hit by a branch from a falling tree. That does happen, you know.'

Jack fleetingly held Fran's hand as she shed tears, and he struggled to hold back his emotions. Fran shuffled down the hallway to the spacious loungeroom and picked up her toddler, Kate, from the playpen, while Jack went to set about hitching up the workhorses to the cart and drew them to the back door. Wally was no heavyweight. He had an ongoing condition that had actually cleared him from being able to join the army before they had left England back in 1913. Jack was able to carry the skinny body to the cart where he covered it with a blanket. He held little Kate while Fran climbed up to sit on the bench seat, and she then settled Kate on her knee as they headed off for the clearing lot.

Jack knew how determined Wally had been to get the trees chopped down. The strong winds of the past few days increased the danger that accompanied the clearing of land in the region. He had promised Wally he would help and be there mid-morning, but knowing his best mate very well, he knew that Wally would probably make an early start. That morning, unaware of the impending tragedy, he had given Elsie, his wife, a quick kiss and a cuddle after breakfast and made his way to the stables. Bess, his honest horse, always pricked up her ears with excitement when she heard him come through the rickety wooden door.

'Hey there, old girl. Ready for a fast trip over to Wally's?'

It didn't take long to make the saddle secure, and Jack was on his way. He admired Wally's determined nature to get things done, but his aspirations were often greater than his physical ability. None-the-less, Jack was always willing to offer his hand. After all, they had begun the 'Great Southern Land' adventure together and were always there for each other. Jack sauntered up to the front door and knocked with his familiar rhythm. Fran opened the door.

'G'morning Jack, we weren't expecting you quite so early.'

'That's okay Fran. I thought the kids would be running around.'

'Ha ha,' chuckled Fran as she gave Jack a sexy look.

'They've gone to school. The neighbour's horse and cart were around here early. Kate's in her playpen.'

As she closed the door, Fran sidled up against the strong shoulder of the man in whom she had never lost interest.

'Hello lovely Jack, we have an opportunity … we shouldn't let it pass us by.'

Jack had been aware of her flirting demeanour over the years, but they had never taken it any further. The absence of the children had been part of the motivation for Fran's intimate suggestions to Jack when he had arrived at the front door. There had been no hesitation as he accepted Fran's hand and followed her down the hallway.

As Jack and Fran laid Wally's body close to the sprawling branches of the largest tree that he had chopped down that morning, they both said prayers and returned slowly to the cart. When they arrived back at Fran's house, there were some tender words between them and then Fran shared her secret with Jack.

'You know Jack, Wally knew I was going to leave him. He knew I hated the farm and I have had contact with an uncle in Ballarat, down south in Victoria. He is expecting me there by the end of the month.'

Jack was in total surprise with her announcement. He knew she had not been happy being a farmer's wife, but for her to leave what seemed to be a loving relationship, he could not fathom.

'Jack, I know my love for you can never be satisfied. You and Elsie are so content and at ease with country life. I told Wally I had to get back to living in a town. He knew I hated the farm but there was no way he was going to change direction and move off the land, so that was when I contacted Uncle Baz and Aunty Rene. They offered their support to help me settle into Ballarat, which is a big busy town, and I was so excited about the idea.' Then, with tears in her eyes, Fran added, 'I would never have thought my reason for moving would be this, as I have loved you Jack, but I knew we could never be.'

Jack gulped. 'So Fran, none of this ever needed to happen.' With his mind trying to handle the enormous load of distress,

Jack rode into Gunnedah to locate the district registrar, the government official who would provide him with a notification form to complete with the details of Wally's death. He would then contact the pastor at the church to organise a funeral service for Wally. He expected the pastor would also arrange for a hearse. He then returned home to Elsie, to give her his version of the morning's catastrophe.

CHAPTER 2

Wally Hammond had grown up on a farm in England. He and his very good friend from schooldays, Jack Franklin, who was also a farmer's son, were always excited to hear news about Australia. For them, it wound up the thrill of adventure in setting off overseas to a strange land. Any news from the Great Southern Land was always of interest to them and when the government encouraged emigrants from England to be part of Australia's agricultural development, the idea of sailing to the south seas, appealed to them both.

In 1913, when Wally was nineteen years old and Jack was eighteen, they packed their bags, boarded a steamer for Sydney, and left England with healthy bank accounts, courtesy of their parents. There had been a fear of war developing with Germany since the turn of the century and, although as teenagers they considered joining the defence force, the two young men were not accepted because of health issues. From an early age, Wally had suffered from a gastric ulcer. Doctors were aware of his symptoms, but other than suggesting changes in his diet, there was little they could do for him, so over the years he had learned to live with the bouts of pain. Jack was also not accepted because he had limited sight in his right eye. While playing with a sling as a small boy, a stone hit his eye and damaged his sight permanently. So, the two young men left England, focusing on a future whereby they could add to the strong British presence in the new country down under.

On arrival, they sought rural labour positions in agricultural work and were subsequently sent to the Liverpool Plains region in central New South Wales. For a time, they both worked on the same property, planting, and harvesting. It took them some time to grasp the extent of the Aussie properties that were so much larger than their parents' back in England. Since they had both learned to handle tractors and other farm machines back home, they were encouraged to assist in that way, and even became responsible for the training of others. Wally and Jack worked hard and valued the experience. Both aspired to buying a property of their own once they had become accustomed to the outback environment and the different climate patterns.

The year 1914 was the year that Germany invaded Belgium, and as a result, Britain declared war on Germany. There were times when the young men received some negative comments and white feathers from locals because they had not joined the overseas force to fight for the mother country. However, both young men set about adjusting to the demands of outback life. They were responsible and reliable, and their skills, particularly those of operating and servicing both steam and petrol-powered tractors, were welcomed in the agricultural community. Always making themselves available for any essential work meant that they not only became well known, but their bank accounts grew steadily. As people began to find out about their health issues, Wally and Jack found that their feelings of guilt were subdued by the support of local families throughout those trying times.

The number of young country girls around the area not only attracted them, but the young men themselves were considered interesting consorts. Wally Hammond was rather skinny because of his persistent ailment, but he had a lively and gushing personality that never failed to be a beacon of attraction when they turned up at garden gatherings, often arranged by farming families at regular intervals. Jack Franklin, however, was a tall, good-looking, introverted soul. His polite and quiet nature in contrast to that of Wally's, meant that sitting and talking was the more comfortable approach he had with young ladies.

Before long, Wally had entranced Fran, quite a beautiful young lady, two years younger, and the daughter of a local tradesman who had moved to Gunnedah in recent times. Their wedding in 1917 was a simple affair since there were no family members from England who were able to attend. However, the local people considered the couple with great regard. Congratulations and sheer delight were showered upon Wally and Fran on their wedding day, and two years later in 1919, his friend Jack married Elsie.

During the war years, Jack and Wally had talked about the possibility that they would each purchase a farm and, at the end of hostilities in Europe, the two couples bought neighbouring properties. Elsie was the only one who needed to be persuaded to agree to agricultural land rather than pastures for sheep. Fran didn't have much of an opinion apart from the fact that she didn't want to live on a farm. Although they had had close contact with sheep rearing since their arrival on the Plains, neither Jack nor Wally was interested in becoming a pastoralist. Instead, they became corn growers.

From the early days of marriage, Fran did not like farm life whereas Elsie considered no other lifestyle. Wally continued to have his health problems and it was difficult for him to keep up with the work commitments associated with the management of his farm. As often as he could, Jack would lend a hand at peak harvesting and seeding times. At the same time, he would not only have to meet his own deadline, but work with Wally to get the harvesting done and follow it up with preparations for seeding. Of course, both fellows hired labour, but overall, management was not only time consuming, but physically taxing.

The situation became unbearable for Fran. She had never adjusted to the role of a farmer's wife and never would. The demands of their growing family, along with Wally's passion for the land, created a tremendous rift in the relationship. By 1925, they had had three children, Robert, their only son, affectionately known as Bob, was born in 1920, then Betty, and the youngest child, Kate, in 1926. With the pressures of child rearing along with hard physical farm work, and coping with Wally's continual medical condition, Fran made up her mind to leave Gunnedah and move to Victoria. Wally could not persuade her otherwise and he refused to go with her. Fran's decision in 1927, to move to Ballarat, was based on the continuing correspondence that she had been having with her favourite uncle and his family, who had lived in the lively, go-ahead city for many years. The town had been first settled by sheep farmers in 1838 and then it developed, at a frantic rate after gold was discovered in 1851. She was certainly reluctant to leave her mother and father, but they were quite empathetic in regard to her extreme discomfort with farm life and knew she would be well looked after by her uncle and aunt.

A few months later, once Wally had been respectfully buried and Fran had organised the move to Ballarat, Jack received a notification from a Tamworth Justice of the Peace that Wally had left a will. It had been prepared in quite recent times but made no mention of Fran and the children. Wally's way to thank his good friend was to will the entire property rights to Jack. This was done in a very private deal and the document, signed by Wally and witnesses, was accepted by the authorities at that time. However, once he was aware of the will, Jack made an arrangement for Fran and the children to have a bounty awarded to them based on the overall value of the property. It was all done with legal supervision and Fran was very grateful for the generosity shown by Jack and Elsie. However, once she had moved to Ballarat, Fran made no further contact with Jack and Elsie or any other friends in

Gunnedah. Any effort Jack made, even when he knew they had been notified of his contact request through a network of friends and associates, was met with silence. Their location was very private. He and Elsie had no idea where the family had settled. Even when they approached Fran's extended family in Gunnedah asking them to inform Wally's wife and children of their desire to communicate, there was no interest from anyone. As the years went by, the families never had any further connection until Betty, the Hammond's eldest daughter, made contact.

Jack and Elsie were totally absorbed by their farm life and had three children: Ted, Dorothy and Sarah. Ted was passionate about farming and shared his father's interest for cropping. He married the love of his life, Mary, in 1950, and with great satisfaction he worked alongside his father on the family property while raising their children. After their marriage, Jack had encouraged Ted and Mary to move onto Wally's property and he named it *Ted's Place*. The two farms continued to develop as one. Ted's sisters both married city men and apart from an occasional Christmas or birthday celebration, spent little time at family gatherings. After Wally's death, with a realisation of the good fortune the family had had bestowed upon it by Wally's generous will, Jack transitioned the management of the new property to be part of this own. As Ted became a solid farm worker, the responsibilities were shared with the guidance of his father. Ted and Mary had three children: John, Anne and Rosie.

Fran settled down as a single mother in the social life of a rural city. She made no effort to communicate with anyone in Gunnedah, and by 1934, when she and the children had been there for seven years, Ballarat was a major rural city and Fran loved it.

CHAPTER 3

It was 1982, and for Rosie, the most satisfying thing about being back in Gunnedah was the time that she could now spend with Chas. Rosie Franklin and Chas Anderson had known each other since school days and their families had been friends for years. Before she left the Liverpool Plains to study at Sydney University, Rosie had felt a sense of camaraderie with Chas that was light-hearted but focussed on determination and motivation to achieve their own ambitions.

Although Rosie and Chas did not have an intimate relationship, they had dated frequently as good friends. There had always been holiday time back home in Gunnedah while doing her studies in Sydney, but while at university, Rosie missed the constancy of Chas's good humour and adventurous exploits. It did not surprise her when he called to see her out on the farm, just a few days after she had returned home. In a cheeky, short embrace, Chas whispered, 'Life has never treated me so well. It's great to know that you're here to stay now, Sweetie.'

CHAPTER 3

The Franklin farm had flourished. It was fifteen minutes from Gunnedah, just off the Kamilaroi Highway. Gunnedah had been named after the local Indigenous people and Kamilaroi was their language. Originally, the town had been called The Woolshed. It reflected the development of the wool industry in the region in the mid-nineteenth century.

Three generations of the Franklin family had been developing the property. Jack and Elsie's two younger daughters had fled the bush in their early twenties and were married and happily settled in Sydney. Jack and Elsie both passed away in the mid-1970s, and Ted then moved back to the Franklin homestead. When his son John married Sally in 1976, they were able to move into the updated cottage on *Ted's Place*.

In his declining years, Jack's greatest pleasure was to watch his grandson John grow up and leave school with only one focussed ambition, which was to work the land with the same true spirit of his father and grandfather. The Franklin property certainly had a sense of history, even though the homestead had been renovated and the farm was very much part of the modern agricultural trend.

Anne had married and moved to Tamworth and the youngest daughter Rosie had aspired to be a teacher from her early school days. Now as a graduate teacher she was so happy to be back in beautiful Gunnedah.

'Let me get you a lemonade, Chas, and we'll go and sit out under the trees. I can't wait to hear your news.'

With big smiles, holding hands and carrying drinks, they eagerly made for a favoured shady spot in the garden. The questions flowed back and forth. Rosie expressed how happy she was and how ideal her job was going to be. Eventually she changed the subject to ask, 'So Chasie, back to you. How's the flying going?'

'Oh, I've had some pretty good fun lately. I've really got the hang of aerobatics. Hey, Rosie, let me take you for a fly!'

'You mean in the old Tiger Moth that you bought just over twelve months ago? How often have you flown it?'

'Awe c'mon, I get out in it quite often.'

'So you know how to fly it?'

'Well, yes. I am an experienced pilot, you know,' Chas replied in a jocular tone. Rosie knew that he liked to tease her.

'Of course, Chas, but aeroplanes are all a bit different, aren't they? Have you flown this one very often?'

'Yep, I've been doing quite a few displays and I even did a few stunts in it last year at air shows around here. You know, spins, rolls 'n' stuff.' Chas looked at Rosie and slowly shook his head and smiled as he continued, 'I would not put my sweetie in any danger. I've had my endorsement on it and my licence is ridgy-didge. You'll be quite safe. You'll have strong belts to keep you in your seat and a helmet to keep those golden curls under control in the wind. I'd love to get you up in the sky on such a beautiful day. C'mon Rosie, it'll be straight and level, I promise. Let's get down to the airfield this afternoon.'

Rosie did know what a competent pilot Chas was. 'Yes, okay Chas, sounds like fun.'

'Whoopee!' With elation, Chas jumped up to make his way to the car as Rosie took the glasses inside and said 'goodbye' to her mother, explaining briefly where she was going. She returned to see Chas holding the car door open for her and they set out for the airport. Chas figured this was a fantastic way for them to celebrate her return home because they had spent so much time apart since she had begun her studies in Sydney. They arrived at the airport and parked near the hangar.

'It's a great afternoon to go up, Rosie. Will you come and help me push the Tiger out of the hangar?' Rosie followed Chas into the enormous shed, and they walked up to the rather sparky, two-seater biplane. The red and white paintwork had a striking effect. The seats were placed one behind the other and both the pilot and the passenger would be out in the open during flight. It looked very small in contrast with the agricultural aircraft around the hangar.

'Okay, you go over behind the left wing and just push gently.' Rosie did as she was asked and walked around to the other side, placing her hands on to the hard edge of the wing. Straight away her fingers bent over and pushed slowly into the flat, soft surface. She tapped with her fingertips several times to check.

'Chas, is the wing just fabric?'

'Yep, that's right. Wood and fabric.'

'Oh my, gosh, you mean that's what is going to keep us in the air?'

'Of course, it's a light aircraft, and very well designed. They've been flying for over fifty years now, even before the Second World War.'

Rosie's nostrils flared and she gritted her teeth until she remembered and came to terms with the fact that Tiger Moth aircraft had a solid reputation. She continued pushing, masking her underlying anxiety, and instead, considered the adventure she was about to undertake. It was not the first time she had been flying in a light aircraft, but in the Tiger Moth, sitting in an open cockpit, she anticipated a more exciting experience and put all her confidence in Chas's skills.

'Okay, here's your helmet, hop in and I'll do up your straps.' Chas tenderly put his arm around Rosie's hips to help her onto the wing. As he did so he could not help thinking how alluring she smelt. 'Now just swing yourself into the front seat.'

'The front seat, Chas? Aren't you the pilot? What's with the helmet?'

'Don't be a worry-wart. The pilot sits in the back where he can see the passenger in case you fall out.' She glanced at him with wide eyes. 'Joke, joke,' he said, far too late for her liking. 'The helmet will keep your head warm, and you'll hear me better on the intercom without the wind blowing in your ears.'

Grasping the helmet like some sort of lucky mascot, Rosie stepped over into the seat and Chas leaned over to fasten the straps. It felt strange having no canopy over her head. The heavy cotton twine belt pulled her back tightly into the seat.

'Well, I won't be going anywhere in a hurry. You've got me, Chas, hey?'

With a sly look and a wink, Chas replied, 'I sure have! You're just goin' to have fun, Sweetie.'

Chas pointed to the intercom. 'That's your communication device. Just keep your helmet on and your sentences short.'

Sitting in the open at the front of the aircraft as they taxied

CHAPTER 3

down the strip, Rosie felt an amazing sense of freedom. There was no cover over her head and the wind was gusty around her. It was rather unnerving not being able to glance across to see Chas at the control column as she was used to doing when they went flying in the Cessna.

As they set off down the runway, the speed of the plane increased and Rosie clasped her hands tightly as they became airborne so quickly, compared with a Cessna. After the aircraft climbed for barely a minute, it levelled out and she heard Chas on the intercom, 'Okay Rosie, seat belts tight. We're going to bank steeply, and you'll be able to see the ground easily.' With the earth stretching out below her and the air rushing past, Rosie yelled, 'It's fantastic Chas!'

'Well just hold on 'cos I'm going to pull up sharply and then we'll go into a dive to touch the trees.'

All Rosie could say was, 'What?' as Chas began the climb. They soared upwards interminably into the clear blue sky and Rosie could look out and see that they were leaving the earth behind.

A quick call from Chas, 'Hold tight, we're heading down'. With that, the aircraft changed position, the horizon tilted, and the nose dropped down so Rosie could now see the trees. The ground grew closer very quickly, and she had no time to decide whether to shut her eyes or to scream; instead, she just looked down at the trees getting larger and basked in the scary dive. As they levelled out, Rosie felt a euphoric web overwhelm her and she heard a call from Chas. 'You okay Rosie?'

'Yep, for sure. This is sensational. I know I want to do it again.'

'Great stuff, we will for sure. We'll go and check out your farm and take a bit of a turn over it before we go back to land.'

Rosie Franklin, a slim, fit, attractive young lady, had graduated from Sydney University at the end of 1981. While she was doing her teaching qualifications at the university, Rosie had found adapting to city life a little difficult. Although she had had a good boarding house for accommodation, she was hypersensitive of the number of people, the traffic, the city noises day and night, and the grimy air of the inner city. To be posted back to Gunnedah was her 'dream come true'. Even though her school days would be routine and made up of regular classes, she planned to establish an out-of-school gymnastics club and spend time at the local swimming pool, coaching potential champions for the school swimming carnival.

She had been a confident and self-assured student but was now about to use those characteristics to provide a role model for young people embarking upon the physical challenges of a sporting career. After completing her teaching degree majoring in physical education and sports studies, she applied for a position at her old school, Gunnedah High School. Arriving there in the New Year, she considered herself most fortunate to have been posted to her hometown where she would be able to put her skills to work as a physical education teacher. The teaching staff had also welcomed another young teacher, Carly Kent, a colleague of Rosie's from university, who was a year older than her, and who had also been posted to Gunnedah as an art and English teacher the year before Rosie's return. Carly and Rosie were happy to be close friends again.

CHAPTER 4

Chas and Rosie shared a sense of adventure. Just to be airborne was an undeniable thrill for Chas. The reason he was in the air, did not matter. His mother often told the story that his first word was not 'Mummy' or 'Daddy' but 'plane' and, when a plane was passing overhead, it could be any sort of aircraft, a Qantas passenger jet, his father's crop duster or a helicopter, and little Chas would jump around pointing to the sky saying, 'Plane, plane.' He was fortunate that his father had been a pilot for many years. Bill Anderson was the local crop sprayer/duster pilot who regularly attended to the crops on properties in the area. He also had a flying instructor rating so, apart from the fact that Chas was able to get many free rides on board his father's crop-sprayer, he was also able to get flying lessons. He started his training at fifteen and had all the qualifications for a private pilot's licence at seventeen years of age.

As a young aviation enthusiast, he followed in his father's

footsteps and had been crop spraying, under his guidance, for several years. While keeping up with his regular job as a motor mechanic at the local servo, he was often granted time off to help his father. Chas's passion for aerobatics had developed from his solo time in the crop sprayers when he realised that there could be even greater freedom in an aircraft that was built for steep dives, loops and rolls. When, early in 1981, he heard that a friend of his father's in Tamworth had a Tiger Moth for sale, he took his father with him to check it out. Chas decided it was for him and, with his savings, he arranged a deposit on it immediately. Being a tail-wheel aircraft, his father flew it back to Gunnedah while a rather disappointed Chas had to drive the car home. His father gave him an endorsement on the Tiger over the following week. Bill Anderson, also an experienced aerobatic pilot, was happy to make time for his son to get the required aerobatic instruction that he could put to good use on the Tiger Moth.

Chas had bought the aircraft at a very good price but would have a bank loan to pay back. Such an aircraft was originally used for training but, over the years, it had been the aircraft of choice by pilots for air show aerobatic displays for years. Apart from flying his father's crop sprayer, a Grumman Ag Cat, Chas was also a pilot of the Cessna associated with the local parachute club, and he flew the parachutists out to the drop zone most Saturday afternoons. However, he had bought the Tiger because he wanted to use it for stunt flying.

A passion for achieving a goal, and the thrill of physical challenges, made Rosie and Chas soulmates. The hours that

CHAPTER 4

filled Rosie's days were always interesting and satisfying. She had been fanatical about physical challenges since school days and her lithe, slim body took well to the flexibility and agility demanded by gymnastics. As her first year back home got underway, she often arrived at her newly established, weekend gymnasium class before the students, just to give herself some practise. She would then check the record player was ready to play her chosen gym club theme 'Just an Illusion' by the Imagination Group, which she thought was so motivating. The constant background rhythm gave her floor movements continuity. The occasional crescendo of high notes sent her leaping into the air with a kick, and then she would stretch her arms to the floor to somersault, before finishing off with a completely airborne manoeuvre. She loved the magic of being airborne and for sure this was the special connection she had with Chas, even though her experience was somewhat closer to the ground. Rosie's innate sense of rhythm and presentation always guided her as she performed for an awestruck audience. Ballet lessons during her childhood, along with many gruelling hours working out on the balance beam and doing floor routines, combined to win her a number of gymnastic competitions.

With a fervent desire to improve her acrobatic techniques, Rosie quite often spent afternoons in the air, diving at the local swimming pool. Set in beautiful parkland, with family facilities provided on the lawns under shady trees, the Gunnedah Memorial Pool was a drawcard for the youth of the town. Rosie arranged for regular swimming classes there but also loved to spend time diving from the three-metre platform. Such an activity, she hoped, would develop grace and flexibility that she could apply to her gymnastic routine, and, as result of her efforts, she was also once proclaimed a diving champion. Her ability and skills resulted in an enthusiastic team of local swimmers that turned up regularly for her coaching class.

While Rosie had been completing her degree in Sydney, Chas, the tall, good-looking pilot had fast become renowned for his stunt displays on field days in the surrounding region, and in 1981, at the AgQuip Show in Gunnedah. This was when, for a couple of days in August, people from around the area would visit the local show to check out agricultural pursuits, the latest farm machinery, and the rural lifestyle. AgQuip had had a tremendous influence on the development of Gunnedah since it was established in 1973 at the Riverside Racecourse. However, by 1977, when the success and increasing number of exhibitors and visitors overwhelmed the site and threatened severe damage to the grassed racing track, the decision was made to re-site the AgQuip Show to a southeast location, where development would not be hindered. It was also convenient for the occasional gyrocopter and other aerial activities to be observed. When, in 1981, Chas's father suggested that a brief aerial show could also be an attraction, he managed to get a promotion for Chas to do a show from the airport later in the afternoon of the final day. The popularity of Chas's event led to an invitation for him to fly at other neighbouring shows in the region, including Tamworth.

After her first flight in the Tiger Moth, Chas gave Rosie the opportunity to join him when he flew to the occasional air show during January and February. There, she watched him doing

CHAPTER 4

some stunts. As often as possible she would tag along to 'ooh', 'aah' and sometimes gasp with horror at the death-defying feats through which Chas put the aircraft. After having attended a couple of displays, Chas asked Rosie, 'Hey Sweetie, you seem to be pretty good at understanding the aerobatic manoeuvres, how about we get you a microphone and when you come on the display days with me, you can do a commentary for the crowd?'

'Oh, do you really think I could handle that?'

'For sure, and I can give you an idea of what I'll be doing, and you can just say what you're feeling about the movements happening up there. You've heard me use words like, climbing, banking, straight and level, loop, dive and roll, so you just put them in a sentence.'

'Chas, that's a big ask.'

Considering that Rosie had not come out directly to say 'no', Chas continued, 'Listen, sometime before a display, we can sit down and discuss the sequence. I can give you a few words and you just put the sentences together. Shall we try it?'

Rosie answered with a giggle, 'Why not? It would be my way of paying you for the trip to the show.'

CHAPTER 5

It had been a great afternoon for Chas. He had been able to get time off from the servo to finish a spray job for his father. As he taxied along the runway towards the hangar and then made his way to the park spot, he noticed an unfamiliar guy watching the aircraft. When he closed down the engine and jumped from the wing, a brawny, sure-footed fellow walked up to introduce himself.

'Hi, I'm Barry Moyle. Looks like you've had a busy day.'

'Yeh, it certainly has been. Pleased to meet you. Chas Anderson. How can I help you?'

'Oh, I'm new in town Chas, just finished my first workday in the hangar.'

'A pilot?'

'No, not at all. I'm an aviation fabricator and LAME. That is a Licensed Aircraft Maintenance Engineer, as if you didn't know, and an enthusiastic 'meat bomb'.'

Chas, with a quizzical expression, asked, 'Crickey, now that's something I don't know.'

'Geez Chas, ya haven't heard that? It's the common name for parachutists around Ballarat. You've gotta land right or a 'meat bomb' is exactly what you'll be.'

With a guffaw of laughter, Chas replied, 'Well, you've come to the right place. I've just had a day out over the paddocks and I'm really hanging out for a drink. Want to join me and fill me in on your pranks?' With that, the two young men arranged to meet in fifteen minutes at the Regal pub, a popular meeting place in town.

Barry Moyle arrived in Gunnedah from the southern state of Victoria in March 1982. He wanted to check out the place because his family, in Ballarat, had had connections to Gunnedah in the past. Although not looking for work initially, when his experience and qualification as an aircraft fabricator, LAME, became known while chatting over a drink at the pub just after he had arrived, it was suggested that he see Phil Jennings the senior engineer at the airport. Phil was impressed with Barry's qualifications and work experience and offered him a job at the airport hangar. It was not a difficult decision to accept the offer, but Barry did indicate some uncertainty as to how long he could stay. However, it provided a good excuse for him to extend his time in the area so as he could explore the history of the arrival of his grandfather, Wally Hammond, back in the early 1900s.

Barry's arrival in Gunnedah was the beginning of a wild new experience. His Uncle Bob had already touched his life and provided the motivation to make a career in aviation and in particular, engineering. Meeting and befriending Chas Anderson was to be one of the most important turning points in his life.

Phil Jennings welcomed Barry warmly when he arrived, right on time, on his first day. The hangar was spacious and obviously well utilised. Once he had been shown around and viewed various projects, Barry was convinced that he would hang around for a while and see how things turned out. It would seem much of his work would be maintenance with attention also to be paid to the machines on the crop-spraying aircraft; something a little different for him.

As the Grumman spray aircraft landed on the afternoon of his first day at work, Barry had been curious to find out more about crop spraying, so he welcomed the opportunity to chat when Chas suggested they meet up. During the next hour or so with beers in hand, they each shared bits of their story. Chas was interested to find that Barry's grandfather, Wally Hammond, had been one of the migrant farmers who had settled in the Gunnedah area before WWI. It seemed Barry's parachuting interest followed on from family tales of his Uncle Bob, who had been killed during WWII. Bob Hammond, Wally's son, was nineteen years old when the war broke out. After joining up, he trained as a wireless air operator, and was then sent to England. Some air crew members were given parachute training, purely as insurance, should their aircraft be set to crash. It was during the low-level raid on Eindhoven in 1942 when, in the midst of an aerial conflict, the aircraft Bob was in was so badly damaged the crew were all directed to parachute from the plane. It was unfortunate that Bob received enemy fire on the way down and did not survive the jump.

Barry was invigorated and passionate as he told Chas about Bob and a letter that his Aunt Betty had received from Bob, her brother, about an earlier aircraft incident during his training as a wireless operator. When Barry met Betty in Brisbane on a trip as a teenager, she read Barry that letter. The words, *Gee Betty, I was shit-scared when we had to jump, but oh boy, floating down felt so bloody good*, had motivated Barry to take up parachuting when he got back home to Ballarat.

Chas knew a very competent Victorian parachutist, Eddie Edwards, and during their chat, mentioned the name to Barry. That really created a bond between the two because Barry had crossed paths several times with Eddie, and it was he who had inspired Barry to continue to train as a parachute instructor.

Chas was impressed, 'So you're a mate of Eddie's? Wow, I've met him a few times when we've been out at competition drop zones. He's a really great guy.'

With that, Chas asked, 'Are you interested in helping us out here? We desperately need a parachute instructor, as anyone wanting to get started must take basic training elsewhere.'

'Aw yes, I reckon that sounds pretty good. You know, I've just been given a maintenance job here in the hangar.'

'In that case,' said Chas, 'I will certainly have opportunities to call on your expertise in times ahead. There are always changes and maintenance required on both the crop sprayers and my Tiger Moth to keep them safe and reliable.'

Chas told Barry about the work he did as the pilot of the

Cessna that was used by the parachutists occasionally, as well as the air displays. 'I don't think there are any shows for a while but perhaps you'd like to come along next time? I'll let you know more about it later, okay?'

Barry was delighted with the invitation. 'Hey, for sure, count me in.' He couldn't imagine a better way to develop a friendship than with someone who had similar interests in aviation. As they shook hands, Barry added, 'Oh, and Chas, if there's any way I can help you out, do let me know.'

'Yeh, will do. Hey, you know there's a Gunnedah Parachute Club social next Saturday night. Why don't you come along and meet a few of the jumpers? We usually get to the Regal pub at about 6.30 pm for a few drinks and a burger. We don't generally have a jump day each week but if you're interested, a weekly jump session could be quite popular. The drop zone is just down the end of the runway and I'm happy to get the Cessna out for a couple of drops.'

'Thanks. Yep, that'd be great. I'd love to get involved with the club. I'll be there for sure.'

Once Barry was introduced around on the following club night, Chas could see that enthusiasm for growth and development would get underway. The club night was always a good social occasion that, with an open invitation, any locals were able to attend. Rosie always went along with Chas and enjoyed a night of talking, dancing, and meeting new people over a glass of sparkly wine. As they sat at a table for two, Chas explained his meeting with Barry.

'You know, I reckon Barry will be able to get the club really going again. It needs its own instructor and I think he'll be a good guy to work with. Do you want to try him out Rosie?'

'Listen, there's no way I want to jump out of an aeroplane that's working really well. Why don't you do a jump?'

'They need me to fly them to the drop zone. I don't care where I am, what I'm doing or when I'm doing it, but I do know how I feel, as long as I'm in an aeroplane. It doesn't matter if I'm flying methodically up and down rows of crops, fleecing the clouds with my Tiger, or taking the jumpers, straight and level, to the drop zone, so long as I'm in a plane, free of earthly bonds and particularly, if I'm with you, I'm happy.'

'Chas, I know exactly what you mean 'cos that describes my passion for gymnastics precisely. You know, we do make a great team. I can relate to all your stories from up above and I am never bored listening to the tales. Of course, being up there with you is even better.'

'Rosie, our relationship just adds to my happiness. Watching you tumble and soar in a floor routine, intertwined with amazing dance movements, just sets my heart on fire.'

However, the idea of a parachute jump did not attract either Rosie or Chas. From time-to-time Rosie had indicated admiration for the wing walkers that were part of the early days of aviation. She often ambled around the room in the pub where the club met, perusing the historic photos of parachuting, wing walking and ballooning that were displayed on the walls. It was not so much the story and pictures of Otmer Locklear, who actually climbed from the wing of one aeroplane to another while they were airborne, that attracted her, but other stunts that were popular in the 1930s. Checking photographs of Gladys Engle and Juanita Jover from the 1920s, balancing and stretching on an aircraft wing, gave Rosie a picture of herself standing on a balance beam with nothing underneath and a rush of air around her as she stretched her arms to capture the space. Then the thought of doing a handstand on the wing of an aircraft, knowing she was secure and safe in an atmosphere of total freedom, captured Rosie's imagination.

She picked up her glass, and with a cheeky grin across her face, Rosie suggested to Chas, 'You know I might not want to jump out of an aeroplane but maybe you could strap me onto a wing and take me high in the sky.'

Chas was sure she was only joking but played along with her suggestion.

'Rosie, you went on the roller coaster in Sydney, and you told me that was scary. How do you think you would feel standing on the wing at 2000 feet, with the wind and just nothing all around you?'

'The roller coaster was scary Chas but that was also what made it so much fun. I reckon wing walking would be thrilling and I'd be safe if you were my pilot.'

'There have been regulations imposed on commercial aviation organisations in Australia since WWI. The idea was to maintain a clear reputation for safe air travel. There weren't too many rules around when wing walking first became popular but there were many accidents. As a result, stringent regulations were developed to encompass particular aerial feats like wing walking. I was lucky that, when my interest in display flying developed a few years ago, the limits that had been placed on some activities had become somewhat relaxed, but wing walking is still included in the regulations even though it is not actually named. It is simply an activity that must be controlled, not because of accidents that have occurred, but simply because the regulators don't want accidents.'

The parachute club, operating from the hangar, was a favoured sporting venue for just a few town folk but it had never appealed to Rosie. Her brother, John, some years earlier, had literally thrown himself into parachuting, and had helped establish the club. His efforts to persuade Rosie to join him fell on deaf ears and proved his sister was not interested. She preferred to work on improving her balance beam manoeuvres and floor routines. When Barry began some instruction sessions on Saturday afternoons, the popularity increased and a regular parachute drop each week was set in place. Rosie occasionally turned up at the hangar, greeted her brother and joined Chas and Barry for a few drinks when it was all over. The thread of conversation, however, was constantly tied to parachutes, drop zones and instruction techniques, so before long she would head for home.

Rosie preferred to go to the hangar early, on a Saturday afternoon, to chat with Chas before he prepared the Cessna aircraft for an afternoon of jumping. Barry Moyle was always there with several parachute enthusiasts. On one occasion, as the instruction began and Rosie was leaving the hangar, she noticed Lisa Jennings, a young local nurse, among the parachutists. Rosie had only recently met Lisa, as the family had arrived in Gunnedah while she was studying in Sydney. Lisa's father, Phil Jennings, was the senior engineer in the hangar, who had employed Barry. Lisa was listening to Chas discuss weather conditions and Rosie noticed that her rather inflated enthusiasm showed a definite flirtatiousness. Rosie stood by the door and when Chas finished speaking she could just hear Lisa asking him a question, 'Chas, how many girls have you taken up for a jump?'

Chas replied, 'Well Lisa, you will be the first one to jump here in Gunnedah.'

'Oh really, so I'm rather special?'

Chas replied quickly, hoping to give Lisa the feeling that she was a welcome member of the group, 'Everyone is special when they are jumping out of my aeroplane, Lisa. I'd like you to remember that when your jump time comes.'

Rosie could tell that Chas was keeping his conversation positive without brushing off Lisa's comment and wished she could intrude. Instead of leaving the hangar, she decided to sit and watch the proceedings from a back office and then she really became aware of Lisa's coquettish behaviour.

A few weeks later, Rosie joined up with her teacher friends for a weekend luncheon. She always enjoyed sharing time with Carly Kent. They considered it most fortunate that they had crossed paths at university.

As they went to the table to be seated, Rosie was surprised to be introduced to Lisa Jennings, who had been invited to the luncheon by another teacher, and was sitting next to her. As lunch began, Carly, who was sitting across the table, raised her coffee cup and called out, 'Coffee cups clinking everyone, let's welcome Rosie back home.' There were some high-spirited cheers and Rosie, taken by surprise, gave a small speech.

'Thank you everyone. I can tell you I am so pleased to be back here. I am sure I will be spending more time relaxing or working in Gunnedah than before I went to Sydney.'

More comments came from around the table, 'Oh Rosie, we'll find something to keep you busy.'

'Gym competitions are still out there, girl.'

'You won't be sitting on your hands, that's for sure.'

'As long as you keep drinking your coffee, you'll have energy for anything Rosie.'

Rosie was renowned for her energy and enthusiasm, and it was common knowledge that she blamed her cup of coffee for her energy. She had always felt that the caffeine gave her a boost. Her coach, in her early days of competing, had suggested a strong cup of coffee just before a competition. Along with some research, Rosie then found that caffeine, before an event, could provide an energy boost with a concentrated focus that also improved her co-ordination when she performed.

A conversation about upcoming local sports events soon engaged the ladies around the table, and the revitalisation of the Parachute Club was of considerable interest. Although not a jumper, most of her teaching friends knew that Rosie had a close association with the club through her friendship with Chas Anderson. There were many jokes and questions for Rosie, and Lisa soon became aware of her connection with Chas. The rather skittish young lady then expressed an overwhelming desire for information.

'Oh, Rosie, how often does Chas take the jumpers out to the drop zone?' Another question really rocked Rosie. 'Oooh, I do like Chas. Does he take friends flying in his Tiger Moth?' Lisa then continued, 'I saw you at the hangar a while back Rosie. Do you go parachuting with Chas? Do tell me what it's like. Is Chas a good pilot?'

'Lisa, if you want to know so much about parachuting you should do it, instead of just talking about it. Just concentrate on your lessons with Barry. Is that your intention? Perhaps too scary for you?' Rosie then, with a shrug, directed her conversation to her friends around the table.

Within a few weeks, it was common knowledge that Lisa, the flirty little nurse, was making parachuting jumps on Saturday afternoons. Rosie knew that the boys would always head for the bar after a busy day in the hangar. Since John would often go to the pub on the days he did a jump, he would casually drop Lisa's name, or mention her flighty behaviour just to tease his sister. 'You know that Lisa girl was real pushy today. We were practising getting in and out of the aircraft door and supposed to be doing it by ourselves, but she had the cheek to try to get Chas to help her. She gave a little scream to attract his attention and slipped from the door. Chas went over to her and offered his hand. She then picked herself up from floor and just said, "Thanks, I'm fine now."'

CHAPTER 6

With the promotion of Barry Moyle, in his role as an experienced jump instructor, the number of people interested in the Parachute Club was growing. The club social night at the Regal was also very popular. Chas often invited Rosie out on the dinner nights where occasionally, after her favourite meal of chicken parmigiana, they would join up with friends from the hangar to finish off the night.

One evening, Chas was telling Rosie about Barry, 'I'm so glad we got Barry into the club, and it turns out we've got a mutual friend.'

With that, Rosie stopped, her hand with the fork in mid-air, and quickly looked across the table to Chas. 'What are you telling me?'

'Just that Barry knows him a lot better than I do. It's a parachute guy at Ballarat, Eddie Edwards. Barry reckons we should go and see him do a display jump in Melbourne.'

With a slight sense of relief in her voice that it wasn't the flirty little nurse who was the mutual friend, Rosie replied, 'Why would you go all the way down there?'

'Well, he has been selected to do a jump into the Melbourne Cricket Ground for the opening of the Commonwealth Games in a couple of weeks in mid-August.'

'Yeh, I guess that would be pretty interesting for you guys.'

The conversation continued about Barry's work with the club and then Rosie approached Chas with her current concern,

'You know that flighty nurse, Lisa, who has been attending jump classes? She is twisting you around her little finger. Do you really have to pay her so much extra attention Chas? I have seen her chatting you up in the hangar on several occasions.'

'You're imagining that something untoward was happening, Rosie. She's just a 'newbie' and needs encouragement.'

With a touch of rancour in her tone, Rosie continued, 'Yep, she makes sure that she has your attention, hey?'

'Rosie, I haven't even noticed the woman. Listen, how about you coming to Melbourne with us? I'd love you to come. I'm flying down with Barry and Jim in a couple of weeks' time on August 14th. We'll leave early Saturday afternoon, stay at a motel for the night, and then go to the MCG the next morning to watch Eddie parachute into the stadium. He'll then deliver the Queen's message in a baton to the marathon runners for the start of the Commonwealth Games. Will you come with us?'

Rosie presumed it was to be a boys' adventure, so being happy for her seat to be taken by a third jumper, she replied, 'Thanks for the invitation, Chas. It's great that you can get out to events with your brother, Jim, and of course Barry will think it's a tremendous opportunity, so I think you'll find someone more appreciative of the offer than me.'

When Chas, Barry and Jim made their plans days later, and Rosie heard that Lisa was taking the third seat, she was furious. She wanted to discuss it immediately, so she phoned Chas at the servo. 'Do you think I am so dumb, Chas, that I have no idea that Lisa is chatting you up?'

'Hey Rosie, what are you on about?'

'You've given her the third seat on the Cessna.'

'Listen, she is really keen to see some professional stuff and she approached Barry when she heard that the seat was available. He asked me, so how could I say no?'

'Chas, she just wants to find some free time with you and even have the opportunity to spend a night with you. She is trying to get under you, not under a parachute. Wake up.'

Chas was getting fed up with Rosie's accusations. 'Rosie, go have a glass of water and just relax.'

'Get lost Chas.' With that, she slammed down the phone.

Over the week ahead, Rosie refused to accept Chas's phone calls.

The group was to leave at midday the following Saturday for the five-hour flight to Melbourne. Late on Friday evening, Chas decided to make a quick visit out to the Franklin's farm. It was 8 pm but the light was still on in the lounge room, so he felt comfortable about visiting at such an hour. The sharp ring of the doorbell vibrated through the house in the hush of the evening and Rosie's mother, Mary, met him at the door, 'Hi Chas, you want to see Rosie? She's rather tired 'cos she's just got home from a training session, but I'll give her a call.' Mary called loudly as she knocked on the bedroom door, 'Chas is here to see you, Rosie.'

Half asleep, with her dressing gown pulled around her, the rather disoriented young woman dragged herself down the shadowy hallway to the front door. Leaning against the door frame and avoiding eye contact, Rosie mumbled, 'What are you doing here?'

Chas was aware that he was not welcome, but he just had to see his sweetheart before the trip to Melbourne. 'I just wanted to say "G'bye".'

'You know that is not necessary. Just go Chas. Safe travels.' With that, Rosie stepped back and closed the door. She really did not want to acknowledge, or recall, any other association with him. She felt betrayed.

With a deep sigh, Chas turned and dragged his feet as he returned to the car, remembering how Barry had put out the word at his last class that there was a seat available on the Cessna for the Melbourne jaunt. It seemed most of the jump group had commitments over the weekend, except for Lisa, who by chance was not on the hospital roster and could take the seat. He figured he had simply been helping her to settle into the club and considered her enthusiasm and chatter in the hangar to be an effort to relate more to the jump lessons. However, Rosie was disturbed about something. He told himself he would have to be a bit more aware of the time he spent around Lisa.

Chas arrived at the airport the next morning rather disconsolate. Rosie's words had been so dispiriting. Barry was there waiting with Lisa and Jim, and because he knew Chas to be rather fanatical about details and punctuality, he could not help commenting.

'Gee, what have you been up to mate? You're all of ten minutes late.' There was no answer from Chas, simply the words, 'All aboard for take-off.'

Chas couldn't wait to get into the wide blue yonder. After his pre-flight check they took off in the Cessna 180, at 10.30 am, with the scheduled time of arrival to be around 4 pm. Once airborne, his spirits lifted, and Chas became more amiable. For him, it also helped that for the flight south, they had a tail wind, and after an uneventful trip, they arrived in Melbourne at 3.45 pm. They found a conveniently placed motel and the three guys shared a room while Lisa had hers all to herself. After a meal at a local café, when Chas was a little disturbed by the proximity of Lisa sitting next to him at the table, they all bade her a flippant 'goodnight' and left her at her unit door.

The next morning, after a leisurely breakfast, they took a taxi from Essendon to the MCG and were at the venue an hour before the expected jump and the following Aussie Rules Football (AFL) match.

With the stadium packed for the anticipated parachute jump and the delivery of the Olympic baton, it took the group of four a while to find some seats and then they all became aware of the rather unsettled weather conditions. They knew how unnerving the strong winds could be for a parachute jumper. However, to the delight of the crowd and, amidst robust cheering, they watched the plane fly over the stadium. As Eddie jumped from the aircraft, the crowd subdued its response, and watched agog as the solo jumper manipulated the parachute through the currents of air. The visitors from Gunnedah held their breath and followed Eddie's movements intently, particularly Chas and Barry who, understanding the difficult conditions, were confident that Eddie, with all his experience, would overcome any problems. There was much applause when Eddie landed accurately on a white cross marker set out on the ground in the centre of the stadium. Jim was less aware of Eddie's ability and was astounded by his accuracy. Lisa watched but showed no real emotion other than asking Chas, while pointing to the small group in the centre of the stadium, 'Chas do you know who those VIPs are?'

'No, Lisa. Just watch.'

As he released the straps of his parachute, Eddie was congratulated for his jump by various dignitaries and film crews. He then handed over the baton to Ron Clarke, Australia's champion long-distance runner. Ron immediately headed off for a lap of honour around the oval before starting the marathon through the streets of Melbourne. Clarke was the first of the four marathon runners, who had been chosen to share the run to Brisbane over the following days.

When Chas hailed a taxi for the trip back to Essendon, they all agreed it had been a memorable occasion and, having planned a fuel stop at Corowa on the return trip, they were now looking forward to discussing the historic day with the man of the hour. Although Eddie had to take part in a parachute competition later that afternoon in Corowa, he had agreed to have a brief chat with his friends Barry and Chas when they landed there on their on their way home..

Once they were on the ground in Corowa with Eddie, each armed with a cup of coffee, the questions flowed thick and fast. Barry's was the first, 'And how about that bloody wind, mate? I bet you hadn't planned for that?'

'Yep, it was rather daunting, I must say. It took a bit of planning and good luck, to be 'on time and on target' as my demonstration motto suggests.'

Jim, listening intently, was intrigued with the degree of accuracy that Eddie had shown, 'How did you manage to achieve your landing right on that cross? Did you drop out a drifter to gauge the distance you would travel from exit to landing?'

'No, if you drop a drifter in the city it can tangle up power lines and cause problems. I got the pilot to fly cross wind to assess the drift and wind strength.'

Jim was amazed at the resulting precision. While Jim continued speaking with Eddie, Chas was surprised to hear Lisa mumbling and asked her what was wrong. 'Oh, this talk is just stuff that hasn't got any relevance for us in Gunnedah.'

Chas was rather shocked at her comment and quietly said to her, 'Lisa, jumping's a learning process just like any other skill. Listen and learn.'

Chas then broke into the discussion with questions related to Eddie's explanation of the role of the aircraft and the pilot's decision in executing the drop. However, Lisa trying to impress, then asked, 'What were you expecting on landing, Eddie?'

'Oh, I guessed there'd be a few cameras and VIPs but not

so much for me as for Ron Clarke and the baton hand-over. I couldn't believe that they'd reserved me a seat to watch the semi-final footy match and they were a bit taken aback when I said all I needed was a carton of beer and a taxi to take me back to Essendon, where the plane was waiting to get me here.'

Lisa had the final question, 'Eddie how did you get interested in parachuting?' It turned out that Eddie's reply was of interest to them all and Chas covered his smile, considering it could have been Lisa's way of responding to his mild rebuke by coming up with a very relevant question.

'Oh, I was working in New Guinea several years ago and my mate, a New Caledonian fellow, who was quite a parachute star, suggested I should give it a go. It was with his encouragement that I ended up becoming a professional parachutist and have since been sponsored to do displays. You know, delivering the Queen's message for the opening of the Games has been my most famous display jump as a professional.'

After a bit more chatter, Chas said, 'To be sure Eddie, there will be many other occasions where your name will be an inspiration for all aspiring parachutists, like young Jim and Lisa here. Thanks so much for making time for us today in your busy schedule.'

Chas then directed the group to their aircraft and, once on board, they took-off into a head wind, for the four-hour stretch home. There was not much talking during the trip but while the two guys in the back seat dozed off, Lisa, sitting in the front, asked Chas a few questions regarding his family and background. 'How long have you lived in Gunnedah, Chas?'

CHAPTER 6

'Oh, my family has pretty well lived there for years since I was a little kid.'

'Have you ever wanted to leave the place?'

'No.'

'Will you live in Gunnedah when you get married?'

'Yep, I reckon so.'

'Would you like to have lots of kids when you have a family?'

'Who knows?' Chas felt the questions were becoming rather personal and apart from simple answers, he was reluctant to say anything. He sensed that Lisa had no desire to get into any details regarding the day's events and considered that the interest she had shown for parachuting, one could hardly call enthusiasm.

When they arrived in Gunnedah at sunset and rather tired, someone thought a take-away meal was a good idea and Chas suggested they meet up at his conveniently located flat, for dinner and drinks. Barry and Jim had their own cars, but Lisa had left her car at Barry's place and had travelled to the airport with him on Saturday morning. While eating, they sat around the TV set and watched the news programs. Being the first night heralding the weeks ahead of the Commonwealth Games, the various channels were choked with the day's events.

Eventually, the guys sat around the table with only an occasional glance at the screen, talking non-stop. Barry was adamant, 'Gee Chas, we've gotta get Eddie up our way. If we introduced him to the locals with a bit of a display, we could really create some interest in the club. Whatdaya reckon?'

Chas nodded and gave a laugh, 'You're just hankering to

increase your student numbers, Barry. But yes, I agree. It could be a big boost for the place.'

Jim offered an idea, 'Why don't we have competitions and open them to other locations?'

'I think that is certainly a great idea, Jim,' Barry continued. 'We could actually prep contenders for the national competitions.'

A soft, sulky sounding voice interrupted the conversation. It came from the sofa where Lisa was sitting alone. They had not paid her any attention, thinking she was quiet because she was tired. However, Lisa had just kept refilling her gin and tonic glass, and lost track of the number of drinks she had tossed down.

'Chas, did you hear me? Do you have any more cushions?'

Chas turned to look at Lisa with an expression of surprise, suggesting that he may have forgotten she was in the room.

'Sure Lisa, I'll get you a couple of pillows.'

Without answering, Lisa got up to follow him.

'No, no, wait there, I'll get them for you.'

'I can come and help you find them Chas.'

Chas left the room quickly, but Lisa was close behind. After picking up a couple of pillows from the spare bedroom he handed them to Lisa and turned to return to the lounge room.

'You've hardly said two words to me tonight, Chas.'

'Awe c'mon Lisa, it's been such a great day. We're all fired up. Why don't you just join in the chat?'

As they walked into the room the others watched with quizzical expressions. 'I think I need another G and T. Could you pour me one please Chas?'

CHAPTER 6

The three guys kept talking. They could envision a lively future for parachuting in Gunnedah and extended the discussion to consider other towns in the region. Chas and Barry also discussed the upcoming AgQuip Show. Barry had been giving Chas some help with a brand-new stunt he was going to perform at the Gunnedah Show but they didn't really want to talk about the details in front of the others.

Before long, Lisa had passed out on the sofa. The boys continued chatting around the table. No one noticed the little lady was out of the conversation. As they all said good night and observed the rather limp state of Lisa lying on the sofa, it was the general opinion that Chas should just leave her there and cover her with a blanket, as there was no way she was going to be able to get into Barry's car and then pick up her car to drive home. Together they all tried to ensure that she was comfortable, said their 'goodbyes', and left as the clock ticked towards midnight.

It was eight o'clock in the morning when Chas trudged through the lounge to answer the doorbell. The state of the room from the night before and the outline of Lisa's body under the blanket on the sofa annoyed him. He opened the door and almost choked as he greeted Rosie, 'Sweetheart, how good to see you.'

'Oh Chas, I'm just off to the swimming pool for the early morning class. I felt so bad about my nasty words on Friday evening when you called in to say g'bye, I thought I would make up for it and get off to a good morning start by saying....' Rosie stopped suddenly, a look of suspicion shadowing her face. With wide eyes filled with dread, and raised eyebrows, she redirected her line of sight from behind Chas's head to meet him eye to eye. 'Forget it,' Rosie said through gritted teeth. 'Goodbye,' she added, then turned and walked away at a fast pace.

'But Rosie, what's up? Hey come back, let's talk.' By the time he realised that she was not going to turn around, he looked back into the lounge with the disarranged furniture and empty glasses scattered around the room, just as Lisa disappeared into the kitchen. It then registered with him what Rosie must have seen when she observed the unkempt situation. Chas raced to the gate but was not in time to catch up with her before she climbed into her car and drove off without a glance behind. When he returned to the doorway, he realised there could be no question as to what Rosie would have been thinking when she turned to go to her car. Lisa was now standing unsteadily and leaning on the dining table, her clothes rumpled, her hair dishevelled, and she had a distinctly detached look across her face. Rosie would have assumed the worst possible scenario as far as Chas was concerned. He put both hands to his head and yelled at Lisa, 'Get your gear, get a taxi and get out of here, now.'

CHAPTER 7

The events of the morning, when Rosie had left him with such disdain, haunted Chas all day When he sat to have his coffee, or took a few minutes rest between jobs at the servo, Chas would put his head in his hands and memories of her words just drained his emotions. She had declared, months earlier, that they were a great team and then had told him how her passion for gymnastics matched his for flying. He could recall the fervent look on her face when she had talked about wing walking, and he now wanted to believe that she was serious. *Should I just lay low or perhaps knock on her door?*

It was 4.30 pm and Rosie would have arrived home from her day at school so he decided to act impulsively. He picked up the phone at the back of the servo and decided to call his sweetheart. After a couple of rings, he heard Rosie's lively voice, 'Hello, Rosie here.'

'This is Chas, Sweetie. I love you. Can we talk?'

'I don't want to talk. I don't want to see you. Just get lost Chas.' The phone connection ended suddenly.

Chas tried to put himself in Rosie's position. *How would I feel if the situation were reversed? Could I walk away from the overwhelming sense of togetherness that we share?* He held no deep feelings for Lisa. She was not a part of his life. *How could she be to blame for Rosie's admonishment?* Chas realised an explanation was in order. Once he got back to his flat that evening, he had a bite to eat and put a favoured record on his gramophone. He loved the LP album *Bridge over Troubled Water* by Simon and Garfunkel. It had been released in 1970 and he remembered his mother playing it during his teenage years. Rosie and he had often spent times together listening to an hour of the soulful music. Now he sat at the table and put his favourite photo of Rosie, showing a close up of them as a couple, sitting on the wing of the Tiger Moth, in front of him. Her beaming smile and dreamy eyes gave him inspiration to put pen to paper. With an initial declaration of his love for her, and mention of the song he was listening to, he then, taking care and caution, tried to explain the circumstances of the dinner at his place, the night the group had returned from Melbourne.

Dearest Rosie,

You are the only person I love, and I believe you to be my soulmate. We have shared so much since school days. How could there ever be anyone else that I could love as deeply as I love you. I would do anything for you and, yes, I would be your pilot if you wish to wing walk. I also believe I would sing

CHAPTER 7

the song to you that I'm listening to right now, Bridge Over Troubled Water, if I could sing, but I can't.

Rosie, Saturday night was just as you often say, 'a boys' night'. Lisa had been a rather disinterested member of the event and for the whole day showed some disdain for the group. She had wanted to stay for the take-away meal but did not contribute anything to the conversation and simply tossed down innumerable glasses of gin and tonic before she passed out into a deep sleep.

There was no delicate way we could handle the situation to get her home. Her car was at Barry's. The guys suggested to just leave her there with a blanket and send her packing in the morning, which, my dearest, I wish I had done before you arrived. Anyway, check with Jim and Barry, they will vouch for my words.

I really did become aware during the trip that her technique was just as you said. Believe me my dearest, thoughts of her have never occupied space in my mind and it is inarguable that my heart belongs to you.

Please, let's meet.

Goodnight, my dearest love.

Chas.

If he posted the letter, Chas knew it would not arrive for two or three days, so he decided to drop it into the school letterbox. Rosie would have it tomorrow, Tuesday morning.

The absence of Chas in her life had hit Rosie like a bolt of lightning. As teenagers, they had always considered the other to be a partner along their path in life. Rosie was a couple of years younger than Chas but had known him since early school days. It was not until he was seventeen, and getting to the end of Year 12, that they began enjoying time together out of school. Sometimes they would see each other at the swimming pool and then call in to the deli for a smoothie and a chat, while they waited for Rosie's father to pick her up. Rosie often thought of the first question she ever remembered Chas asking her, 'Rosie, what is your life's dream?' She sort of thought that he wanted her to say, 'A relationship with you,' but instead she replied, 'Chas, I want to be the best gymnast I can be.'

Then there were occasions when Chas remembered times before Rosie left Gunnedah for university, when he and his father would land the crop sprayer on the rough airstrip at the edge of the Franklin property. Rosie's dad, Ted, would arrive at the strip, pick them up and take them back to the homestead for a cup of coffee. They were friendly afternoons and Chas was always eager to talk about the flying lessons he was getting from his father. 'Will you come flying with me when I get my licence, Rosie?'

'Maybe I'll be too busy doing my acrobatics.'

'You know, one day I'll be doing acrobatics in my aeroplane too, except we call them aerobatics.' At that point, Chas had a firm conviction that he would be saving his money for his own aerobatic aeroplane. Before long he had his pilot's licence but when he left school, he did a car mechanics course and got a steady job at the local servo.

Rosie had always had the desire to be a teacher, particularly a physical education teacher, and during her last two years at school her ability as a gymnast really developed. Whenever she was in a competition, Chas would go along to watch. He got so engrossed in the movements she performed that he automatically related her acrobatics to his aerobatics. She surprised him one day at the end of her last year at school, when she told him of her plans. 'I'm sure I'll get a successful Leaving Exam result Chas, and then I'm heading off to Sydney in the New Year. I'm going to train as a physical education teacher.'

'Wow Rosie, how long is the course?'

'Three years, and I'll only be coming home for the holidays.'

'What? It's going to take three years. That's a bit much. Can't you just set up a local gym club or something?'

'Well Chas, if you think my life choices aren't as important as yours then that is something you are going to have to come to terms with. You're always checking out the new things you're going to do and don't ask me what I think, so now I'm just doing what I want to do. I'll miss you but we'll have fun at holiday time.'

Thinking about those early days made Rosie angry with herself and with Chas. It seemed okay for him to do what he wanted without any repercussions, whereas she had had to supply reasons to him for her choices and argue the relevance. The following years at university had introduced her to Germaine Greer, one of the major voices of the radical feminist movement. Since 1970, when her first book 'The Female Eunuch' became an international bestseller, Germaine Greer had encouraged young women to resist the assumed submissive role that males forced upon them. Rosie took heed and understood that she had every right to define her own values and decide what was important in her life and how she wanted to live it.

How could Chas now play her along while keeping company with Lisa Jennings? Seeing the pretty little nurse appear in Chas's loungeroom on Monday morning, just passed her limit of tolerance, but then Rosie realised that she had to show more resolve. However, she wanted to make it clear to Chas that the hurt and apparent secrecy of his actions was something that she neither understood nor would blindly accept. Sharply hanging up on Chas when she answered his call on Monday evening felt quite justifiable as far as Rosie was concerned. She could not imagine how she and Chas would ever spend time together again.

As she walked into the staffroom for lunch the next day, the front office receptionist handed Rosie a letter that had been in the letterbox that morning. Taken totally by surprise, Rosie took the letter hesitantly. It had no stamp so she guessed straight away that it was from Chas. She then quietly excused herself and went to sit on the bench outside on the veranda. It was a few moments before, with a deep breath, she tore open the envelope.

It surely was a bridge that Chas was looking for. The tears in Rosie's eyes came with her memories of the nights they had played *Bridge Over Troubled Water* and she reflected upon the words in the first verse of that familiar song. *When tears are in your eyes, I will dry them all.* After considering the words in Chas's letter, Rosie began to feel his loving nature beckoning to her. Yes, as a young teenager, Chas had expressed some rather chauvinistic, narrow-minded views but that was not unusual for young guys in the 1970s. The role of women, and

CHAPTER 7

their acceptance as individuals, was certainly something that had been developing in recent years, and as Chas and Rosie's relationship had grown, so had a loving understanding between them. She believed what he said in the letter. He wanted to renew the relationship, but she wasn't sure she wanted to. She needed time to think it through. Rosie tucked the letter away in her pocket and returned to the staffroom.

After dinner that evening and at the end of a busy day, Rosie retrieved the all-important letter. In response, she decided to reply to Chas in a similar manner, by letter. She tried to lay the burden of sadness on him but before she had finished, she realised that there was much she had to delete. Her reply was only a few lines. If she posted it early, on the way to work, he would be sure to receive it by Friday

Dear Chas,
I believe you. I am considering your explanation. It is hard to erase Monday morning. It rocked me to consider that the man, the most important person in my life, was so thoughtless. Perhaps we can meet at the swimming pool coffee shop at 10.00am on Saturday?
Rosie.

If the nurse was definitely out of the picture, then she would agree to consider a reconciliation.

Chas routinely checked his mail from the letterbox. It wasn't until Friday that the rigid muscles of his face broke into a relaxed, wide grin. There was a letter from Rosie. At least she had replied. He raced to the garden seat on the patio and ripped open the envelope. It was short, almost note form, but he felt that her suggestion, that they meet at their favourite café at the swimming pool, seemed rather conciliatory. All he could think was, 'roll on Saturday morning'.

When Saturday morning came, it was a rather toned-down reunion, but both greeted each other with smiles. As they approached the counter to order, Rosie, with a soft voice, simply said, 'I've missed you Chas.' They found a table in a quiet spot near the window overlooking the park with its beautiful pink dogwoods in bloom.

Chas then merely touched on the calamity of the past weeks by saying, 'I'm sorry, Rosie. The last thing I want to do is make you unhappy. How about we sort of start off from when everything was hunky-dory?'

Rosie looked up at him, 'Chas, a lot has happened, I think we need to continue slowly.'

'Perhaps you're right Rosie, but it is always great to be with you, and it can only get better. Every time we do stuff together it works out well, let's remember that.'

With that, Rosie was not all that surprised when Chas began talking about the AgQuip Show, marked on the calendar for three days from Tuesday, August 24th to the Thursday.

The AgQuip days were certainly a highlight of the year for Gunnedah. Rosie presumed he was trying to carry out a more artful resumption of a normal conversation, but recognised the fervour in his voice when he started to tell her of a stunt that he and Barry were working on for the display.

CHAPTER 7

'Barry is very keen to throw himself into what we've planned as a rather deceptive little stunt. You will do the commentary for us, hey? You know, the ones that you have already done for me have been great, but this one is going to require a bit of preparation and there's only a week to go. How about we three get together tomorrow afternoon to give it some thought?'

He was hoping that Rosie would fortuitously pick up on the reference to her usual role at the air shows.

With a discreet smile, Rosie said, 'Oh, I may well have a job to do on the afternoon of Thursday week.'

A wave of disappointment spread across Chas's face. *So, she wasn't yet ready for them to work together again.*

'Oh, that is disappointing. I'll miss your presentation, as will the spectators.'

With a little giggle Rosie explained, 'Of course I'll come Chas. But I'll have to get permission to leave school a bit earlier, it's the commentary for your display that is the job I must do. Anyway, it is the end of the term so I shouldn't have any problems leaving at about 2.30 pm. I'll come with you tomorrow to see Barry and do the prep.'

'You little devil. You really know how to get to me, hey?'

The camaraderie between Barry and Chas had developed easily because of the time they spent together in the hangar. Chas had begun his preparations for the Gunnedah AgQuip Show some weeks before and, when Barry had become interested and questioned the possibility of a parachute drop being included in the display, that really started something rolling. Before long, they had put together a routine that, with the approval of the

AgQuip organisers, could encourage local people, and visitors who had to drive home on Thursday, to stay to see a couple of scheduled air events at the airport. The aerial show was planned to be a tremendous crowd pleaser.

After coffee with Rosie on Saturday, Chas spoke to Barry, and they set up Sunday afternoon at the airport to introduce her to the plan and presentation. Once all three were sitting at the office table in the hangar, the details unfolded. Rosie had to create the dialogue to fit in with the sequence but because of a fake emergency, they would also bring an official on to the microphone to create a sense of concern and realism. There was much excitement and a sense of fulfilment about the development of their ideas. To finish off their afternoon Chas went to get a couple of beers from the fridge for Barry and himself. 'What would you like Rosie?'

'Um, are there any cans of cider?'

'Yep, for sure.'

While Chas was busy, Barry put his hand out to touch Rosie's hand on the table and said, 'So pleased Rosie, that you and Chas have made up. He's been in a bad place for a few days.'

Rosie glanced across, caught Barry's eye, and whispered, 'Thanks Barry.'

Chas delivered each of the drinks and the conversation continued. It was a very satisfying meeting with all issues resolved.

The following Thursday afternoon was the last day of AgQuip. Rosie had been given the afternoon off and, as she and Chas

CHAPTER 7

roamed around the displays before the planned air show, they managed to catch up with several friends. Word of Chas's display at the airport later in the afternoon was already current news. The air show was to be held at a convenient time for visitors so they could enjoy the morning's activities and then see the flying event before heading off home to the surrounding regions. The well-advertised three air display events had created considerable interest so as Chas and Rosie went off to the airport to begin the preparation, Chas was pleased to find so many people who had remained to see the show. Flying gave him the utmost pleasure. It did not matter where, when, or how he flew, but he was happy once again. The announcer was broadcasting information about the ag-aircraft and then Chas's father flew the Cessna to give the crowd a thrill to see three parachutists land precisely in the drop zone at the end of the airstrip. Rosie then made her way to the trailer used for announcements.

After a few minutes and a notification from Chas, the announcer was ready to introduce Rosie.

'Good afternoon, everyone. We are now about to begin another very interesting part of our wonderful AgQuip Show day. First of all, let me introduce you to Rosie Franklin, who will tell us all about what is happening next.'

'Thank you, and good afternoon to all you kind people who have stayed around after the fantastic AgQuip Show to see the air display. I am sure you have heard that Chas Anderson, our local stunt man, is here to fly one of his amazing displays and he will be in the air very shortly. Of course, there are always checks and double checks to be made before take-off.'

Suddenly she could hear a loud commotion coming from the hangar at the end of the runway. Rosie ignored it following the cue of the planned sequence, and began making some regular announcements with the announcer, regarding the display. The appearance of Chas's Tiger was then to be seen coming from an unexpected direction and Rosie's voice reached a fever pitch.

'Oh my goodness, what is happening? Hello again everyone. I have just received information that a stranger is in Chas's aircraft. It has been stolen and has taken-off and is now in the air.'

The siren of a police car could be heard over the radio. Shouting loudly, people called out to others, and bunches of spectators rushed to a cleared area. The crowd grew rapidly along the fence.

The plane was flying in a rather unpredictable manner, which continued, as it climbed steeply. Rosie described the unsteady movements that changed in surprising ways, indicating the instability to the crowd. There was a steep turn and then another sideways movement in the opposite direction. In the meantime, the aircraft was climbing erratically with the nose moving up and down. Rosie then changed her tack, 'Where is Chas? The aircraft is not under control. Ladies and gentlemen be wary. I am now handing over to the official who will advise you.' One of the chief organisers then took over the microphone as had been planned by Chas, and in an official manner, continued to report on the incident until he handed it back to Rosie. While controlling her own excitement, Rosie presented an account of the manoeuvres until the aircraft began to fly away from the gathering crowd and gained more height at a slow rate. The official then indicated he wanted to speak again so Rosie handed him the microphone. He was continuing to explain the possible outcome with some rather nonchalant comments, when a woman came up behind him and jabbed his backside with an umbrella. 'How can you be so offhand when that man up there is in so much danger and so are we?'

The crowd then gasped in unison as the plane turned upside down and a body fell out. A parachute opened and the crowd could see a police car rush to the drop point. While descending, the plane continued to fly erratically and was headed for a tree-covered hill. The official brought some urgency to the broadcast, and everyone was now watching the aircraft. Rosie, standing close to the spectators, overheard the words of two distressed women standing in front of her. As one of them held tightly to the other, she heard, 'Oh, but it's out of control. There's no pilot. It's going to crash. How can it land safely?' The other woman, seemingly a little less anxious, replied, 'Don't worry dear, it's all radio controlled.'

The next shock was the boom of a distant explosion and to all intent, the spirals of smoke, above the trees, indicated that the aircraft had crashed. There were screams and shouts from the spectators and then the official delivered words to conclude what had been a most effective and enthralling act. He then handed the microphone back to Rosie. 'Ladies and gentlemen, please do not be concerned. If you look to the east, you will see the aircraft flying straight and level. Our renowned pilot, Chas, is now preparing to land here, on the runway. He and his parachutist, Barry Hammond, have just completed an amazing stunt and both are safe.'

Within a few minutes, the aircraft flew low over the AgQuip ground and landed, to taxi quickly past the crowds. It then stopped briefly at the far end of the runway to pick up the parachutist before it slowly moved back in front of the spectators. Barry sat high in the front seat and, together with Chas, they both waved heartily to the crowds. The general feeling hanging over the mass of people, although it could have been sensed as shock and horror, was one of great enjoyment instilled by the thrill of the event.

Word spread throughout the region of the outlandish stunt that Chas and Barry had performed and each Saturday afternoon the hangar was a popular place to hang out. Barry would give some general parachuting instruction and then work with individuals to concentrate on their particular needs. Lisa was often there, and attempted, although somewhat reluctantly, most exercises that Barry gave her. For those about to take to the air, Chas would remind them of their exit procedure. Jim, already an ardent jumper along with Steve Jennings, Lisa's brother, never missed a day. A teaching colleague of Rosie's, Jeff Dane, and her brother John occasionally added to the numbers, and all were keen to give it a go. The Parachute Club had become a social set-up for Gunnedah with its dinner nights and weekends away.

Feeling very happy and satisfied with his first months in Gunnedah, Barry was convinced that his decision to actually settle in the place had been a good one. He had only ever been to the town once before, years earlier, in 1972 when the family was travelling north on the inland highway to Brisbane. On that occasion, his mother had mentioned something about her father, Wally Hammond, emigrating from England with his friend, Jack Franklin, and settling on the Liverpool Plains. Barry had heard of the Liverpool Plains, but their location and productivity had never been of any interest to him. Now, ten years later, he wanted to satisfy his curiosity and unravel his grandparents' story. He was aware that Rosie was a Franklin, but did not wish to approach her yet about the Franklin-Hammond relationship.

In 1978, Barry's father, Ken Moyle, had a fatal car accident while on one of his exhausting trips, out of Ballarat, as an agricultural agent. There was only one surviving relative on his father's side that could be contacted and that was Ken's sister, Betty. They had visited her some years earlier when his father drove to Queensland via the Liverpool Plains. His unmarried aunt, who was sixty-eight years old, still lived in Brisbane. When Barry's mother, Kate, contacted her and gave her the sad news of the death of her brother, Betty made her way to Ballarat to spend time with the family. Aunt Betty was a godsend for Barry, who as a twenty-two-year-old, was shaken badly by the loss of his father. She had always had a strong interest in history and, on many an evening, during her stay in Ballarat, she told some more remarkable stories of the Hammond family history and the war years. She had kept much of it to herself as the extended family had never seemed at all interested.

Barry's arrival in Gunnedah was the beginning of a wild new experience for him. His Uncle Bob had already touched his life and provided the motivation to make a career in aviation engineering. Meeting and befriending Chas Anderson topped it off. Gunnedah became even more important when he realised that Rosie Franklin and he had such close historical ties.

Barry felt a desperate need to get to the roots of his family's story. He was prepared to accept the fact that his grandmother and mother had never felt any attraction to farming and that his father, Ken, enjoyed being associated with the business of agricultural machinery but not farming, and that even he, Barry Moyle, had no desire to be a farmer. *However, was there some heritage that am missing out on?* That's when he planned to visit the Liverpool Plains and see for himself.

CHAPTER 8

The air show following the AgQuip Show had been an overwhelming success. It was certainly putting the Gunnedah Parachuting Club right out there. The day after the show was the first day of the third term school holiday break and Rosie imagined the two weeks ahead would be very busy. She had some Gym Club commitments as well as preparation for upcoming swimming events. Ending the week with Rosie by his side and his friendship with Barry strong and innovative, gave Chas a sense of fulfilment that provided steps to achieve his greatest dreams of love and flying. Chas did feel his life was returning to what he liked to think of as normal and that he and Rosie would resume the pattern of their lives. However, he knew that the immediate future had to also encompass the requirements of his father's business.

On Monday morning, knowing Rosie was on holidays, Chas decided to invite her over for a meal during the week. Although she had not been to Chas's for dinner very often, on the occasions she had, they had shared a tasty take-away. Chas therefore decided it was time that he convinced her that he did have some culinary ability. As he dialled her number, he was hoping Rosie would pick up the phone.

'Hello, Rosie here.'

With a soft sigh of relief, Chas replied, 'G'day gorgeous girl, you're on holidays, hey? Do you need a healthy, appetising meal, maybe on Wednesday night?'

'Oh Chas, hi, yes, that would be nice. What do you have in mind?'

'Well, I'd like to show you what I can do at a kitchen bench. Would you like to drop over around five?'

'That sounds a nice idea, for sure. Am I allowed to know what is on the menu?'

'Listen Sweetie, if I don't know your favourite food by now, then I have not been a very observant swain. It'll be a surprise, okay?'

'Okay, that'll be great. Thanks Chasie. See you then.'

Well, Chas thought, *that went well, particularly as she hasn't called me 'Chasie' for weeks.*

It was a balmy evening on Wednesday, so Rosie planned to wear a dress she had bought a few weeks earlier that would be ideal for the casual occasion. It was in the new bohemian style that allowed her to sit in a relaxed and easy manner, while looking rather avant-garde. When Rosie arrived, Chas couldn't take his eyes off her. He invited her in and the blue floaty fabric of her dress wafted gracefully around her as she moved towards him and pecked him on the cheek.

CHAPTER 8

Taking her arm, he led her to the kitchen and before asking her to sit at the kitchen bench, his arm slipped from hers and moved around her slender waist. She turned to face him and was a responsive willing partner in the warm embrace. As their lips met, Chas could feel her body tremble, and Rosie, feeling his eager manliness against her, stepped back to eye him coquettishly. Attempting to keep her quavering voice under control, she suggested, 'Chasie, maybe I need to be tempted by your cooking before we get too involved.'

Chas beckoned her to sit on the stool at the kitchen bench. 'Rosie love, sit here while I just finish off a few things and then we'll find a more romantic spot to eat.' As he placed a glass of Chablis in her hand, Rosie's eyes widened in pleasant surprise. Chas wasn't sure if it was because the wine was her favourite or if it was that he used the word 'romantic'. While he dished up his chicken cordon bleu, Rosie couldn't resist commenting, 'So, who is it locally that cooks up delicious chicken cordon bleu and makes such a beautiful dish available for take-away, Chas?'

With a quick glance across to Rosie, he caught her eye and then said, 'Yes, I am available to make it for take-away.'

Chas had decided they would eat al fresco at the small round table for two under the pergola. By leaving the loungeroom window open, the music from his record player would softly drift through the doorway. The evening was off to a good start. It was so pleasant sitting under the pergola and talking non-stop. There were a few general comments about life in Gunnedah and AgQuip, and then an excited conversation about future plans.

Rosie relished the meal. 'Well done, Mr Pilot-come-chef, that was my favourite dish – chicken cordon bleu with the best Dijon mustard, cooked to perfection.'

'So glad you enjoyed it Rosie, but I'm afraid dessert is simply an ice-cream on a stick. Would you like chocolate or vanilla?'

'Oh, vanilla thanks. It has been a delicious meal, Chas. It was a lovely idea for you to invite me over.'

Chas suggested they sit on the casual sofa and listen to the music. Rosie took a guess and said, 'Would that be Simon and Garfunkel?'

With a hearty laugh, Chas replied, 'Sweetie, we've built the bridge, let's consider the future. I now have another surprise, Neil Diamond's album, *Jonathan Livingston Seagull*. I haven't played it all through yet but when I heard a couple of the songs on the radio, I figured I had to have the LP.'

'Oooh, why Chas?'

'Well, after a bit of research I found out that the original story, by Richard Bach, is based on the belief that living an adventurous life can give you a great sense of freedom, and I thought that applied to us.' Chas went inside to set up the player and once it started, he returned to the sofa and took Rosie in his arms. They spent the next hour within the grasp of the music and lyrics. The first track certainly set the mood and then, as Rosie explained, with the words and Diamond's melodic voice, she felt completely under a spell. Chas's gentle touches were like a charm that elevated her to a level of romance she had not experienced before. *Oh my God*, she thought, *If this is love, I've got it.*

'Just what did you think that record would do, Chas?'

'Well, do you still want to do a 'Jonathan' using my wings?'

CHAPTER 8

After the quick reference to wing walking, Rosie began to get ready to leave, with a promise to think over her aspiration to wing walk. 'I must do a load of research Chasie boy.' She went on to explain. 'My vision of the exploit has to match the actual experience. I feel that it must be a mindset not just an exercise. Give me time, Chas. I need time to think about it.'

Having observed Rosie on countless occasions doing her balance beam and floor routines, he understood that she had to be totally absorbed by the activity, with a complete disregard for the surroundings. Recalling her last regional competition earlier in the New Year when he had watched her compete, he knew exactly what she meant.

'Gee ... I'm not sure I want to drive home after such a delightful evening.'

With some concern, Chas asked, 'You sure you're not too tired? You could spend the night here.'

'I'm sure, I'll be fine. Thanks for such a lovely time, Chasie.'

Chas moved closer and as he took Rosie into his arms, she stretched her arms gently to hold his face as they kissed. After a long look into each other's eyes, they kissed again before saying, 'Goodnight'.

As she drove home, Rosie could not get the music, or Neil Diamond's voice of the *Jonathan Livingston Seagull* songs, out of her head and it was all tied up with Chas's loving moves earlier in the evening. It seemed all so enchanting. She rolled down the window and in the dark night she could feel the air rush past her as she imagined herself standing on the top wing of the Tiger Moth, just above Chas in the cockpit.

On Thursday morning, Rosie looked out over the paddocks as she was driving into town. They were swamped in the green shoots of the springtime wheat crops. It was true, the countryside, the great open spaces, beckoned her to venture forth and achieve a dream. She planned to check out the community library and then, if that could not satisfy her appetite for accounts of aerial adventures, she would telephone Ben, a friend who lived in Sydney, whom she knew to be absolutely remarkable in digging up rare information.

Chas also was going to find out what he could about the requirements for wing walking. He knew that Rosie was quite passionate about the prospect and, as there had been developments in wing walking since the 1920s, he knew there would be many ideas and actual reports to read about.

CHAPTER 9

The calm, sunny spring days, which were becoming more frequent after the unreliable winter months, had the parachute enthusiasts at the airport every Saturday afternoon. Rosie had spent the morning with her gym club girls and was preparing to set off to meet Chas in the hangar before the jumps began. She was taken by complete surprise when Carly suddenly appeared.

'Rosie, sorry I didn't make it to gym today, but I knew I'd catch you here with the girls and I wanted to ask a favour of you. I'd like to check out all this parachute stuff. I heard from Jeff that there's a new instructor out at the airport. Would you be able to introduce me?'

'Wow, Carly, of course, but you don't really want to climb out of an aeroplane that is up in the sky, do you?'

'Well, I just thought it could give me a new perspective for some of my artwork. I mean, seeing the surface of the earth from a few thousand feet up above could give me not only a different view of things but also a rather 'out-of-there' feeling. You've done loads of flying with Chas, so what do you think?'

'Ha ha! Sitting in the plane with a pilot that is so in control and then gazing out onto the beautiful landscape is not quite the same as trusting a white sheet over your head.'

'Awe, c'mon. Anyway, I want to go and check things out.' The two young women then headed off for the airport.

Barry, in his role of instructor, was very popular. His research was telling him that the conventional method of the style and accuracy approach to jumping was losing favour to that of freestyle. Also, the fact that women around the country were being encouraged to participate in the sport meant it was all getting quite exciting.

He was pleased to see Rosie arrive early. 'Hi Rosie, good to see you.'

'Hi Barry, yes, this is Carly Kent. She's an art teacher at school but more importantly a friend of mine. She's just going to watch today but who knows, you may have another learner.'

With that, Rosie left the two of them and went to find Chas. Barry explained some of the preparations required for the day to Carly and then told her that Lisa Jennings was his only other female student. He then suggested she have a chat to a few of the jumpers as they arrived. Barry did not suggest for her to have a meeting with Lisa, although of course, they did know each other. Lisa had a marked lack of enthusiasm for jumping, which was counteracted by her eagerness to climb into the aircraft with Chas, and Barry did not need her relating any negativity about the jumping experience. He also knew of the rancour that Lisa and Rosie held for each other.

Chas was doing his flight check and his face lit up when he spotted Rosie. 'Hey, good to see you. Jumping today?'

'Oh, Chas, you know the answer to that, but Carly my workmate, is thinking about joining Barry's group.'

'That's a surprise, but I'd really like to get you down here on a regular basis now that summer is coming. Have you given the wing walking anymore consideration?'

Rosie lifted her eyebrows and closed her lips in a suppressed smile. 'Of course, Chasie. Let's have a talk about that later.'

'Actually yes, I agree. This is not the place. I really don't want anyone to know we're even considering the idea, so do keep it to yourself for the time being. Okay?'

When Chas finished his prep, Rosie went back to the group and saw a very animated Carly in a deep discussion with Jeff Dane, also a teacher, who had been jumping for a while. Jeff was a geography teacher and the local football coach, so Rosie was wondering what could be keeping them so engrossed since Carly was an artist and passionate about painting and sculpture. Anyway, she said 'G'bye' to them both, and set off for home.

That evening, on their regular Saturday night dinner date, Chas decided to broach a couple of sensitive subjects with Rosie. 'You know all this talk about wing walking? As I said today, we should proceed with caution.'

'I agree, but why do you say that, Chas?'

Chas continued with some circumspection. 'Well, you know it's not actually legal. I figure that we can do all the basic planning and then get a couple of trustworthy mechanics on-side to handle the strapping, etcetera, before we approach the Air Transport Bureau.'

Rosie seemed alarmed, 'What do you mean 'not actually legal'?'

Although hesitant, Chas replied, 'Er well, after the accidents in the US, the Aussies have reacted rather strongly. Anyway, I reckon we can sidle around it all. You know it would be much easier if we moved in together and then we could have our little get-togethers without any fuss.'

'As much as I would love to be up close and personal Chas, that is not something we should do just yet.'

'Yep, I understand Sweetie.'

'However, I do want to read up a bit more on what wing walkers have been doing in the States. Ben, my research associate in Sydney, has found that it has been predominately women who have got out on the wings. He told me a funny story about Jessie Woods, a woman who has really done lots in aviation. She had nothing to do with wing walking but carried out a sort of a crazy stunt like yours. Apparently, she and other pilots would use animals in their air shows. Someone would go out and find a stray cat before the show and then they would strap it up with a little parachute and drop it from a plane. When it landed, it was picked up and then offered to a lucky person in the crowd who could give it a good home. One day they had a big strong tom cat that was dropped with an orange parachute. When it landed it didn't wait to be picked up, it just went helter-skelter over the airfield with the chute flying out behind him. I hope he found someone to love him.'

CHAPTER 9

Chas let out a laugh and said, 'Well, that is a bit different.'

'That's for sure, but although it's an original idea I can't say that I like it, the poor cats must have been terrified. But have you heard about Martin Caidin?'

With his hand on his chin, Chas slowly replied, 'Yep, that name is familiar. Isn't he some American aviation enthusiast?'

'Well, yes he is, and I have some notes about him.' Rosie scrambled around searching her bag for a moment and, holding a crumpled page, continued. 'He's famous for the story *Marooned*, which is about an American astronaut who is stranded in space and it was made into a movie in 1969 starring Gregory Peck. He also has written lots of aviation stories about World War II and is regarded as, and I quote, 'an authority on aeronautics and aviation'. Also, I found out that on November 14th last year, he was pilot-in-command when he organised nineteen people to walk on the wing of his fully restored, and oldest surviving Junkers 52 aircraft called Iron Annie. I wouldn't have a clue what sort of aircraft that would be, but it must have been a big one. Surely Australia can keep up with America?'

'That's really interesting for sure, but listen Rosie love, you and your friend are coming up with some brilliant research, but how about concentrating on equipment and technique, then you decide what you want to try, and we'll sort out what we can get away with, safely.'

With wide eyes, Rosie said, 'Chas, are you for real? I'll delve a bit deeper and once I know exactly what I would like to try then I'll hand it over to you. I gotta go. G'night Chasie.'

After an extended sleep-in the next morning, Rosie got up

to have a quick breakfast. She just needed a bowl of muesli, a cup of coffee, and a quiet spot in the tiny study she had been allotted to use for her daily class preparations. As she left the kitchen, her father was right behind her

'G'mornin' sweetheart, can I have a word?'

'For sure Dad, what is it?'

'You would have met Barry Moyle, I'd say.'

Rosie instantly stopped and turned to face her father. 'For sure Dad, that's all it's been I'm afraid. I don't know much about him.'

'C'mon, he virtually lives at the airport I'm told, and you are always there to see Chas.'

'Okay, what do you want to know?'

'Rosie, he's contacted me, wanting to visit and have a chat. I know he's a mate of Chas's and that he arrived in town earlier this year, but why would he want to see me?'

'All I know, is that he came here from Ballarat for a visit and to look into his family history. Apparently his grandparents settled here somewhere at the beginning of the century. When he mentioned that he was an aviation mechanic, Phil couldn't get him into the hangar fast enough. Chas got to speak to him ages ago and it turns out he's also a parachute instructor, so he's kept pretty busy with the club.'

'So, it's nothing to do with you?'

'Oh my goodness Dad, are you for real? Do you think there's something between me and him? No way, that's for sure.'

Ted gave a sigh of relief. 'Oh, okay then. I did hear you telling your mum that you met him and talked about doing some parachuting a while back.'

'Oh yes, a couple of weeks ago. I thought I might give it a go. It was just a short enquiry for information, Dad.'

'Alright, all good, but we'll see what he has to say this afternoon.'

Knowing she had only one week of holidays left, Rosie made her way to her desk and began organising some books before getting started on preparing her programme for the term ahead. She was certainly rather curious about the expected visit from Barry.

Ted had an office that he had used constantly since his two older children left home. When they amalgamated their farm with Wally Hammond's way back in the early 1960s, Wally's house needed a great deal of renovation, so Ted and Mary worked on it slowly over the years. When John married Sally in 1972, Ted suggested that they should move into Wally's small, updated colonial house. John had taken over a lot of the physical activity on the farm and Sally cooked the most delicious meals when Ted and Mary were invited for dinner. Although Ted liked the outdoor activities, he spent much of his time on accounting and administration. He also handled the vegetable garden so there were always fresh vegetables available. Why a newcomer to town would want to visit him, Ted had no idea. Although when Rosie mentioned that he was researching family history it did sound interesting, but he would just have to wait until 2 pm.

CHAPTER 10

Mary answered the doorbell. She knew it would be Barry Moyle as John had told her that he had arranged a time for Barry to meet with his father a few days earlier. One Saturday afternoon, not long after Barry had arrived in Gunnedah, he had questioned John Franklin as to whether his grandfather, Ted's father, was Jack Franklin. John confirmed this but Barry didn't follow with any further questions. John was just left thinking that the fellow had an interest in local history. Soon after, Barry asked John if he could arrange a meeting for him with Ted. Mary was expecting the visitor and greeted the tall, muscled man at the door, 'Hello, you must be Barry. I'm Mary, Ted's wife.'

The visitor extended his hand and said, 'Yes, I'm Barry. Pleased to meet you, Mary. I'm here to see Ted. Is he okay?'

Mary replied with a chuckle, 'Oh yes, as long as he is not in the paddocks, these days Ted is up for anything. Come in and I'll take you to his office.'

CHAPTER 10

The twenty-six-year-old Barry instantly became a little circumspect and felt rather awkward. When his father died in 1978, Barry became the only remaining male in the line of Wally Hammond's descendants. He knew that Jack and Wally had been great friends and today was the day he hoped to find out if he had missed out on something.

As Ted heard the footsteps coming down the hall, he opened his office door and, with a lively bellow, called out, 'G'day, so you're Barry Moyle. Ted Franklin. Come and sit down.'

'It's nice to meet you Mr Franklin.' With a quick handshake, Barry settled into the chair offered to him.

'Nah, nah, make that Ted.'

Mary nodded and the two men closed the door after she left the room.

'So, to what do I owe this pleasure? I believe you're a keen parachute enthusiast.'

'Well, yes that's so Ted, but I'm not here to get you into the air, I believe we may have some ties from further back down the years.'

'Really, how so?'

'I believe your father, Jack Franklin, and my grandfather, Wally Hammond were great mates.'

Ted's jaw dropped. 'What? That's amazing. How did ya know that?'

'Well, my Aunt Betty knew your sisters, Dorothy and Sarah, when they were all little kids living here in Gunnedah. You might remember her?'

'My goodness, yes, I do. She was a few years younger than me, and I do remember Kate and Bob. Bob was like a big brother to me when I was a little kid. He was a WWII hero, wasn't he?' Ted's mind was flashing back to his childhood days and memories of kid pranks. 'This is quite amazing that you've been able to trace the connections here to Gunnedah because you're from Ballarat. Isn't that so?'

'Yes, I was born there. My grandmother, Fran Hammond, left Gunnedah in the 1920s, my mother Kate, married Ken Moyle. I know about my Uncle Bob who died in 1942 and Aunt Betty, who, after travelling around Queensland for years as an outback nurse, settled in Brisbane. My father, Ken had taken us to visit her once or twice when I was a teenager, but it wasn't until my father was killed in a car accident in 1978 that we became a lot closer as a family. Aunt Betty, as I call her, has a passion for history and, as far as family history goes, we have her to thank for all the stories she has uncovered, some go back a hundred years.'

'Barry, that is truly astounding. Yes, your grandfather Wally, and my father Jack, were the best of mates and were Pommy settlers in this wide brown land. I know they were very young when they left England and that they both had a landed-gentry heritage. Oh well, maybe not 'gentry' but a farming heritage. At least their families gave them a pocket full of cash to set themselves up here.'

'Yep, I heard that too. I was hoping that you could tell me where I could find the Hammond farm.'

'Well at the time of your grandfather's death, Barry, your grandmother left the farm for a town life. Fran, your grandmother, hated farm life. I remember my father saying how she was a big town girl and couldn't wait to get out of the isolation of rural life. But Wally was accidentally killed just before she left Gunnedah. All we knew was that she had gone to the state of Victoria and didn't want any more contact with anyone around here.

'He and my father got on really well, and because their farms were next to each other, they shared the workload on both the farms. Apparently Wally often got depressed, and his health just continued to decline over the years, so because the property was just next door, it was easy for my dad to help him quite often. On the morning of his death, Dad went over to help him chop down some trees and he and Fran found him dead in a paddock he was clearing. Apparently he was killed by a falling tree while cutting some trees down by himself.'

Barry asked to know more about the change of ownership. 'Aunt Betty told me that Wally had left the property to your father in his will.'

'That's right Barry. It was certainly something that took us quite by surprise at that time.'

Barry did not quite know how to respond to the information. He was pleased that he now knew where the property was, but he also felt despondent that what could have been his, now belonged to someone else. Ted watched Barry's face and noted the change of expression. His eyes opened wide, and his hand went from holding fingers to his cheek and chin to being spread to cover an open mouth, as the words, 'Okay, so you actually own my grandad's farm now?' came spluttering out.

Ted continued, 'Barry, my father had no idea that his best friend had arranged to leave his farm to the Franklin family. We knew nothing about Wally's intentions, only that he was very upset when his marriage floundered, so my dad apparently just kept the property maintained until a few months after his death, thinking that because he could not get in touch with Fran that she would contact him. Even her parents made no effort to find out what was going on. When my mum and dad were notified and shown his will, they were very surprised, but Jack did arrange for a considerate amount to be paid to Fran as a token of respect.'

Ted could see an admonishing look on Barry's face. 'Hey c'mon lad, it was all done legally. You can check out the paperwork. I'll give you the name of the legal company in Tamworth.'

After a few more comments about the hard times on the land during the Great Depression and WWII, the two men drew the conversation to a close. As he stood up to leave, Barry offered an apology. 'Look I'm sorry Ted, but it's hit me a bit. But thanks for the info. If you don't mind giving me the name of the legal guys in Tamworth, I would like to check it all out.'

Ted stood up and offered his hand. 'Sure Barry, here's my number. Give me a call in a few days, and in the meantime, I'll check and update any info I can. I understand it's all a bit of a shock for you but go ahead, follow it through and come and see us again. Maybe you could give John a call. I'm sure he'd show you around the place if you want.'

After Rosie heard her mother and father take Barry down the hall to the front door and say 'goodbye' in rather formal

CHAPTER 10

tones, she made her way to the kitchen and put on the kettle. As her parents entered the room she asked rather nonchalantly, 'You ready for a cuppa?' With their agreement, and each with a cup in their hands, the three of them moved out to the back veranda. Mary was the first one to make a comment, 'He left rather brusquely, Ted, I thought you'd ask him to stay for a cuppa?'

'Yep, I think he heard more than what he wanted to hear.'

'What do you mean? What do you think that was Dad? Tell us what you talked about.' Rosie was curious that Barry should have unnerved her rather calm and gentle father so much.

As Ted's conversation with Barry over the past half hour unfolded, both Mary and Rosie listened without interrupting. All three reacted with a sense of disbelief that another family story could become so much a part of their own. Ted wanted to assume that once Barry had come to terms with the situation he would return, and they would resume the conversation.

Hesitantly, Rosie asked, 'Dad, do you really think you should drag John into this?'

Ted replied with a sense of exasperation, 'They'll work it out.'

CHAPTER 11

Barry called around to see Chas after his meeting with Ted Franklin and poured out the story of his grandparents that he had learned from Ted. Chas listened closely. Wally Hammond was remembered as an early settler in the district and Chas knew there had been a connection to the Franklins, but the details of the families from a couple of generations past was news to him. 'So, you realise Ted Franklin is Rosie's dad?'

'Oh, for sure, he's a nice guy, but oh boy, it took me by surprise when he told me that he now has my grandfather's property.'

'How's that?' Barry went on to fill Chas in on the details. He was certainly considering the circumstances in a more rational vein and explained that he did want to follow up on the legality of it all.

Chas nodded. 'Good onya mate. I'd say it's all above board. The Franklins are a great family, and they'd probably welcome you around anytime to fill you in with more of the story.'

Chas was juggling the extra workload supporting his father

and the crop dusting at this busy time. A great deal of preparation always had to be carried out early in the season to ensure all equipment was operating correctly. Spray nozzles on the aircraft required particular attention because of their importance to distribute the spray evenly onto the crops. All pumps and containers needed to be checked for leaks, and washers ordered as spares to minimise any downtime. During the average season there was a need to control insects, diseases and weeds, and the right amount of chemical had to be considered along with seasonal timing and planning. A good plan was essential to ensure the chemicals were used safely and responsibly. Also, if there were considerable savings, not only financially, but in the amount of chemical use, it raised the reputation of the company. From the beginning of September, his father began to timetable his son into the contracts and Chas was then able to get an agreement from his boss at the servo for changes in his weekly commitment.

Early on Monday morning, as he was about to leave for work, Chas got a phone call. It was his father. 'Hi Dad, what's up?'

'G'day son? You want a job?'

'Yeh sure, I'm available. What have ya got for me?'

'Well, a new customer has come out of the woodwork and wants a quick dust on a crop of five hundred and fifty hectares, which should be about four to five hours work to keep you going for an afternoon. He wants it done as soon as possible and I just don't have the time. Could you check him out? The Grumman will be available from Friday if that suits him.'

It lifted Chas's spirits to be able to help his father so, after getting the name and number of the farmer, and the location of the property, he immediately followed up with a phone call. There was a gruff voice at the other end. 'Hello?'

'Hi there, would that be Tom Groves? This is Chas Anderson. I'm the pilot who will be doing your dusting for you.'

The gravelly voice replied, 'Oh Chas, good onya. Can ya make a start as soon as possible?'

'Okay Tom, sure, the aircraft will be available Friday afternoon. Tell me the layout of your paddock. I know it's location but what about fences and power lines?'

Tom Groves continued while Chas made notes. 'There are fences around the entire paddock of five hundred and fifty hectares and power lines running down the southern and western sides. Okay?'

'Yeh, got that, anything else?' Chas was quite satisfied with the information and knew that his father had already discussed the spray requirements.

'No, that's it, Chas. Give me a bell when you're about to head out this way on Friday. Thanks.'

Chas had already got a clearance from his servo boss to take a couple of days off and turned up at the hangar at 8.30 am on Thursday morning to prep the aircraft for the job at Tom Groves'. Barry and Phil were already there. Barry had volunteered, for a price, to be the marker on the crop to make each run more accurate. After a thorough briefing, Barry left the hangar to drive out to the farm with the instruction to call Groves and tell him that he was on the way and that Chas would be there a little before the first run at 1.00 pm to check the layout of the property from the air, as Tom had described it.

CHAPTER 11

Phil and Chas had a quick chat in the hangar over lunch and then Chas jumped into the Grumman and set off to taxi down the runway. Once airborne, his mind was in gear for what was ahead. The beautiful still day was ideal, and he played the planned sequence over in his head. As he approached the property, he did a circuit to check the crop, neighbouring trees, and power lines before he spotted Barry in his white overalls. The overalls stood out like a beacon amidst the green of the young crop.

A quick plan for following the crop strip included a check of the power lines and an allowance was made for the effect of wind drift on the spray. Then Chas dived in for the first run. After several runs, he was approaching the far edge of the crop, when there was an horrific jolt and he felt it. The aircraft lurched and began a roll to the left. He got no response from punching the stick to the right, so with right rudder he stopped the roll. *Shit!*

Chas could smell smoke and heard worrying noises. There was no chance of climbing over the fence, so he accepted a crash, straight ahead onto the rough surface and the crop. With the throttle closed, he held off to brace for the inevitable crash. It came a second later; the wheels dug in; the aircraft jolted and, in another instant, threw itself forward onto its back.

Amid the noise and violence of the final second, Chas had a ridiculous thought. *The crop is dry., I might burn, but I won't drown!*

It was not until about 3.00 pm that Chas was aware that something had happened.

As Barry watched the plane crash, he fumbled with his radio

to call Phil at the hangar. 'Phil, there's been a Grumman crash at Tom Groves' property. We need an ambulance ASAP.'

Barry then raced down the crop strip to the aircraft, hoping to rescue Chas before the wreckage burst into flames. Fortunately, there was no fire. The aircraft was mangled but the cockpit was secure. He could see that although Chas was not bleeding, he did not appear to be conscious. He began talking to him and then there was a very slow response as Chas lifted his head and Barry could see that he was breathing. With strength that he had no idea he possessed, Barry began moving the pieces of the wreck away, as well as earth that he knew would make it easier for Chas to be removed by the paramedics. Twenty minutes later, the ambulance was at the scene.

Barry experienced immediate relief when he heard the paramedic examining Chas say, 'His breathing's steady and he's conscious. There are a few bruises, but he'll get the attention he needs as soon as he is in emergency.'

Barry radioed Phil again, 'Phil, Chas should be okay. Contact his father. We'll see him at the hospital in about half an hour.' He then followed the ambulance to the hospital.

After the initial examination, Barry and Bill Anderson were allowed to sit at the bedside with the assurance that Chas was in good shape and resting. Within a few minutes Chas opened his eyes and immediately recognised his father.

'Oh Dad. Hi.'

'Gee son, so glad you've come through okay. How are ya feeling?'

Cautiously, Chas moved his arms and body, but with a few

CHAPTER 11

grunts. 'Oh, aches and pains, but I'll be fine.'

Bill suggested that as Chas was now communicating, they should contact Rosie before she left the school, rather than waiting until she got home, because she would then have to drive back into town.

'Yep, I'm onto it, Bill.'

Barry made his way to the information desk, where he requested the phone. On contacting the school, he asked to speak to Rosie Franklin as it was an emergency. The receptionist explained the last bell had rung and staff were heading home but she was sure Rosie was still around. Within a few minutes Barry recognised her voice.

'Hello, Rosie speaking.'

'Hi Rosie, Barry here.'

'Oh, hi Barry, what's up?'

'Listen Rosie, Chas is okay, but this afternoon there was an aircraft accident. He's in hospital and conscious. He'll ....'

'Oh Barry! Oh no, can I see him?'

'For sure Rosie, he'll be okay, but just get here as soon as you can.'

Rosie was in the car on her way to the hospital and at the reception desk within minutes.

'Please, I need to see Chas Anderson.'

'Yes ma'am. But who are you?'

Rosie quickly explained that she was a close friend and was then directed to Chas's room. The on-duty nurse opened the door for Rosie. As she approached the bed, Barry and Bill stood up and beckoned her to the bedside. Chas smiled as he recognised Rosie. 'Oh Rosie, it's great to see you.'

'Chasie darlin, whatever have you been doing? Oh, it so good to see your lovely eyes looking at me.'

'No worries. I've been a lucky boy. I'm okay, have just a bit of a daze and a few bruises and painful spots.'

As Chas slowly began to explain to Rosie what had happened, Bill and Barry looked at each other, said goodbye to Chas and left him alone with his sweetheart. They would return the next day to get more of Chas's story, but in the meantime they both wanted to return to the scene while it was still daylight.

Alone with her dear Chas, Rosie leaned forward to kiss him softly on the lips and said, 'Oh, Chas, I love you so. Please don't do such a thing ever again.' She then found his hand under the sheet and held it tightly.

In what seemed only a very short while, the on-duty nurse returned to ask Rosie if she would leave the patient to rest. Rosie smiled, kissed Chas gently and said, 'I'll be in to see you tomorrow, Chasie. Have a goodnight darlin'.'

Rosie left the room, saying to the nurse, 'Thank you for letting me see him even if it was just for a little while. He will be fine, won't he?'

The nurse looked at Rosie and said, 'You seem to know Chas quite well.'

'Yes, of course,' and with a little giggle, Rosie added, 'He is my boyfriend.'

With some surprise, the nurse replied, 'Oh, really? This afternoon, when I took over from Lisa Jennings, and Chas was knocked out with medication, she told me to take good care of him 'cos he was very special to her. She implied he's her boyfriend.' After raising an eyebrow, the nurse continued, 'Interesting.'

Rosie looked askance at the nurse, and without a word made her way to the exit and left.

As she drove home, the nurse's words kept coming back to here. *Whatever was that woman, Lisa, doing? Why was Chas special to her?* Rosie was convinced that it was Lisa doing all the pushing because after the previous Saturday night, she was assured of the loving bond that existed between her and her dear Chas. She brushed the angry thoughts aside and spent the rest of the drive thinking positively about how she could help Chas with his recovery.

Rosie called the hospital the following morning and was relieved to hear that Chas had had a restful night and that she could see him during the morning. She planned her Saturday while driving into town. She would make a quick visit to the hospital when she first arrived in town and then attend her gym club for a couple of hours. After lunch she'd see Chas again and then spend time at the library to do some wing-walk research before she set off for home. She guessed it would be a while before Chas would be taking off again to soar into the sky on his next adventure, but it could be a good time for them both to relax together.

CHAPTER 12

Lisa took care not to draw attention to herself as she pushed the Saturday morning breakfast trolley to Chas's room. She had persuaded the kitchen assistant to give the trolley to her with the excuse that she had to attend his bedside. Her heart missed a beat as she saw from the doorway that he was already awake.

'G'morning Chas,' she chortled as she twirled the trolley to drag it behind her. 'You are looking real good this morning,'

Chas was rather taken aback to see the flirty nurse making her way to his bedside. 'Hi Lisa, yep, I slept okay and my checks this morning came up just fine.'

'Oh, you will enjoy your breakfast then.'

'Yep, I'm hungry. Wow, eggs on toast, looks good.'

'Chas, do you remember what happened? There was no way we could communicate with you yesterday when you were admitted. If you want to talk about it, I'm all ears.' Lisa helped him sit up and placed his plate on the bed tray.

CHAPTER 12

'Lisa, I don't want to talk about yesterday. I want to eat my breakfast and think about today.'

'Of course, Chas, I will make sure that there is something tasty that I can bring you for morning tea and we'll see how you are feeling then.'

'Lisa, just cut back the pressure. You don't have to bring me anything.'

'Oh you poor man, you still sound like you are in shock. That is understandable and I will make sure you have a peaceful day.'

'Lisa thanks for the attention but just leave me alone please.'

Reluctantly, Lisa turned and left the room a little disgruntled, asking herself why he would be so grumpy but blaming the medication.

Before she headed off to the hospital, and knowing how much Chas loved the *Jonathan Livingston Seagull* record, Rosie decided to check out the local bookshop for the book written by Richard Bach. Tucked away on the top shelf she found it in the 'B' section of the fiction authors. As she browsed through and read the cover information, she realised it would be a good story for Chas to read while he was recuperating. Bach was a pilot and it seemed he used his own aviation experiences to illustrate stories and express his philosophy of overcoming physical limitations, as in *Jonathan Livingston Seagull*. With the book in her bag, she set off for the hospital to visit her dear love.

Chas was sitting up in bed reading the newspaper. 'Oh Rosie, sweetie, this is a lovely surprise.'

'This is no surprise, Chas. You knew I would be here as soon as I could. You do look bright and are you feeling pretty good?'

'Yep, really good. I've just had a long chat with Barry and Dad about the prang. It seems I connected with some bloody power lines that old Tom did not tell me about. When they questioned him, he told them that he hadn't mentioned them to me because they aren't used for anything anymore.

'Oh really! So will there be an investigation?'

'Nope, probably not 'cos it's my fault, but due to the lack of information I was given, I can't be held responsible.'

'Have you got a good doctor? Has he said how long they'll be keeping you here?'

'Dr Johnson seems a great guy and always listens to what I have to say. It seems that the concussion is what they're worried about, so I'll probably have two or three days in bed here with doctor check-ups and then just rest at home for a while. I'm going to miss you.'

'Well, I am on holidays for another week, so I'd say we'll have lots of time to talk about walking in the clouds.'

As she dragged the book from her bag, Rosie said, 'I've something here for you that I am sure will keep you totally absorbed.'

Chas was truly delighted with the book. As he flicked through the pages, tossing some of his own memories around, he said, 'When I've finished this it will be time to go home.'

After further chitchat, Rosie knew it was time for her to leave. Reluctantly she picked up her bag. 'Well, I'm off to the library when I leave here. My friend in Sydney has suggested some areas that might help with my wing walk research. Apparently quite a bit has been happening in the US even though there are still restrictions.'

'Yep, I believe they have established a requirement that any stunts have to be on the upper wing section because there have been more accidents resulting from stunts on the bottom wing of a bi-plane. So that's something to check out.'

'Will do, Chas darlin',' she cooed as she kissed him.

He stroked her cheek and whispered, 'Love you, Sweetie.'

Rosie smiled to herself as she made her way along the hallway, then suddenly stopped as an officious-looking Lisa passed her and grinned as she said, 'I'm just about to check on Chas, see you.'

As Rosie made her way to the carpark, she certainly realised that she had a sense of foreboding with the manner of the flirty nurse, but she knew that she had no cause to fear any approaches Lisa would make to Chas. He was her love and unwaveringly she knew she was his.

The gymnastic session went very well, and she was pleased to have such enthusiastic participants, particularly as their talents kept her motivated to continue her own progress. Carly was always there, willing to take over a mentoring role. While sharing a takeaway lunch with her friend, and giving her an update on Chas's progress, Rosie explained that she was always busy and how she was always looking for extra time to share with Chas. It was her excuse to cut lunch short and make her way to the library. With her head down and her mind transported, the hours passed quickly before she realised the visiting hours at the hospital were nearly over. She managed to get to Chas's bed for a half hour visit and was able to give him a rundown on her research before the time was up. Feeling a little guilty, Rosie kissed him goodbye and said, 'I promise tomorrow will be an easier day Chasie, and I'll be spending more time with you.'

'Anytime I'm with you passes too quickly, Sweetie.'

As she parked the car for a short stopover at the supermarket, Rosie spotted Barry parking a few spaces away. She waved to him and as he stepped from the car, he called out to her, 'Hi Rosie, I was hoping to catch up with you.'

'G'day Barry, good to see you.'

'Yep, you too. I saw Chas earlier. How about we have a quick coffee?'

'Yes, that'd be nice, I've actually just been to the hospital.'

They walked quickly down the path to the café and found a spare table inside. Barry started asking questions straight away. 'I've been wondering how you've been coping?'

'Oh, I'm fine, particularly now that Chas is chatty and not showing any distress. You saw it all unfold Barry, which must have been devastating for you?'

'Yep, I – I – I just couldn't believe what I was watching. He was a lucky guy to make it out as well as he did.'

'Oh, that's for sure. He'll thank you forever for getting to him so soon.'

'D'ya know how long they're going to keep him in hospital?'

'Apparently only a few days but I don't think he'll be flying for a while.'

Barry chuckled as he replied, 'Awe, okay, I guess I'd better cancel jumps for a few weeks.'

CHAPTER 12

'Hahaha, I'd be a little careful about giving a time for restart. I reckon Chas will be out to the airfield sooner than you think.'

With a wide grin, Barry sat back in his chair and nodded his head. 'Yeah, if a pilot's had a crash, it means we must be wary. By the way, I had a great chat with your dad the other day. It seems that my grandfather actually willed his property to your grandfather.'

'Oh heck, I do recall hearing something about the relationship between our grandfathers. I hope it doesn't make you feel too bad. John works that property most of the time.'

'I don't feel bad. It's the way of life. Things happen for various reasons, and you just have to make the best of it.' Barry raised his eyebrows and hesitated before asking another question. 'Rosie, do you think John would show me over the place and tell me a bit about its history?'

'I'm not sure. I'll check it out and get John to give you a call.'

The coffee time went well, and Rosie was pleased to have Barry ask a few questions about her airborne aspirations, including the possibility of taking a parachute jump, however, she was careful not to divulge any wing-walking information.

Being holiday time and having no work restrictions, Rosie was able to visit the hospital each day. She preferred the morning sessions as they seemed longer, and Chas seemed brighter. With Chas out of action, the weekend parachute drops were on hold for the next couple of weeks. The accident was news about town so apart from a few of the jumpers calling up Barry, it was a foregone conclusion that the club would not be undertaking any activities until further notice. The opportunity to have some free time at the weekend gave Barry the incentive to take a trip to Tamworth to check out the details of the transfer of his grandfather's property. Ted had sent him the legal details and he had already searched out the possible current outlets in Tamworth that would have been around some forty years earlier, so he planned to leave Gunnedah on Friday after work. Without telling anyone else of his plans, he simply mentioned to Phil that on Friday afternoon he would be leaving town to do a bit of touring around the region for a couple of days.

Chas was progressing well. On Monday, he mentioned to Rosie that when Lisa was on duty, she always made a point of asserting her presence and that he tried desperately to ignore her as he found her attention irritating. The other nurses and Dr Johnson were very pleasant and helpful. Since his headaches were decreasing and his aches and pains were definitely under control, Chas felt confident that he would be able to go home soon.

After Rosie left on Tuesday afternoon, Lisa approached his bed with a huge smile. 'Hi Chas, it's my job to help you with your shower this evening.'

Chas looked up from his book, and smiling amiably said, 'Lisa, I don't need any help. I'll wait awhile and have one after dinner.'

'No Chas, orders are you must have it now and I'm here to see you are okay by yourself.'

Chas mumbled to himself, put his book aside and climbed into the wheelchair. Once they were in the bathroom, Chas said, 'I'll be fine now, thanks.'

Lisa leaned back to close the door behind her, ignoring the

CHAPTER 12

comment and said, 'Well, let's get you up and moving.'

Chas was furious. 'Lisa, if I needed help, which I don't, I wouldn't have you holding my hand. You are not my aid. You could try and catch Rosie. She'd do the job if it were necessary. Now just get out of here and let me get on with what has to be done. I'll face the music if I have to. Thank you.'

With one enormous sigh and a huff of her shoulders, Lisa left.

Rosie visited Chas on Wednesday and, when she heard the account of his medical examination that morning, she was rather irritated. Apparently, Lisa had reported from the night before that Chas had shown signs of weakness while taking a shower, and his unsteadiness could not be explained. After he told Rosie a little of Lisa's involvement in regard to the incident, she asked Chas, 'Have you explained to the doctor, how at times she has pressured you in some way?'

'Not really, but I did say that I wanted her out of the bathroom yesterday. I just want to get out of here, Rosie.'

After undergoing a neurological test and receiving a clear chart from Dr Johnson on Thursday morning, Chas was to be discharged on Friday afternoon. Rosie, being on holidays, arranged with his father that she would pick him up because they had already planned that she was going to Chas's to prepare their evening meal. Chas was happy to get back to his flat and rest up. With an easily prepared dish of chicken pesto pasta on the coffee table, the couple sat side by side on the lounge and made easy talk of the past week. The most animated discussion resulted from Chas's comments on Richard Bach's book.

'Thanks Rosie, that really was a great read. It confirmed my belief that flying can be interpreted as another sense. After all, the seagull knew flying was his life, not just a way to find his tucker. Are you going to read it?'

Rosie took his empty plate and placed it on the long, low table as she gazed lovingly into his open questioning eyes.

'Of course, Chas darlin'. I will, but not just yet.' With that, Rosie stretched her arms to hold Chas's head as she moved to snuggle closer to him on the cosy lounge and take her lips to his. It was an evening both had longed for over the past week. In fact, from Chas's viewpoint, it was even longer overdue. 'Rosie, this sort of evening should be available to us every night. There's so much to do.'

'Whaddya mean, lover boy? What are the other things that have to be done?'

'C'mon, there's the washing up of the dinner plates and sweeping the floor but that could all be included in the arrangement.'

'Chas, just what are you on about?'

'Rosie, how about you move in here with me? You'll be able to help me get independent again while we make the most of together times discussing the future. You can be my carer.'

It was a question Rosie had been expecting for some time and the current circumstances seemed to make it a consideration.

'Chasie, just exactly what do you mean, 'discussing the future'?'

'I'm simply referring to getting our heads around the wing-walking project.'

'Oh really? Okay, I guess that is for real.'

'Oh Sweetie, what say you move in, and we save on the laundry by sleeping in one bed?'

With an uncharacteristic girlish giggle, Rosie tightened her arms around him, and replied, 'Is that an offer, Chas?'

Chas stood up and took her hand to lead her to the bedroom. They slowly climbed onto the bed as Chas said, 'Well, you know me. What say we take this for a proposal?'

Rosie gasped. She had always expected to marry Chas and here it was happening now. She felt a tingle go through her body. His words excited her whole being. At the same time, she could feel he was aroused too. Gently, but persistently, he turned around to pull down her panties and roll on top of her. They made love spontaneously and passionately.

God, I'm so glad I've been on the pill for months. It all seemed so natural and uninhibited, so absolutely marvellous, for Rosie it was better than her dreams or imagination had envisaged. Chas knew exactly what her body needed. *No virgin on her wedding night could have felt so sated.* She drove home an hour or so later with plans to return the following morning.

CHAPTER 13

When Rosie arrived home, her parents were relaxed in front of the TV. In her usual cheery manner, she greeted them as she entered the lounge room.

'Hi Mum, hi Dad, I hope you've both had a good day.'

Mary replied rather wearily as she lifted herself up in the armchair, 'Yes honey, so how is Chas? You picked him up from the hospital, didn't you? I bet he's happy to be home. I guess you had a bit to do to get him settled. Did he like your dinner?'

'Yes, he's sure happy to be home, but he still has to take things easy, and you know Chas, he doesn't like doing that. Anyway, he'll have to contend with me to make sure he makes a good recovery. I'm going to move into his flat over the weekend. I'm going to be his carer. Being holiday time for another week, it will be quite convenient for me to help him get back on his feet.'

Both her mother and father turned away from the TV to give Rosie an eyeful. Her mother's exclamation did not surprise her.

'Oh no Rosie, what are you doing? Is it just for the weekend?'

CHAPTER 13

'No Mum, I've got no idea for how long at the moment.'

'That can't be. You're not even engaged.'

Her father's comment was somewhat more rational. 'Well, I guess that was on the cards.'

The conversation was then livelier for the next twenty minutes or so as Rosie put forward her argument between her mother's rather antagonistic comments.

'Mum, I am twenty-two and have known Chas for always. We are a unit and a team. He likes to know 'how' and 'why' I do things and I like to know 'why' and 'how' he does things. Mum, we love each other. Getting a bit more familiar will help us realise how much we want to be together forever.'

Rosie's words cut short a tirade from Mary. 'I guess my days of telling you what to do are well and truly over. I just hope you realise the implications of your decision.'

Ted was a little more consoling as he softly suggested, 'It's your decision, sweetie pie.'

Rosie woke up the next morning, excited but wary. *What will I pack?* When she broke the news to her mother and father the night before, the reality of the move came into focus. Fortunately, her things did not have to be moved very far, but Rosie had to think carefully about what she would take to Chas's. Ted and Mary both offered their help and by mid-morning her car was packed. In a somewhat conciliatory tone, Mary asked Rosie, 'You will have a cuppa before you leave, won't you? I've just called your dad.'

The family group went outside and sat around the table on the veranda. Immediately, Ted said, 'It's a big step you're taking

Rosie, so just remember you can always come home if it doesn't work out so well.'

'Thanks Dad. It is quite a step I know, but at least I'm not far away.'

The conversation continued in a supportive manner. As she picked up the cups and plates to take to the kitchen, Rosie announced that she had better get going. As she turned to leave the kitchen, her mother took her arm and led her aside and said softly, 'Rosie you are taking precautions, aren't you?'

'What d'ya mean, Mum, I'm okay.'

'Rosie, you're on the pill, aren't you?'

'Well, that's something that I found out all about at uni. You know, the pill is actually great for skin care. You remember Mum, I used to have a load of pimples from time to time? When I got to uni, the girls talked about how good the pill was in helping with acne to head off bad skin days, and it works. It's all about balancing out the chemicals in your body. I've been taking it for a while.

Mary's frown was a look of surprise and sort of relief. Rosie gave her mother a kiss goodbye, went to the veranda to pick up her last bag, and waved to her parents, who were so very important in her life.

Rosie was surprised to see Chas open the front door as she pulled up in the driveway. He had apparently been watching for her from the window. 'Wow Sweetie, I didn't expect you quite so early.' Chas greeted Rosie with a tight hug and gentle kiss as she met him at the door. 'Let's get your gear inside.'

'You are supposed to be resting, Chas. You know my role here

CHAPTER 13

is as a carer so I think you should be in bed, or relaxing. You are not going to help me. I packed the car at home so I am sure I can manage this stuff. You can sit on the lounge with your feet up and tell me where to put it.'

It still hadn't registered for Rosie that this was now home. Chas's flat was part of a duplex. It was rather modern with two bedrooms and a large living area. Directly off the kitchen, along the side of the building, was a long patio that was ideal for outdoor living. This was something Rosie was keen to utilise. The proximity to town meant that she would have more time on her hands, meeting the early start time at work, the trips to the pool, the after-hours commitments, and Saturday mornings at the Gym Club. Chas was quite independent when it came to cooking and housekeeping, but Rosie knew they would learn to share the responsibilities.

'Now that everything is out of the car Chas, I'll park it around the corner in the side street. I don't want to crowd up your driveway.'

'Good idea Rosie. I'll go and organise a sandwich each for lunch, okay?'

When Rosie got to the kitchen, she insisted that Chas just sit and watch as she made the sandwiches. Before they sat at the table, she pulled a couple of easy chairs out onto the patio, and they sat outside enjoying the early summer day.

'When do you think you'll be back in the cockpit, Chasie?'

'Well, I sort of hope in a week or so, but I guess the doc will give me a good idea on Monday. In the meantime, we can spend time deciding how we're going to get you on the wing, all legal like.'

'Actually, it'll be good for me to tell you all about my research and you can tell me all about the mechanics of getting me up there. I really am so excited Chas, I feel it is a creative project for me, and the idea of being safe and able to experience such a literally unearthly feeling is so compelling.'

Time passed quickly as the couple spent the afternoon sitting on the sofa talking and having a comfortable cuddle. Chas was impressed with the tales Rosie told him of wing-walking ventures and how they could build on the experiences of safe adventures from past years. Rosie was nodding her head as he suggested, 'You know, for our first effort, I think we might just strap you on to the top wing in a standing position and do a lazy bit of straight and level for you to get the sensation. You are sure to feel exposed and vulnerable, but the knowledge of the straps will give you confidence that you are safe and simply in a different location.'

'Yeh, I know what you mean Chas. Just standing there, I will be able to appreciate the extent that I will be able to move.'

'And Rosie, there will be a thoroughly rehearsed procedure to make you aware of upcoming aircraft positions, whether it's a turn, a climb or a dive.'

'I will have a helmet on and communication through earphones, won't I?'

Before he could answer in detail, the doorbell rang and Chas replied with a quick "Yes" and then, 'Sorry, I'll just check who that is.'

Rosie stayed on the sofa sipping her coffee until she heard a familiar female voice through the open kitchen door. As she made her way down the hallway, she could see Lisa with her arms full of boxes. 'But Chas, I've only come to drop off a couple of prepared meals for you. I knew you would be convalescing alone, and I thought it would be helpful.'

As Rosie appeared beside Chas, Lisa's eyes opened wide and her voice went to a higher pitch, 'What are you doing here?'

'Well Lisa, Rosie is my carer, and she has moved in to be sure that I eat well, sleep well, and have any of my needs taken care of.'

'You are supposed to be resting, Chas.'

'Exactly, and that is why Rosie is here.'

A rather agitated Lisa replied, 'I think I had better let the doctor know that you are not following your recuperation directions.'

Rosie could not help herself and had to reply, 'Lisa! Chas doesn't need your attention today, and in fact considering the times you tried to involve yourself with his medical condition when he was in hospital, I think we could consider your actions harassment. Maybe you'll be the one that we inform the doctor about.'

Lisa's reply shocked both Rosie and Chas, 'Me, harassing Chas? You, Rosie, are responsible for Chas's deterioration. You have occupied his space so much that he now feels he must do as you say. You are ruining his progress.'

Chas had now heard too much. 'Shut up Lisa. Thanks for your thoughts, but you can take the food and get out of here.'

Chas started to close the door as Lisa scowled at Rosie and mouthed the word, 'bitch'.

'Get out of here Lisa,' and Chas slammed the door. He turned around, and without a word, Chas swept Rosie into his arms, and they kissed slowly and passionately.

Apart from the hours that Rosie had to spend at the gymnasium and the pool on Saturday and Sunday, the rest of the weekend was relaxing and most enjoyable. If they weren't having an animated conversation about wing walking then it was either about flying or gymnastics, and they would exchange information and ideas in a professional manner. Rosie took on the responsibility of housekeeping to be sure the laundry was done, and the place was kept clean. Chas loved to cook, and he was more than pleased that Rosie was not insisting she should also do the cooking. The week ahead was going to work well. Although Rosie had to prepare for the next term, there would be real time for the two of them to work together. Chas assured her that he would be making phone calls and setting out a plan of action to ensure their wing-walking objective could get underway.

CHAPTER 14

Barry's visit to Tamworth over the weekend had settled a few things in his mind. The legality of the transfer of his grandfather's property to the Franklins was a fait accompli and, although it had happened some forty-five years earlier, he had no option but to accept the fact that he could not question the situation.

His first decision back in Gunnedah was to arrange another meeting with Ted later in the week. He then explained that his time in Tamworth had given him some reconciliation and time for reflection. For Ted, Barry's conversation provided him with a deeper understanding of the circumstances that had been troubling the young man, and between them they could now talk of future possibilities.

Barry had no desire to become a farmer. He liked country life and appreciated the natural environment, but apart from caring for animals, the idea of growing crops did not appeal to him at all. His discussion with Ted drew him closer to the

Gunnedah community and, over a glass of beer they developed a friendship. Ted also explained that his parents had named Wally Hammond's farm, *Ted's Place*, as Jack had considered Ted to be the future owner. Barry was grateful for Ted's interest and candour, and liked the suggestion that he should catch up with John, who now considered *Ted's Place* to be his responsibility. He had not had any response from his earlier query to Rosie about checking out the farm, so he took matters into his own hands and phoned John. As a result, John agreed to take him around the farm to show him some of the beauty spots.

Work at the airport was almost back to normal. Bill Anderson was flat out keeping up with his bookings using the alternative crop sprayer aircraft and it would probably be another week before Chas could be around to assist. He would also have to wait for a while before the insurance came through so that he could purchase another Grumman, but Phil hoped Chas's confidence had not diminished in any way because of the accident. Barry was busy with several regular servicing jobs in the hangar but Steve Jennings, Phil's son, was completing his apprenticeship experiences so Phil encouraged him to move on to more challenging tasks. The Cessna 180 and Chas's Tiger Moth were not in great demand while Chas was out of action, so Barry made time, introducing engineering aspects of those aircraft to Steve.

On Tuesday, Rosie stayed at home doing some schoolwork while Chas headed for the airfield. He wanted to check the contact phone number for the Department of Transport, Air Transport Group, to start making some enquiries about prepping the aircraft for Rosie's first venture and safety issues. As he entered the hanger, he could see the two engineers with their attention on the engine of the Tiger. 'All okay, guys?'

'Wow, here's a stranger, but I know that voice.' Barry cleared his head from the aircraft engine and put his hand out to Chas. 'It is great to see you back on-board, mate.' As they shook hands Chas smiled and said, 'Hi Barry, which aircraft has been okayed for take-off?'

'You're kidding me! You're not taking off today, surely.'

'You're right. I'm just a bit overconfident but I'm pretty sure I'll be in the queue next week.'

'Awe, that'd be great for sure, Chas.'

Chas then turned to Steve. 'Hi Steve, ya got it all under control?'

'Yep. Good to see you up and about, Chas. Barry's been so much help and he just fires me up with answers to my questions and then questions me. He does make it hard work but I'm getting the message.'

'Any jumping happening?'

'Awe c'mon.' Steve gave a wry smile and did a thumbs up. 'You're the one we need in the cockpit.'

Rolling his eyes and turning with a bit of a snort, Chas made his way across the hangar to the office. Once he had the phone number for the appropriate contact at the Air Transport Group, Chas decided to head for home. He really didn't want anyone overhearing the discussion, at least not just yet.

That afternoon, Barry set off to do some shopping. The supermarket was rather quiet and as he pushed the trolley slowly around the corner at the end of the aisle, the wheels decided to do their customary trick of remaining steady and rolling straight ahead. He then had to use some pressure to force the trolley to turn. Unfortunately, his strength, coupled with the irritation, forced him to collide with another customer's trolley, and it was being pushed by none other than Rosie Franklin.

'Oh! Hey, I'm awfully sorry lovely lady.'

'Ha ha Barry, one of the hazards of supermarket shopping. Hey? All is okay. These trolleys really like to do it their way.'

Feeling a little apologetic, Barry asked Rosie to join him at the neighbouring cafe when she had finished shopping.

'Well, there are no fines for such a collision, but okay Barry, a milkshake is just what I need after a day with my head in the books. I'll finish here and see you there in about five minutes, but I'll have to make it short.'

'Sure, that'd be great.'

Barry considered a bit of flirting was not anything untoward as far as Rosie was concerned. He was quite unaware that she had moved in with Chas. When Rosie saw him, Barry was sitting at an outside table, so she walked over and as she dropped the grocery bag under her chair, commented, 'This is a pleasant end to a shopping spree. Have you been busy today?'

'Not really, things have slowed a bit since Chas had his prang. I just wanted to have a quick chat with you.'

'Oh yes, okay. I guess you saw Chas this morning and you know he's doing pretty well and has been discharged.'

'Yep, I had a bit of a chat with him today. When he came into the hangar, he was keen to check out the aircraft. I guess he'll be back in the cockpit before too long.'

Rosie was a little taken aback. 'That was cheeky of him. He's supposed to be resting. That's my job now. I'm Chas's carer and I must make sure he does take things easy.'

'What do you mean "your job"?'

'Ha ha, I'm still teaching of course, but I moved out of home and in with Chas last weekend.'

'Really? You've changed abode?'

'Chas needed someone to be with him, so it seemed a legit reason to move in.'

Beginning to feel a little uncomfortable, Barry quickly set about thinking how to change the subject as the waitress delivered the two milkshakes he had ordered.

'You'd be lucky to see Chas taking things easy. Anyway, I wanted to tell you about my trip to Tamworth last weekend.'

'Tamworth, what was that all about?'

'Oh, I thought your father would have told you that he'd talked to me about my grandfather's property becoming your grandfather's.'

'Dad did mention you were going to call in. He said you were surprised about the family farm.'

'Well Rosie, apparently my grandfather, Wally, transferred his property to your family in his will and that was done by a law office in Tamworth way back in the 20s. I just wanted a quick chat to tell you what happened in Tamworth. It seems that your brother's property could have been mine if it hadn't been for some slip-ups my family made down the track.'

'That must be a bit hard to handle, Barry. Your family in

Ballarat had no idea about any of that? So, what's going to happen now?

'Well, your dad suggested I contact John, and when I gave him a call, he told me he'd show me over the property next weekend. It will be great to have that chance to see the land.'

'Are you interested in buying the farm Barry?'

'Oh, I don't think so, no way, I'm no farmer.'

'Are you looking for something for nothing?'

'Hell no, Rosie.'

'Well, that situation could get under John's skin a bit.'

'Whaddya mean?'

'Just that. I don't think he'll want you seeing up close and personal what should or could have been yours.'

'Oh Missy Muff, you're assuming a bit much aren't you?'

'I don't think so. I'd be a bit tactful if I were you, Barry. Anyway, I best head off. Thanks for the drink. See you soon.'

Barry knew his comments did not sit easily with Rosie. He had been hoping that she would have supported his side of the situation and given John some assurance that all he wanted to do was check out his family history.

That evening, after telling Chas about Barry's trip to Tamworth, Rosie tried to temper her reaction. Chas pointed out that the whole reason behind Barry's move to Gunnedah was to delve deeper into his family's history, so surely a visit to the property would be high on his list. However, as far as Chas was concerned, he had more important things to discuss with Rosie. 'I was out at the airport earlier today and I got a number to contact at the Air Transport Group in Sydney. It's for the Superintendent of Operations. You know the Department of Aviation was only renamed in May this year and it has the responsibility for air safety. I reckon that we might be able to get some support to show a carefully planned and pro-safety proposition. It would be great if they could give us some sort of assurance that we can get something established along with a load of checks before we put anything into action. My plan is to strap you on the top wing with a pattern of straps to hold you secure so that even if the wings fell off, you would be held firmly in place. The feeling of freedom with straps around you could be something like the sensation one has when parachuting.'

'Oooh, okay.' Rosie then continued with some hesitancy, 'but does that mean I'll have to become familiar with parachuting?'

'Well, just a couple of jumps p'raps, so you know what to expect. However, we need to draw plans for the location of a platform to stand on, the attachment of the straps to the wing and details of the harness type, and how it will be attached to you. All simple really, but we will have to get advice from an approved and experienced aeronautical engineer while preparing the plans for the Air Transport Group.

'Sounds good Chas, so what do I need to do first of all?'

'Yeh, well, I suggest you have a talk to Barry about your jumping requirements. You're not going to do the full course, but you do need to get an understanding of how gusts of air can influence your movement and location.'

'Okay, but I don't know that he's going to be very empathetic after our last meeting, but I'll make a time to meet up.'

'Good onya and I'll have a chat with him as well regarding

the straps and harness. I think he'll probably get Steve to do the job because Barry is always busy in the hangar. The straps will have to be well checked out for different uses and locations and could be a bit expensive, so we'll just keep a separate account for things related to the exercise, okay?'

'For sure, and I guess I only need to wear a shirt and trousers, and some tough boots, is that right?'

'Yep, but not baggy. Just make sure they are a nice tight fit, um, yeh, I think tightfitting, and must be approved by me.'

'Oh Chas, you do go on!'

Chas then added, 'I've been doing quite a lot of research myself and I will have to run you through a regime of hand signals and some pretty important instructions on breathing techniques. You also must become familiar with the implications and limitations of the harness as well.'

Rosie then went off to prepare dinner and Chas got out a pencil and paper to start making a few notes.

The next morning, between yelps of surprise and a strong response from Barry, Chas gave him a brief outline of the wing-walking plans. He then explained how Rosie would be in touch with him to set up a program for an introduction to jumping. Barry was most interested and supportive. He offered a few other ideas and suggested a couple of contacts for Chas to follow up. Being Wednesday, Rosie called him when she got home from school, and in a brief conversation, asked if she could join in on the Saturday afternoon jumping session. Barry was more than happy to help and wanted her to meet him at the hangar the next day. He thought a quick scout around the hangar, a look

CHAPTER 14

at the Cessna and a beginners' prep session, would set her up for Saturday afternoon.

After getting off the phone, Rosie asked Chas, 'Will you come with me to the hangar tomorrow afternoon? Barry wants to show me stuff.'

'Sorry Sweetie, I've already made arrangements to see the boss at the servo at about 4.00 pm. You don't need me anyway. Barry just wants to show you the gear and review what I'm sure are things you already know.'

Chas was feeling fine, and with the doctor's support was planning to start work, although he wouldn't be flying for another week or so. Rosie was rather uneasy about meeting with Barry, but with his positive and pleasant approach on the phone, she accepted the situation.

Barry greeted Rosie with a big smile and a pat on the back. 'Wow, so you are taking to the skies at last dear lady.'

'Well yes, it's not quite what I imagined but I guess to achieve a goal there are steps that have to be taken. I'm not afraid, it's just that I don't see the point of jumping out of an aeroplane that is flying okay. However, if to achieve my great ambition to walk in the clouds, I must float through them, then so be it.'

The afternoon went well. Barry explained some basic terms around the aircraft and their use in the jump procedure, like the struts, the step and the static line, and then also some basic vocabulary including the importance of the word 'Go'. Rosie's enthusiasm and confidence built in response to the reality of what was going to happen on Saturday.

Barry's offer came unexpectedly but quite innocently. 'Let's have a cuppa before you go.'

'Oh thanks, Chas won't be home for another half hour, so I may as well.'

After making a coffee at the machine, they sat down on the outside bench. Rosie attempted an apology for her comments about Barry's visit to the farm. 'John tells me he is going to show you over the place. I am pleased that he has agreed to take you around. I am sure he'll be able to fill you in on a few good stories from the days when our grandparents were working the land.'

'Yep, thanks Rosie. I accepted his invitation to visit on Sunday. It'll certainly be a historic revelation for me. To think that I can be walking on the land where my grandparents worked means a lot to me.'

'You probably should keep some notes of what you see and what you feel.'

As he slowly shook his head, Barry replied, 'No, not me. I'm not really into writing, but I'll be taking some photos for sure.'

The conversation continued amiably, and once the coffee was finished Rosie stood up and held out her hand. 'Goodbye Barry. Thanks for the afternoon and I'm looking forward to Saturday.'

Barry lent forward to shake her hand with two hands. 'You're welcome, Rosie, and Saturday will be a great day for you.'

Rosie made her way to the carpark, relieved that the meeting had gone along without any hitches.

CHAPTER 15

It was calm and sunny on Saturday afternoon as the Cessna took off on the first jump flight for the day. Bill Anderson was the stand-in pilot for his son. Rosie shivered a little as she sat on the floor of the cabin reacting to the tight straps of her parachute. She had prepared herself with a strong cup of coffee, as she had always done before a competition. Barry's voice was strong and reassuring, 'This is a day you will always remember Rosie.'

'I'm sure I will. I think it is the freedom of the fall that I'm fearful of. Something that will be so new, but gee Barry, thanks, you have given me so much confidence.'

'A lady who is totally her own person has only herself to thank. You will achieve whatever you want, Rosie.'

Jim and Jeff, the other two jumpers, offered their encouraging words and Rosie put her mind into gear in preparation for the jump.

As she had left the hangar, Chas had given her a quick kiss

and said, 'Goodbye and good luck, Sweetie. I'll see you at the drop zone'.

The cabin had been cleared of seats, so Rosie, along with Barry, Jim Anderson and Jeff Dane all sat closely together on the floor for the take-off. The nose of the aircraft then rose, and the aircraft climbed slowly upwards. In minutes they were high enough for Rosie to familiarise herself with the layout of the airport from above as Barry indicated the jump zone to the west of the airport. The earlier introductory session had given her a load of confidence, but she still had an underlying sense of fear of the unknown.

Chas watched intently as the aircraft took off from the airport runway. He was not aware of the presence of Lisa, standing beside him, until he heard her question. 'You are not going up today, Chas?' Although her voice was soft, it had a definite sense of wanting to know his movements.

Chas felt angry because he considered Lisa was again intruding in his space. Wanting to preserve the growth and popularity of the parachuting club and his reputation, he replied, trying to dispel any possible antagonism, 'No, not today, Lisa, but it won't be long. I've gotta go. I've gotta get to the drop zone.'

'Maybe we could have a coffee before you head off? It'll be about ten minutes before they jump.'

'I don't think there's time Lisa. It's a few minutes' drive and I want to be there to see my dad's approach.' Chas turned to head for the carpark.

'Oh Chas, I've missed you. How are you feeling?'

'Really good, thanks Lisa.' Chas turned to Lisa, shrugged his shoulders, and replied firmly, 'Heck Lisa, I've gotta go. See ya later.' He then walked quickly to his car, relieved by the easy getaway.

As the aircraft approached the drop zone, at the exit height of 2,500 feet above ground level, Rosie watched anxiously as Jim and Jeff moved to the open door, each of them checking that their static line was attached to the aircraft, then jumped one after the other. Barry now pointed to Rosie, who moved to the gaping space. With his strong and instructive words echoing in her ears, Rosie stepped into the blast of air, unwaveringly reaching forward for the strut as she carefully placed a foot on the step. She had each hand on a strut. As she had been trained, still holding on with both hands, she kicked her foot from the step and her body was flying in the gust of wind. *What a wonderful feeling!* She glanced at Barry, and he shouted, 'Go'! With a deep breath and a body full of confidence, she let go. Her awareness from gymnastics made the fall seem natural, and a second later, as she felt the tug of the static line pulling open her parachute, her eyes opened wide as she let out a scream, not of terror, but of sheer thrill. The robust movement and mind-boggling awareness on leaving the aircraft, quickly settled into an exciting and satisfying sense of *I've done it!* A second later, she looked up to ensure the canopy had deployed correctly. *Wow!*

Chas had pulled up in his car near the drop zone at the far end of the airport to watch his father approach in the Cessna, manoeuvring the aircraft for the jump in exactly the same way as he would have done. Jim and Jeff left the aircraft, one after the other. Chas waited and watched intently for a vision of Rosie, and there she was. The chute burst out over her head, and he could see her floating down and drifting in the gentle breeze. With bated breath, he kept his eyes on the chute as she dropped close to the drop zone. The two guys landed and left their chutes on the ground to make their way to what they anticipated as Rosie's landing spot. Chas then left his car and raced across to welcome her. Having put the landing technique and tumble into practice, Rosie jumped up, exhilarated. She used the quick release box to get rid of the chute, and exuberantly yelled out her thanks to her jump mates as she spotted Chas and raced to his open arms.

'Oh Chas, that was dreamsville.'

Chas held her tightly, and feeling her excitement at having fulfilled another step in her dream, he said, 'And Sweetie, there's more to come.'

Together they packed up her parachute and walked quickly back to the car while Rosie continued chatting about her experience. Chas made a quick suggestion. 'Let's get some fish and chips and go up to Porky's for an early dinner.'

'Chas, that'd be great. I haven't been up to Porcupine Lookout for ages, and I reckon a visit there will just revitalise my jump sensation.'

On such a clear, sunny afternoon, the view from the lookout was beautiful. Chas collected the take-away bundle of fish and chips from the backseat of the car, and they wandered over to the picnic table. 'You know Chas, I have flown over this beautiful country with you so many times and looked out over all the sights, that I feel I know it so well, but dropping gently and quietly through the air, and feeling closer to the clouds while scanning the view below was like sitting through the most fantastic movie. I almost felt I could touch the few little bunches of fluff that I passed by.'

'What did you think when you were standing ready on the step?'

'Well, I was entranced with what I could see, and Barry had to give my hand on the strut a bit of a bang for me to let go. At first, I felt I could not breathe but I was able to let out a very unearthly scream. Then once the aircraft sound had gone and the initial gust of air had passed, the static line released the chute and floating through space just seemed so peaceful.'

'What was the best part of the experience for you, Sweetie?'

'That's a tricky question. I just felt my senses were all being tested at the same time. The air was so fresh and clean. It sort of smelt sweet, much like it is here at the lookout, and of course I could feel the temperature change as I floated lower. I think the silence, after the gushing sound when I jumped and the aircraft had moved on, seemed to be an unbelievable form of peacefulness. It was so quiet there was just nothing to hear. Certainly, getting closer to the ground I could hear voices so clear that I could understand what was being said.'

'Could you pick out anything familiar on the way down?'

'Once I got my bearings, yes. I scoured a bit for our farm and then I picked out the Namoi flowing slowly, and Yarrie Lake, which still has a fairly high water level. Oh Chas, it was a picture wonderland. I felt so close to the clouds. As the different shades of green across the plains and the rising ranges of hills all got closer, I felt absolutely charged up that this was home.'

With a winsome smile passing across his face, Chas asked, 'So now that you've passed your initiation test, are we going to pursue the wing-walking adventure?'

Rosie answered with a teasing scowl, 'Of course, of course, I can imagine my senses will be on even higher power for that. When do you think you'll be back in the air?'

'I'll have another check up on Monday and I reckon Doc Johnson will give me a clear chart so, by the time I check out with my boss at the servo, I think next Saturday I'll be doing the chute drop.'

'Whoopee for you. Barry did ask me to catch up with him tomorrow for a debrief. I wonder if he will want me to do another jump next week.'

'I guess that's possible. We'll go out to the hangar about 3 o'clock and see what he says.'

Somewhat hesitantly, Chas asked, 'Rosie, you know I might not need a carer, but I still want to live with someone who cares. Whaddya reckon?'

With a cheeky laugh, Rosie replied, 'Okay, we'll see how it goes.'

That night, after they returned from Porky's, Chas suggested, 'How about we have some bickies and cheese with a glass of wine?'

'Oooh that does sound nice,' and the conversation then continued as to how they would approach the next step for wing walking.

After a late start in the morning, Rosie called Barry to say that she would see him for the debrief in the hangar at 3 pm. She asked Chas if he would join her and maybe they could talk to

Barry about the wing-walking plans. 'Uhm, you want to do that now? Actually, I've gotta run over some stuff with Dad so we'll make a time during the week to sit down with Barry. Just let him check out things with you and I'll see you at dinner time, okay?'

'Well, yes, that'd be fine. Of course, it's the start of the new term tomorrow. It'll take a while to talk about all the technical stuff with the straps and everything so I'll find out which afternoon would be the best to fit in with my after-school commitments and his plans.'

Barry was obviously pleased to see Rosie and gave her a hug, with exuberant congratulations on having made such a great first jump. 'Are you going to do another one?'

With a little hesitancy Rosie replied, 'Maybe, but I think I'd prefer to get things moving with the wing walking.'

'Oh yes, I guess you're really keen to get that rolling. However, having done a couple of jumps will definitely increase your confidence and I think you could use the fall time to expand your sensations, since it won't be a first time. You could try to get your mindset into the stability of the experience that remaining on top of the aircraft will create.'

'Well now, I guess I could, and for that matter I should do another jump, hey?' Rosie agreed to attend some preparation sessions in the hangar and take another jump in a week or two. The discussion continued with her asking some rather astute questions regarding the preparation for the wing-walking requirements and after about an hour or so, Rosie decided to head home feeling satisfied with the day's proceedings. Barry seemed a little disappointed that she wanted to leave so soon.

'Hey, let's have a quick cider before you head off, or a cup of tea, if you wish.'

'Yeh, okay, maybe I'll have that quick cider.'

After Barry retrieved a bottle from the refrigerator and poured out a couple of glasses, he led her to the bench under a shady tree. He quickly referred to his recent trip to see John and Sally on their farm, *Ted's Place*. 'You know, sightseeing around the property really gave me a sense of belonging, and when John took me to the old homestead, he explained the history of how, after Wally's death in 1927, when the property was willed to Jack, he gave Ted and Mary the opportunity to spend the early years of their marriage on the Hammond property and gave it the name *Ted's Place*.'

Rosie's memories kicked in and she replied, 'Yes, Mum and Dad were still living there when all of us kids were born, and then in the 1970s, when grandfather died, Dad moved us back to the old Franklin farm and encouraged John, who was about to marry Sally, to takeover and maintain *Ted's Place*. They had a very comfortable first home.'

'Yep, that's for sure. Although when John took me back to the homestead, Sally did talk about the changes they had made to the house over the past five years. They were very kind, invited me to share afternoon tea and then told me more of the story, and honestly, it just increased my sense of wanting to become more familiar with the place without being responsible. I did think how great it would be if I could live on what had been my grandfather's property.'

'I don't know if that would be possible, Barry.'

CHAPTER 15

'Well, I did ask them if they would consider selling me a small parcel of land on which I could build my home. It did knock them off guard a bit.'

Shaking her head and frowning, Rosie asked, 'C'mon Barry, are you serious?'

'Yeh, of course, I don't want any commitments from them or your family. If I had a block, somewhere out of the way, I'd take care of all the financial aspects regarding having a house there. Whaddya reckon?'

Rosie was beginning to feel a little anxious. She felt it an intrusion on her family's livelihood and history.

'What did John say?'

'Well, he said he'd look into it for me and did say that there were a few private spots around the place that would probably suit, but he thought a building block under those circumstances would have to be more than an urban house block size. He seemed pretty encouraging though and is going to check it out. Rosie, would you like to come out to the property with me and offer me some suggestions?'

'Are you serious?'

'Of course, I am. I thought you might know of some places that could be ideal.'

'Barry, really? I'm in no position to encourage you or to make any suggestions. Please don't bring me into the situation, and for heaven's sake, don't tell John that you've been talking to me about it all.'

Grabbing her bag from under the bench, Rosie jumped up and said, 'It's getting late, I must be going. Thanks for the cider.

I'll see ya round Barry.' She then hot-footed it to the carpark without a glance back.

'Oh my gosh, Chas. I really do think Barry is taking his heritage interests a bit too far.' They had just sat down for dinner. Since she had returned from her catch-up with Barry, Rosie had felt her irritation grow and Chas was aware that something was bothering her.

'I thought something was up with you. Was he positive and helpful in regard to your jump?'

'No problems with that.'

'So, what day will we catch up with him? I reckon I'll be able to do the drop next weekend.'

Rosie felt she had to fill Chas in on what Barry had disclosed. 'Chas, Barry's really started something over the old property. He's been to see John, done a tour around the farm, and was telling me that he had discussed the possibility of buying a block of land on *Ted's Place*.'

'What? How can he do that?'

'Well, he reckons John is going to make enquiries. I can only see trouble brewing. Can you imagine that if a third party has legal possession of a section of what is really your farming property, the implications that could develop?'

'For sure. However, I reckon he'd have to go through reams of legal issues, and it would all cost a fortune.'

'I reckon too. I told him not to mention to John that he'd told me of his desires. I just hope John can get on to something to stop it developing anymore.'

CHAPTER 15

'So, have you made a day to catch up and discuss your wing-walking requirements?'

'No. I'll have to ring him. You're getting your doc check tomorrow so I'll wait until we see each other in the afternoon and then I'll give him a call. Okay?'

Chas lay back on the comfy sofa and patted the seat. 'All good. Now let's just have a lazy evening. I can't bear to think that you are not needed to care for me anymore.'

CHAPTER 16

On Monday morning, Chas's medical report was positive, and he was cleared to fly the following weekend. That evening, Rosie and Chas discussed calling the Air Transport to find out as much information as possible about the restrictions currently placed on wing walking.

'I hope I can get to speak with an official who has a feeling for development and change. You told me about that famous aviation fiction writer, Martin Caidin, who is also an aviator of some renown, and who organised the wing-walking event in the USA last year. Well, I checked him out and that was actually an unofficial event but was claimed as a world record. I really want to put all possibilities upfront and make sure that they know what is happening overseas. Then, they might consider Australia's stance on the rising interest in wing-walking.'

'Wow, what was the record for?'

'Well, Caidin had nineteen skydivers standing on the left wing of a flying Junkers JU52. That is a rather large aircraft,

CHAPTER 16

and he obviously covered all safety issues.'

'That's it,' said Rosie. 'Maybe if we put a great deal of effort into the safety aspects then that may help to convince the Air Transport people.'

'Yep, for sure. As wing-walking became a spectator sport back in the 30s, the performer had no harness or straps, and then with the increasing popularity some straps and frames were introduced, but accidents still occurred. I reckon we just go overboard on safety and set up carefully arranged cables and harness, etcetera, and you dear love, are the ideal performer because you are lean and hungry but exceptionally strong because of your regular gym workouts.'

With a cheeky laugh, Rosie said, 'Ha ha! You have me summed up, Chasie. Okay, I'll go ahead and see Barry later this week and explain what you're up to. I'll probably do one more jump, just to help me with the mindset.'

Chas could not let the opportunity pass in regard to discussing Rosie's accommodation issue.

'So, you have no need to pack your bags just yet, have you Sweetie?'

'Well, I'm happy to stay-over as long as I'm not overstaying, Chasie.'

'Great, that means our discussions and planning can all take place as needs be rather than setting up appointments.'

Rosie met Barry on Thursday afternoon after school. Over a cup of coffee, he explained that there would be no jumping at the weekend. He had heard that the weather report for the next week suggested heavy cloud and showers, so he was going to cancel any activities. He expressed his hope that Rosie was planning to do another jump and she agreed.

'I guess the wing-walking plans are still going ahead though, Rosie?'

'Yes, Chas is currently making calls to all and sundry regarding safety issues. I believe we may have a visit from someone in the Air Transport Group soon to check out our facilities and personnel. That would include you Barry, of course Phil, and probably Steve.'

'O-oh, I'd better do some homework and set up my fabricator paperwork. The big guys will want to take a look over my credentials, I'm sure. Have you worked out anything with Chas yet?'

'Yes, we're really going to push safety in regard to the harness, straps and cables, and also weight and balance, so I would say that will all be 'par for the course' for you.'

'You're right there. Thanks for that, I'll follow it up. By the way, have you seen John lately?'

'No, we don't get to see each other too often. Sally and I often meet up for a cuppa when she is in town shopping, but I haven't seen either of them for a while.'

'So, you don't go out to their place at all?'

'Not very often.'

'I thought you'd probably like to check out their dogs and chickens and get out on the tractor occasionally.'

With a rather flippant giggle, Rosie replied, 'Barry, that's not really my scene. I don't mind an easy garden around the house but I'm just not into crops and tractors. Even Annie my sister tossed the idea of marrying a farmer and headed off to the city.'

'So, you wouldn't even consider living in a rural environment?'

'Oh no, I don't think so. I'm definitely more of a town girl.' Rosie decided it was time to leave. 'I'd better be off, Barry. Thanks for the coffee. See you soon.'

'Awe, you don't need to go just yet.'

'Well, yes, I do. There's prep for tomorrow and it's my turn to cook dinner.'

In surprised acknowledgement, Barry continued, 'So you're still at Chas's? I didn't think he needed a carer anymore.'

As delicately as she could put it, Rosie replied, 'No, of course he doesn't need a carer, but we both care, Barry. See ya.'

As she walked back to the car, Rosie felt that Barry had wanted her to stay longer. However, she was a little fearful that he would continue talking on the topic of *Ted's Place* and that was something she just didn't want to even think about.

Chas and Rosie had planned to spend the weekend relaxing. Of course, Chas was disappointed that the weather denied him the satisfaction that climbing back into the Cessna would have provided. Rosie was also disappointed that her second jump was not to happen just yet. Instead, the disheartened couple kept themselves busy. If it wasn't sitting, talking, and writing down their wing-walking plans, it was taking turns cooking, and Chas loved to surprise Rosie with unexpected dishes that went beyond her expectations.

As she sat reading the Saturday newspaper with the radio softly playing the latest Paul McCartney and Stevie Wonder hit,

Ebony and Ivory, Rosie heard Chas call from the kitchen. 'Hey Sweetie, I'm going downtown. I hope the shops are still open. I'm missing a crucial ingredient.'

'Oh, okay, do you want me to come with you?'

'No, not all,' and as he opened the front door he added, 'Bye, I'll be real quick. No worries.'

Chas left and Rosie slid back into the sofa. She could enjoy the few minutes alone to finish reading the newspaper and enjoy listening to the radio.

With the paper finished and the radio now broadcasting the news, Rosie realised Chas had been gone for over three quarters of an hour for a jaunt that took about fifteen minutes. She set about sweeping and cleaning but soon became rather anxious. The clock showed 5.30 and they usually had dinner on the table at about six o'clock; she was beginning to be rather concerned. She decided to go out to the front yard. It was beginning to get dark and there were a number of cars heading along the main road at the end of their street. After another ten minutes, Rosie was just making up her mind whether to get into her car and go and look for her man or not, when Chas pulled into the driveway.

'Oh Chasie, where have you been? I have been so worried.'

'It's okay Sweetie, I got rather held up.'

'What do you mean? Heavy traffic?'

'No nothing like that. I'd just finished getting my ginger sauce and was walking out of the shop when I bumped into Lisa.'

'What, that bit of baggage? You have set me on a path of anxiety Chas, because of that little witch.'

'Hold on Rosie, I said sorry and went on my way when she

CHAPTER 16

tugged my sleeve and said that she really needed to talk to someone. She did look very anxious so, I reluctantly asked her what the problem was, and she suggested hesitantly that we might sit down outside the tea shop.'

'What? And you said yes? What the heck did she want to talk to you about?'

'Well, according to her, it seems Barry doesn't listen to her about her parachuting problems and she's afraid she's going to do something wrong and have an accident.'

'Oh, what twaddle. She just wants to get under your wing and have you give her your attention. Chas, you can't fall for that.'

'Rosie, she was very distressed. I was just trying to help.'

'Chas, I was here, absolutely off my perch with worry that something had happened to you. You were only supposed to have been away fifteen or twenty minutes. You could have had an accident, a relapse from your injuries, or anything could have happened. I was just about to get into my car and come looking for you. How could you be so stupid?'

'Gee Rosie, it was only a conversation.'

'For sure, but not for her it wasn't. She's going to get an earful from me, that's guaranteed.' Rosie turned her back and walked down the hallway. 'I can't eat anything after that. I'm going to bed.'

On Sunday morning, Rosie woke to a warm embrace and a gentle caress. 'Oh Sweetie, I am so sorry about last night. I know I would have been out of my mind too if you had been so long over the time span. I can see now that obviously I should have told Lisa to catch up some other time or find someone else, cos I was in a hurry to get back to you, my dear love. You are the focus of my life and without you, I don't know where I'd be. Will you marry me, Rosie?'

The endearing words fell on very warm ears.

'Oh, yeh, I guess I'm sorry for what I said too. I love you so much and will say 'Yes' to your question. I do want to marry you, Chasie darling.'

There was no ring, there were no plans and no suggestions as to what the next move would be, but the agreement was settled in their hearts and Chas and Rosie went about life as usual.

Being back at school after the holidays meant Rosie had less time to spend in quiet moments with Chas. He was only working mornings, but her free time was limited to an hour or so in the afternoons. She still needed prep time for school in the evening after dinner.

'Rosie, let's make a time to meet Barry and get him to bring Steve along, so we can work through some of the details during the afternoon.'

'Why do you need Steve? He's still an apprentice.'

'Oh, Barry's suggestion was that it would be a good opportunity to increase Steve's learning curve, and of course Barry would not only be the creator and overseer, but he would be able to double check everything Steve does.'

Rosie replied dubiously, 'Oh really? I'd prefer to keep it all in Barry's hands, after all, don't you think that Steve would assume he could tell his sister all about the project?'

'When we announce that the project, details must be kept within the hangar crew. I am sure Steve will realise the sensitivity of the plans and, if he is found to have released any information, his job and future would be at stake.'

'Okay, but you really must make that clear to Steve.'

'No worries, Sweetie, Barry's a professional, with lots of experience. He'll be doing all the planning, and after all, Steve is the chief engineer's son. I think Phil will be pleased that we are getting him involved.'

'Whatever … I guess he's on a learning curve too,' replied Rosie.

On Wednesday afternoon, they all met at the hanger and Rosie's cheery greeting to Barry rather surprised him. 'Hi Barry, this is going to be great. I'll do another jump at the weekend and then you can work out how I'm going to be safe and comfy catching the clouds.'

'Good to see you, lovely lady. This is going to be quite an adventure and Steve's tickled pink that you've brought him on board, hey Steve?'

Steve's jocular reply sounded quite confident. 'Oh, for sure, I'm stepping out there too, hey? Thanks guys.'

The afternoon went well. Rosie's height and weight were measured, and various harness styles were discussed. The men were all busy measuring and testing while Rosie found a quiet spot and flipped through the pages of an aviation magazine.

'Rosie.' It was Chas's voice. 'Rosie, you wanna come over here?'

'Oh sorry, I've been so engrossed in an amazing article. Is it coffee time?'

Chas held up the cup and they all moved to the table to sit down and have a chat. Barry explained what they had decided upon, 'Well Rosie, we've made a few decisions and Steve and I are going to get the plans set up. You mightn't like the straps. They will be quite broad and tight, but it depends on what is available to suit the requirements.'

The discussion continued and then Rosie wanted to tell them what she had been reading about. 'Have any of you heard about the movie *Flyers?*'

Steve and Chas came out with a quick 'No', but Barry said, 'Yep, I read about that too. It was a thirty-two-minute film that was shown in the Air and Space Museum in Washington DC last August. Apparently, it was quite fanciful with lots of fictional drama.'

Rosie continued, 'Yes, it was a film to promote the IMAX filming process on an enormous screen. It involved a wing walker falling from a biplane over the Grand Canyon. He was then supposed to be rescued by another plane whose speed was slowed by three parachutes trailing behind it. In real life the parachutes didn't work well and Art Scholl, the pilot, renowned for his stunts, only just managed to clear a ridge in the canyon by ten feet as he rescued the parachutist.

'Listen guys, make those straps very strong, and if I hear, as a safety measure for me, that if I fall off the wing you're going to have another aircraft flying nearby for me to parachute onto, I won't be there for the take-off that day.'

The guys let out a few guffaws and Chas added, 'Rosie, there are two wings on the Tiger, so we don't need two planes.'

Rosie's second parachute jump came the following weekend after the bad weather had left the district. As she explained to Chas, 'I am quite accepting of the challenge and thrill of doing it all over again. I will have my cup of coffee about half an hour before I jump.'

'Ho-ho, I'd say that is probably just a psychological boost, Sweetie.'

'Whatever, it seems to convince me that I'm doing my physical best.'

It was to be the first time since his accident a few weeks earlier, that Chas was to fly the Cessna. He was elated and very satisfied that he could be there, in the air, with the love of his life. Rosie was in the second jump load and, along with Barry who was always there as the instructor, she was with Jeff and Carly.

'Hello you two. I'm in this with two experienced jumpers, hey?'

Carly laughed. 'I don't think we could teach you anything, Rosie. I guess you're just getting some practice breathing at a high altitude. Have you had a coffee?'

'Yep, for sure and that's right, I just want to expand my lungs and fill them with the cool clear air up here. You know what I mean?'

They all chuckled and Jeff commented, 'Hey Rosie, you seem to be taking this all very seriously?'

Aware that she was not to even hint that she was parachuting for another purpose, Rosie replied, 'Well, why wouldn't I? It's a pretty serious pastime. This is my second jump and I'm trying to look forward to my acceptance of leaving the open door and enjoying the drift slowly downwards.'

The jump went off perfectly, as she later described to Chas and Barry. 'It was just wonderful. I felt that I had total control.

Hmm, it sort of gives you a mindset. The freedom as you fall through space is almost a sense of autonomy. You have a parachute, but you are self-sufficient and aware that there is absolutely nothing that can get in your way. In fact, I think I will feel even less daunted standing on the aircraft, tied on of course, than jumping out of the door. I think that is truly the scariest part of parachuting. Climbing out of the door.'

CHAPTER 17

When Des Herd, the aviation officer from the Air Transport Bureau, arrived at Gunnedah Airport on the first Friday in December, Chas immediately introduced him to Barry and proceeded to guide him to the office in the hangar. Phil Jennings had also been made aware of Chas's aspiration. He was in the middle of a major operation, but knowing who the visitor was, and the reason he was in Gunnedah, Phil stopped everything and walked over to meet him. Chas offered them all a cup of coffee as they sat down around the table.

Des listened patiently and asked an occasional question about Chas's desire to present a wing-walking stunt for the 1983 Gunnedah AgQuip Show. Chas covered a considerable range of topics in support of the suggestion that wing-walking, as a carefully planned project, had to have the quintessence of safety. He then elaborated the fact that it could create an increased interest in aviation, which would revitalise the reputation and development of associated aviation activities.

'I do understand what you are trying to do Chas, but wing walking is prohibited, as you know. I do agree with you that there are some situations in display flying that come close to the limits of the air regulations, but now you are telling me that you want to carry out an experiment, which plainly goes beyond those limits, along with the support of the Air Safety Transport Bureau. That is a big step.'

Chas took a deep breath before he replied, 'Well yes. However, I do believe that progress in any field in society cannot remain restricted as new techniques, modern engineering and imaginative ideas are brought forward. Wing walking was considered an exciting and thrilling aerial stunt fifty years ago in the 1930s when there was no form of control, and at that time, of course, inevitable accidents. However, the aspiration and skill of a performer, in any activity, can be a highlight for many onlookers holding on to an ambition in a range of activities. I do believe that with meticulous planning, careful construction, and the cooperation of the Bureau, great steps could be made to increase the service, popularity, and reputation of aviation in Australia.'

'My goodness you are enthusiastic about this idea, Chas. You and Bill, your father, certainly have had the respect and support of the Bureau for your responsible and reliable activities over the years, while developing crop dusting in the region. So okay, without any approval implied or otherwise at this stage, shall we say that you go ahead, prepare a written plan that covers the skills and well-being of all participants, both ground and aerial personnel, a full report on the aircraft to be used and the fabrication required to cover the entire range of possible weights and measurements. Maybe we can then have another look at what you have in mind.'

Chas held back any expression of delight but as he said goodbye, he thanked Des for his time and interest.

Chas's news for Rosie that evening brought on a very animated and lively dinner conversation. Rosie was obviously thrilled with the apparent success of the meeting.

'So, you'll have to interview me and release my vital statistics, Chas. Is that right?'

'Yep, that's right, along with all the others. Barry and Phil came out and met Des just as he arrived, and they all seemed to hit it off straight away. So that was good. Phil also showed his interest and support. However, I reckon I'll have to line up some others like Steve and my dad. If I cover all bases, we just might get lucky.'

'So, initially your plan is for me to be relatively secure without much movement.'

'Yep, I think so, but Barry and I will do a load of research to see what is happening overseas and build on that. Maybe some independent leg and arm movements and even freedom to bend forwards and backwards. Of course, your curls will be blowing in the wind, we can't control them.'

Chas had also found some interesting references to a first wing-walking experience in a United States aviation publication. 'The article I read made it clear that a prospective performer should be given a full explanation of the equipment and we're certainly going to do that. However, it also suggested that there should be an understanding of breathing techniques that would provide greater ease on the body. That, I will have to research, but I would say breathing during a physical challenge would be something you would clearly be aware of Sweetie. It also referred to an understanding of the use of hand signals for communication, which would be advisable not only for confidence but safety issues. So, we'll spend the months ahead making decisions and plans, and getting the safety issues documented. Hopefully, we will get the Bureau approval in the new year and be able to go ahead with the aircraft preparation and practice sessions so that they are all completed well before the next AgQuip Show.'

The weeks passed and before long it was the Christmas season, which made Rosie realise just how much had happened during her first year back home and in the workplace. During the coming long summer break, she was looking forward to rest and relaxation, but she knew that much of her time was already committed. She had some new moves that she was going to introduce to the holiday gym team and also a load of additions to make to her schoolwork programme for the following year more exciting. Along with Chas's support, she was becoming more confident and involved with the wing-walking project. Barry and Steve had been kept busy preparing safety documents on the straps and platform construction details. Her vital statistics were part of the overall consideration and she also had to prepare a written account of her physical skills and ability. From time-to-time, Chas had a phone conversation with Des

Herd, who was most helpful and supportive in assisting with the planning and consideration of the requirements for the safety document.

A pre-Christmas party was arranged at the hangar and all aviators and those interested were invited to attend. The limited number of people who knew of the wing-walking venture were asked to hold back on making the information public knowledge. Chas had suggested that they would make a newsworthy announcement if the Bureau granted permission that the event could go ahead. Most of the talk and conversation centred around the growing interest in the parachute club. Phil Jennings gave his Christmas goodwill speech, and extended thanks to the AgQuip personnel and the local council for their consideration and support for the ongoing development of aviation in the region. It seemed that other organisations involved with air services were extending their interests to the area and that meant all-round growth in the industry. Phil also offered thanks to Barry and Chas for the responsibilities they had taken on during the year, and the impact Barry had had on the development of the Gunnedah Parachute Club. The speech was greeted with overwhelming applause.

Barry spent the evening constantly surrounded by people interested in speaking with him. Ted and Mary were one of the first couples to tap him on the shoulder for a chat. 'It seems like you are a popular man around town, Barry,' said Ted.

'Thanks Ted and to you too Mary. You have helped me so much in my search for history. John has been pretty busy lately, but he did say he'll look into whether there is any chance of me buying a house block on the property.' Ted replied with a chuckle,

'Ha ha, yep, he told me all about it. However, you know Barry there would be a few legal hitches to something like that.'

At that moment, Rosie joined her parents to also congratulate Barry. 'Hi Barry, I think it's great that your efforts and support for the Parachute Club over the year have been recognised.'

'Rosie, that sort of comment is really appreciated. Thanks.'

The family group and Barry then began a more generalised and community-based conversation.

Chas had been speaking with Steve about the growth of the Parachute Club when Lisa joined them. 'G'day Chas, it's nice to see you again. Is Steve telling you all about his jumps? You know, he has really inspired me and I'm going to get serious about continuing mine in the new year.'

'That sounds a good idea Lisa, your brother is the best person to motivate you. He has really come a long way and would be your best coach, I think.'

With raised eyebrows and a twisted smirk across his face, Steve replied, 'You're a good sort Chas and thanks for the recommendation, but I'm not putting my hand up, thank you.'

Chas then questioned Lisa, 'Ha ha, what d'ya reckon Lisa?'

'Awe if you treat him well, he can be a good sort, but I reckon you could give me a few words of encouragement.'

'No way, coaching's not for me.' Chas's words were out before he realised what he'd said.

'Lisa, Chas is the best of coaches, but you'd have to make it wing walking not… ahhh sorry, don't know what that's about.'

CHAPTER 17

'What do you mean, wing walking, Steve? I can't see Chas doing that when he does all he wants by just sitting in the cockpit.'

Without a word, Chas waved to a friend, said 'bye', and walked away as Steve mumbled, 'Sorry I've gotta go too Lisa. See ya.'

Chas kept turning over the words Steve had used that ended their conversation at the Christmas party. He explained to Rosie how it had unfolded and fortunately Rosie was positive enough about the slip of words to say, 'Chasie, I don't think Lisa will take the inference seriously. She would have no idea that anyone is considering wing walking.'

'I hope you're right Rosie, otherwise I'll have her breathing down my neck asking what it's all about.'

Christmas came and went, and New Year celebrations heralded some busy months ahead. On the first Saturday jump day in January, there was a group of twelve enthusiastic jumpers, including several newbies, hanging about in the hanger for the prep session. Barry was really chuffed that there was such a strong interest. However, he took the presumption of suggesting that it would be a much better session if maybe those doing their first jump could stay and if the experienced jumpers could make it the next day, Sunday. It was considered a good option by several participants. Barry was about to start on a busy weekend. Before she left the hangar to take up the option to return on Sunday, Lisa approached Barry. 'I really need to talk to you privately about my jumps. Can we have a coffee before prep tomorrow?'

'For sure, Lisa. I'd like to help you. Shall we have a coffee and an early lunch downtown?'

'Oh, yes, that would be so nice.'

After making arrangements to meet, Lisa left, and Barry got ready to get his session underway. Jeff Danes was going to be the ground observer. He had already arrived and then Barry noticed Rosie's friend, Carly Kent, amongst the group, and had a few quick words with her.

'Good to see you, Carly. Doing another jump?'

'Well yes, Barry, I really am excited. It's taken me a while to get back out here and I'm hoping it will give me another mode to think about artistically. Can I stay around today cos I'm busy tomorrow?'

'For sure, that's fine. Look, Jeff Danes is here. You know him. Have a chat to him and then we'll do the prep and I'll put you in the first drop group, okay?'

Chas had arrived and was checking the aircraft for it to be ready for two or three drop flights over the afternoon. He was surprised when Barry said there would be another session the next day.

So, it wasn't Chas that Lisa ended up approaching. When she and Barry met the next day, Lisa wanted confirmation that her interpretation of what she had already learnt about jumping was correct. She appeared nervous and Barry believed it was because she was just not sure of herself. He boosted her confidence by telling her that her previous jumps were good but that she needed to convince herself that everything was okay. After a period of easy talk, Lisa then asked Barry, 'What do you know about Chas coaching wing walking?'

'What? That's nothing to do with parachuting.'

Unconcerned with his reply, Lisa went on, 'Oh, I heard that he was a coach for that sort of thing. I just wondered if there was someone in Gunnedah who was going wing walking.'

'Lisa, lots of stories get around. Wing walking is an illegal stunt, so Chas would have to be very aware of his reputation if he decided to do that. Anyway, I've gotta get back to the hangar so I'll meet you there in half an hour to set you up for an exciting afternoon. See ya later.'

As Barry left, Lisa felt it was the same off-hand type of response she had had to the question when she had asked Steve at the Christmas party. Even her father, Phil, evaded the question.

The afternoon went well. Chas greeted Lisa with a cheery 'good luck' as she got into the aircraft to set off with Barry and two others for another jump. After they had all left the aircraft and Barry had checked their descent, he put his head over the front seat and told Chas what he had heard Lisa say at lunch. Chas's voice crackled, 'Oh, oh-oh no. No way. So, she believes something is happening. She only has to put two and two together and she'll realise it's me and Rosie.' Chas then told Barry about Steve's comment at the Christmas party.

'Yep, I'd say she thinks something is going on. Anyway, we just have to brush her off until we hear from the Bureau.'

When Chas told Rosie that night of Barry's brief chat with Lisa, she was again rather nonchalant and insisted that they just ignore her questions.

'It is better that we just don't react, that way she will probably forget about it. She's just a stirrer, particularly in regard to anything about you Chas.'

CHAPTER 18

Barry had just got home on Sunday afternoon and was planning a lazy and relaxed evening. He had become rather resourceful in providing himself with basic but tasty evening meals. There had been times when he wished that he had the courage to invite Rosie to dinner, but was sensitive enough to know that she and Chas had developed a tight relationship. Although he really wasn't sure of Rosie's opinion of him, he did like them both as friends and they had helped him settle into the community to the point where he was convinced that Gunnedah was a town that he could make his hometown.

As he stirred the pot on the stove, he was thinking about Carly, the bright young woman to whom Rosie had introduced him, and who seemed keen to take on the challenge of parachuting. *Maybe I could get sweet with her.* He sat down to wait for the quick curry to finish cooking and picked up one of his magazines from the pile on the coffee table. He had two major subscriptions, one associated with new developments in aeronautical engineering and several copies of *NSW Farmers*, a magazine that was really helping him to get his head around the agricultural industry.

The telephone rang and interrupted his train of thought. He turned down the gas on the stove and made his way to the hallway to pick up the phone.

'Hello there, Barry here.'

'G'day Barry, this is John. How ya going mate?'

'Yep, all fine here. What's up?'

'Well, I've checked out a few details in regard to the property. I reckon we need to sit down with a beer to discuss possibilities and think it through. You want to come out and have dinner with us Friday evening?'

Barry believed John was speaking with a touch of enthusiasm and was quick to reply. 'For sure, John. I'll probably be out of the hangar by about 5.30, so how about I pick up some beers and see you about 6.30?'

'Yep, that would suit us well. Make sure it's Toohey's New. See you then, mate. Cheers.'

As he put the phone down, Barry was certainly feeling optimistic, but realised he had to hang out until the end of the week with the possibilities of what John maybe offering chasing around in his head.

This was going to be the first week that the wing-walking group would be working together to exchange ideas and confirm the projects required by each member. Although Phil Jennings was not going to be actively constructive, his knowledge and skills as the chief LAME, with a full understanding of the capabilities

CHAPTER 18

of the Tiger Moth, were essential for assisting the work to be done by the others. Barry and Steve were to concentrate on the planning of the harness, straps, and aircraft modifications. Chas was going to record everything and ultimately prepare the document for the Air Transport Bureau. Nothing was to be physically constructed until everything had been checked and then approved by the Bureau.

The programme was arranged whereby they would all get together at 3.30 pm on every second day, beginning Monday, then Wednesday and Friday. There would be an exchange of plans and achievements and then a continuation of their individual projects. It worked well for Rosie because she was on holidays for three more weeks, so she could also turn up in the hangar. Her queries were also to be considered, as were Chas's, for example, Was Rosie to be in the same position for the entire stunt? Some of the questions she had prepared considered her position on the platform above the cockpit, along with the movements she would like to perform with her arms, her legs or even her whole body while remaining in a restricted position.

It was 3 pm. Chas and Rosie were eager to get to the hangar. It was fortunate that all were able to be present for the first pre-arranged meeting. Phil, Barry and Steve immediately gave Chas the leader's seat, and the talks began. For the next step, each individual found a quiet spot to peruse the elements of his or her part in the project and began the documentation ready for discussion at the following meeting.

Towards the end of the session, Barry called Rosie and Steve over to his bench and table in the corner of the hangar. As Rosie sat down, she noticed several magazines at the end of the table. Aeroplane photographs were on the covers of most of them but there was one that stood out. A bright photograph of farm workers clambering over a tractor was on the cover of the *NSW Farmer*. That did surprise her. She wondered why Barry would be interested in a farm magazine.

Barry and Steve both had to have Rosie's height, weight, and some other basic details like waist measurement, to construct the frame that was to support her body. The harness would be tailored to her measurements and fixed so that no adjustments would be possible. This would be an added advantage for the safety issues. Rosie still needed to be sure of the degree of movement she could have.

'Can I still have unrestricted body movement?'

Barry's reply came with a chuckle, 'Rosie, I don't think you'll want that. The harness will hold your body firmly. You'll have freedom to move your arms and legs and make a slight turn of the upper body at the waistline but there can be absolutely no forward and backward movement. The air will be gushing strongly, and your body must remain in one position so the weight and balance will not change, and the pilot can manage the flight.'

'Okay, so I can stretch and bend my arms and legs?'

'Yes, that's right. You can put your ankle behind your head if you want.'

'Ha ha, not quite. Anyway, I guess it won't be until I have my first run that I will appreciate exactly what I can and want to do.'

Steve added a comment, 'Rosie you could turn the air fan up

CHAPTER 18

to maximum and if you stand in front of it, you'll get a feel for a strong air current.'

Barry had to supply an answer for that comment. 'I wouldn't want Rosie to compare the blast of air on the top wing of the Tiger with the gentle breeze coming from an air fan.'

There was hearty laughter from all three.

Later in the week, Rosie let her head loose at the holiday gymnastics session. Trying to keep her body rigid while she stretched her arms and legs into a variety of positions was not an easy task. She wanted her positions to look graceful, but knowing the wind would be challenging, she knew that if her figure could look astonishing, she would achieve her goal. She did come to realise that strength would be her greatest asset, so she set about doing routines on the parallel bars and the vertical pole that would develop arm strength, while floor work was good for general strength and resistance.

On Friday afternoon, as the stunt discussion came to an end, Steve left, and Rosie asked Barry for a chat.

'I've got some news to share with you too, Rosie.'

'Oooh really? What's that?'

Barry told Rosie he was meeting up with John that evening.

'Yep, John phoned to say there was some news about the property.'

'Oh, really Barry, do you think it will be good news?'

'Well, yes, I did get that impression when he spoke, although he didn't tell me anything. I'll let you know over the weekend if something turns out. By the way, do they have any children?'

'Yes, two little girls. Jenny who's four years old and Lorraine who's just two. They are two busy little girls. They'll knock you off your chair if you don't watch out.'

'Oh right, do you think they'll have anymore? I guess a farmer would always like a son to help on the farm and inherit the property.'

'Oh, I really don't think John is concerned about anything like that.'

Rosie then explained that she wanted to show Barry a few of the movements she was considering in the stunt. She was appropriately dressed in jeans and T-shirt as she stretched her arms and kicked her legs. Barry was impressed and suggested they could fit an arrangement of straps on her body so that she would have an idea how the harness would work and feel. It was 4.30, and as Chas came looking for Rosie he saw Barry gently manoeuvring some straps around Rosie's body. In a quiet, doleful voice he asked, 'So, what's going on here?'

Surprised, Barry said, 'G'day Chas,' while Rosie jumped at the sound of Chas's voice and said, 'Oh Chas, Barry's just showing me how I can attach some straps round my waist and then to a post, to give me a sense of rigidity to discover the moves I should make.'

'Yeh OK, but I reckon we've gotta go now. Thanks Barry.'

With thanks from Rosie, Barry wound up the straps and handed them over. 'They'll make a difference to your practice, little lady.'

With a smile, Rosie replied, 'Bye, see you next week and I hope it's a good night for you.'

Chas and Rosie drove home in their own cars, but Chas could

hardly wait to start asking questions once they were at home. 'Rosie, why, after saying goodbye, did you wish Barry a good night?'

Rosie could see the humour in the question and proceeded to explain that Barry was going to see John later in the evening. 'Apparently John's got some info about the farm, and he wants to talk to Barry about it.'

'Didn't you think Barry seemed to be getting a bit touchy-feely with you as he played around with the straps?'

'Oh Chas, no way. He was just trying to help, and I do reckon it's a good idea. The straps were the touchy-feely bit of the exercise, not Barry, and they'll certainly give me an idea as to how my movements will be restricted.'

Barry was out of the hangar on the dot of 5.30 and set off for home. He had to change from his work clothes and searched through his wardrobe to consider what would see him suitably dressed for the hot summer's evening. He was feeling a little sceptical because his conversation with John had been a week earlier, and over the past couple of days, he had begun to doubt his own optimism. By dressing in comfortable but smart clothes, he was hoping to boost his ego. After he had showered and dressed, he set off immediately. On the way to *Ted's Place* he picked up a carton of Toohey's New that he knew was the favoured beer in Gunnedah, and a bunch of flowers from the supermarket for Sally. He certainly wanted to appear friendly.

Twenty minutes later, as he pulled into the driveway, Barry spotted John sitting on the fence. It was a cheery welcome.

Seeing the car arrive, John jumped off and greeted Barry with a strong handshake as he got out, 'Good to see ya, Barry.'

A little girl came running up to John, and as he picked her up, he introduced her to Barry, 'This is our little girl, Jenny. There's another one inside. Her name's Lorraine.'

'Hello Jenny, and yep, thanks for the invite, John. I thought something like this might be useful during the evening.' Barry opened the back door of his car to pick up the carton of beer, which he passed on to John and then stretched along the back seat for the bunch of flowers.

'Ha ha,' chuckled John, 'you've certainly come prepared.'

Sally also welcomed Barry warmly as John led him into the kitchen. 'We're pleased to see you again, Barry. I hope you've had a good week at work.'

'Always, thanks Sally.'

With such a jovial welcome, Barry felt somewhat relaxed. Sally was pleasantly surprised and very thankful for her bunch of flowers. The two guys then stepped outside to the veranda, each with a glass of beer, while Sally stayed to look after the little girls, to feed them and get them ready for bed. An hour or so later, when the three of them sat down at the table, Barry was completely dumbfounded as his hosts raised their glasses and suggested that their evening would be one to remember. John began the conversation by referring to the visit he had made to the real estate office.

'Yeh Barry, I had a good chat to a guy at the agency that had handled our grandfathers' properties way back in the 20s. They are interested in helping us work out something that would suit us both. We can come to a legal agreement about size and location, but it will all cost a considerable amount for subdivision and the registration.'

A little dubiously, Barry asked, 'So, you two are okay with the idea?'

'Well, yeh, but we need to work with you, and none of us can afford to be backward in coming forward with ideas, questions and suitability. It was also explained to me that the whole process could take some time. It's not going to be an easy exercise. However, if after all necessary discussion and initial decision-making, the plan suits both parties, Sally and I are prepared to proceed.'

Although John was speaking a little hesitantly, Barry could understand where he was coming from, and he felt much the same.

'Listen John, I understand exactly what you are saying. I am going along in all this with a fond hope that I can somehow absorb some of the history of our adventurous grandfathers. I understand the legal implications and how it must involve you and your family. As I said before, I will take all financial responsibility and choose an option that would in no way be stressful or uncomfortable for you and your family.'

John listened carefully. 'Yes, thanks Barry. I have heard that over the past twelve months you have settled into the Gunnedah community very well. You're well respected and hardworking, so there's a reputation that can be considered if you are keen to stay here permanently, and in that case, I do believe you.'

Barry added, 'I do want to stay here, and I do want to maintain my job at the airport, however, if there were circumstances John, whereby I could provide assistance in some way, then maybe I could be looked upon as an independent family member.'

'Okay Barry. I know you said previously that you were only considering a reasonably sized house block so, how about you make some plans, and we'll see what the possibilities are? First of all, you must let me know where you would like to settle and how much land you want. You will need to follow up on the financial situation. You don't have to share that information with us until we get the finer details of the land you want and then we'll put a fair price on it. Hey?'

The discussion continued as they enjoyed the delightful meal Sally had cooked. It was a productive and pleasant evening and when it came time to say goodbye, Barry complimented Sally, 'Thank you both for an interesting and enjoyable evening. I must say that I knew of your reputation Sally, because your father-in-law said that you always cook delicious meals for them. Thanks again, you'll hear from me soon in regard to the offer to have another look over the farm.'

As Barry left, Sally and John waved then turned to go inside. Sally's comment to John surprised him. 'So, that all went well. Financially it could make a difference for us too, John.'

CHAPTER 19

Rosie felt that her holidays had passed too quickly. The Gym Club was developing well. It was twelve months since she had set it up and the support and popularity had not stopped growing. Carly had often attended to do some routine gymnastics built on previous experience, but once introduced to parachuting she found the gym to be an exciting diversion. Barry was pleased with her progress and Rosie was not surprised that she had taken several parachute jumps.

Carly approached Rosie one day before the beginning of Term 1 wondering if she could help out with the Gym Club.

'Oh wow Carly, that would be fantastic. Yep, with the increase in numbers, particularly with the younger children, I would really like some assistance.'

Carly was not aware of anything else that was capturing Rosie's time and Rosie was certainly not going to tell her about her hours at the airport. Knowing that once school started she would need to spend a regular afternoon with Barry and Steve in the hangar, it seemed Carly would be the help she needed for that one afternoon a week. The Saturday morning gym session would remain the strongest time and that was no problem for Rosie, so she asked Carly if she could start as soon as possible.

First term got underway, and with lesson preparation and the new year changes and challenges, both women were exceptionally busy with their responsibilities.

Barry had been very helpful by providing chances for Rosie to experiment with the harness he was working on, but it was purely experimental. Rosie would climb up onto the top wing of the Tiger and move and stretch, and pull, while the men observed the positions and stress affecting the harness and straps. It was a weekly exercise for Rosie. Because of their regular work commitments, it took several days for the two men to make satisfactory and safe adaptations for the test period the following week. For Rosie, it was time for her to be imaginative and innovative. For all three, everything had to be recorded and then edited with each change, according to the need to show the safety aspects.

Bill had kept Chas very busy throughout January and that was going to follow into February. It was during the hot summer months that the insects and weeds were the bane of a farmer's life. The hardworking producers were tormented daily by the increase of insects and the insidious spread of weeds, so there were constant calls for aerial spraying. Rosie and Chas were together for the evenings, but the daily pressure meant there was little time spent in each other's company during the daylight hours. Chas was also having to write his account of the development of the wing-walking project. When the other members of the group had completed their reports, he would have to arrange them in a final document. Phil Jennings would have the broader details on the Tiger Moth, Barry and Steve were developing an outline of the finer details of the harness and platform, and Rosie would have a description of her routine. Chas was hoping to get the final report, detailing all procedures and safety aspects, away to Des Herd within a few weeks.

One evening, Chas asked Rosie, 'How's your routine working out? You're still going to the hangar on Wednesdays?'

'Awe Chasie, it's all going well. Yep, I have to see Barry every Wednesday and Steve is usually there to.'

'Do they need you there each week? Surely things aren't changing that much in just a week.'

Rosie was surprised that Chas needed an explanation.

'It's about time you started finalising things you know... I just haven't got time to look over everything, so I hope Barry's fulfilling his responsibility and covering all aspects.'

Chas was more than a little surprised that Rosie was required to be out in the hangar so frequently. 'I thought once you had given them your routine, they would be able to cover all requirements. I just wonder why you have to spend so much time with Barry.'

'Oh Chas, Barry has been fantastic. He really is very supportive, as is Steve, who is also very encouraging, and is there every afternoon as well. Between us all we have changed things from time to time for the better. We all see the routine from a different angle and each person, even including Steve, has contributed to what we are now considering to be a project that the Bureau cannot find any reason to deny us the opportunity to test fly the complete stunt. Chas, there can be very small changes that can have rather broad effects, whether it's the position, the strength, the length or whatever, just maybe because I want to change something or one of us has a better idea. Steve has been really reassuring and encouraging. When I suggest something, he either knocks the idea on the head with a big no-no or puts me into a position where the straps can be adjusted, and I can make it work out.'

Chas's reply was certainly one of conviction. 'Wow Rosie. I do respect what you've said and admit it sounds like you've all done a great job. I look forward to the report. I love you so, Sweetie. I am just not seeing enough of you these days and am somewhat jealous that those guys can spend a whole afternoon with you.'

Rosie had questioned Barry after his dinner evening with John and Sally, but Barry still didn't want to say too much about the ongoing plans. He had planned to do another trip to the farm and examine all possible sites. He was certainly encouraged by the proceedings but had to be sure of the financial situation in which he would find himself. When Rosie noticed her brother at the parachute session in the hangar one Saturday afternoon while she was waiting for Chas, she went up to him and asked, 'John, what is Barry really trying to persuade you to do?'

'Awe, you know he's really interested in putting up his own house on the property.'

Rosie then replied in a very halting tone, 'John, I'd like to talk to you. Can I call out to the farm for a coffee and have a chat to you and Sally?'

CHAPTER 19

'Yep, for sure. Would you and Chas like to come for dinner tomorrow night?'

'Oooh now, that would be really nice. We'll come out about 5.30 and that will give us some time to play with my little nieces before they go to bed. Tell Sally we'll bring a trifle for dessert.'

'Okay li'l sis, we'll see you then.'

Rosie was pleased to think her brother was prepared to speak about the situation. When Chas returned from his last trip to the drop zone, they hopped in the car and headed for home.

'Chas, John has invited us to dinner tomorrow night. Okay with you?'

'Ha ha, I bet he had some encouragement to do that. You just want to talk to him about Barry's interests, hey?'

That was exactly what Rosie was planning. She really did get the vibes that Barry was interested in more than just a house on the property.

It was fun to catch up with her brother and his family. Rosie had missed the early years of John and Sally's marriage and the arrival of the babies. Now she really enjoyed being able to socialise and be an auntie. The evening was pleasant. After dinner they all sat out on the veranda to enjoy the cool summer evening. Rosie then decided to broach the subject they all knew was coming. 'Okay John, so what do you think Barry is going to do?'

'Rosie, it's still nowhere near a conclusion. There's an awful lot that has to happen and Barry does realise that it is going to be a very expensive exercise. He seems very enthusiastic and if he can be satisfied with a house tucked away down near the creek on the far end of the property just off the main road, then that could possibly work out.'

'Yes John, I know what you're saying, but I reckon Barry may well prepare his plans with opportunities tucked away somewhere.'

'Whatever do you mean Rosie? What he pays for is what he'll get.'

'Uh-uh, there could be more to it than money. There could be legal implications tied up with council requirements that might all sound ridgy-didge now but as circumstances change, both within and without family connections, there could be increasing avenues to increase the influence of the smaller property owner. I don't know for sure, of course, but I do think Barry has a deeper need in the way he wants to associate himself with what was once his grandfather's farm.'

'Awe, c'mon. I do believe him to be an honest and straightforward fellow. He is up front and prepared to seek advice.'

'Yes, John. I agree. He is a nice enough guy, but he is extremely disappointed that he has no stake in a family inheritance. Even though he told me that he doesn't want to be a farmer, I do think he realises a future on the land could be in his hands. All I'm saying John, is to be wary. Get advice constantly, talk to the local land agents and lawyers. Yep, it's going to cost you money too, but if it protects you in a process that is not easy for us non-professionals to understand, then it will be worthwhile. If you talk to anyone about anything I've said, it will all be rebuked with people saying, 'Forget it John, what would your little schoolie sister know about such things.' Please keep me out of any discussions. Keep my name out of it altogether.'

'Oh boy Rosie, you certainly did have something to say. I am listening and I will certainly check and double check everything that transpires. I do appreciate your support.'

The conversation continued with both Sally and Chas having words to say. Ultimately, John felt there was some sense in anticipating an inadvertent process that could evolve negatively for him and his family.

During the following week, Chas made it clear to the wing-walking group that their final reports needed to be in by Friday. He wanted to do his editing and presentation over the following week so the report could be sent off to the Air Transport Board during the first week of March.

CHAPTER 20

When the wing-walking report was eventually sent off to Des Herd, Chas and Rosie found they had more time together. Having assistance with the Gym Club during the week was relieving the impact on Rosie's workload, even though she did keep in touch with Carly, offering ideas and suggestions that were very welcome for the novice instructor. Carly had updated her first-aid qualifications and was taking her responsibilities very seriously. She and Rosie had started to regularly exchange information over an iced coffee on Thursday afternoons.

'You know, Rosie, there are a couple of students I'd love to coach.'

'And I am sure I'd probably know which champs you're referring too, Carly. That sounds a good idea and there's an upcoming regional gymnastic championship, so they'd have something to aspire to.'

'Yep, I'll certainly get those details. Barry really is a great jump coach. He has helped me so much, not only in the physical aspects of jumping and preparation, but he really knows what to say to boost a person's confidence and self-esteem. I'd like to take those attributes I've learnt from him and use them to help the young gymnasts.'

'Yes, that's so right, he certainly helped me too when I was doing my jumps.'

Carly then asked, 'Why don't you come out on Saturday afternoons anymore?'

Rosie had to be careful with her answer. 'Oh, I'm sure I will. It's just that I am pretty busy on Saturdays after the gym session in the morning and some other stuff in the afternoons. I reckon Barry wants to hang around Gunnedah for a while yet. Did you know he's even been trying to get a bit of land out John's way?'

'Oh, is that so? Does he want to go farming?'

'Not to my knowledge, maybe you should ask him.'

'Ha ha. I might just do that.'

Rosie felt there was more to Carly's answer than what she said. *Perhaps*, she thought, *Carly might be doing a bit of flirting with Barry.*

When Rosie arrived home that evening, Chas welcomed her with a big grin and cuddle. Rosie had to ask the question, 'Hey ho, something's happened. What's the news Chas?'

'Oh, only that I had a phone call from Des to say that the report had arrived. He hasn't read it yet, but he did say that it looked like all parties have put in a great effort and that he's looking forward to reading it.'

'Well, you couldn't get a better response, hey?'

'That's right Rosie. He sounded positive, so I hope that means we won't have to wait too long for a reply. There's a fly-in over at Tamworth on Saturday. I'd really like to go and take the Tiger, not to talk about the project but just to be out there in the field, so when things do start to happen, we can get a supportive response.'

Rosie's face lit up. 'Oh Chas, that sound's great. I'll be free but what about the jump drop?'

'Oh, I'm sure Dad will help out. I'll see Barry about that.'

The Tamworth fly-in went well. Chas met up with some of his flying mates and was also introduced around, all of which ended up with him accepting some slots for air show presentations over the rest of the summer and even for springtime. Later in his conversation with Rosie, he suggested that those springtime stunts may well include wing walking, though of course, he had not breathed a word of that to anyone during the afternoon.

'I just hope Des gets back to us soon. There'll probably be a few hiccups, so we'll get them cleared up and then we'll be able to start our practising.'

'It is all so exciting, Chas. I know what to expect, and it's all firing me up.'

When they arrived back at Gunnedah Airport, the parachuting had not long finished, and Barry was doing a bit of organising in the hangar. Chas parked the Tiger and he and Rosie were making their way to the carpark when Chas recognised Barry's voice calling to him. They turned and everyone exchanged greetings. A little to Rosie's surprise,

CHAPTER 20

Barry was walking out of the hanger with Carly.

'Hey Chas, we're just heading off to the Regal for a drink and a bit of dinner, why don't you and Rosie join us?'

'Yes, that'd be great, mate. See you at Conadilly Street.'

They met up at the hotel and found a comfortable spot outside where they could enjoy their drinks and order a hamburger for dinner. Carly and Rosie were elated to see each other and with a twinkle in her eye, Rosie asked, 'Well Carly, did you have a good jump today?'

'Yes, of course, as always.'

Barry then offered his opinion. 'This lady just gets better and better. She was right on her landing spot today and Jeff was there to help. She is very good at following his instructions immediately, like, 'Get your hand on the right riser, now'. He always offers good advice for the newbies and does a great job.'

Rosie and Carly continued to chat while Chas and Barry compared notes of their day's exploits. When the men got up to replenish the drinks, Rosie couldn't help commenting in a cheeky voice, 'Carly, so you're getting out and about with Barry?'

'You could say that. We do enjoy each other's company.'

'Have you noticed Lisa Jennings at the jump club? I know she wanted some lessons, but I haven't seen her around for a while.'

'Yes, she was there last weekend. She's always looking for special attention. I've often seen her grab Barry or Jeff for some personal advice before she jumps. You know her, don't you?'

'Not really well. We've crossed paths a couple of times, but she never really seems to regard jumping with any great passion. I think she just likes the environment and uses her charms to get the attention of the nice guys around.'

It was a pleasant evening for all and as they headed off for the carpark there was mutual agreement that they should meet up for dinner more often. Once they were in the car, Chas told Rosie that Barry was really eager to get started on the wing-walking fabrication. He wanted to start ordering stuff and play around with it a bit before actually making the platform and harness. Chas did not think that was a good idea just yet as somebody might see what is going on and start asking questions. Rosie agreed and then repeated what Carly had told her about Lisa's ongoing fraternisation with the guys at the jump club. Both she and Chas agreed that Lisa was the last person they wanted to have any knowledge of the project.

When Chas arrived home from work on Friday, there was another cuddle for Rosie, and with a big smile on his face, he told her that Des Herd had called him and was coming for a discussion on Monday. 'Do you think you'll be able to get an hour or two off work late Monday morning, Sweetie? I want to get the other three guys too, so we'll all be there to hear the decision.'

'No problems Chas, I actually have a free period to lunch time after morning recess, so that should work out well. I'll be there.'

'Des has also suggested that if we have anything that we are going to use or work on, related to the safety issues, then we should have them available for inspection. I guess Barry will be all for that and I think you could have some evidence on what you will wear. Remember, tight fitting trousers, no flapping shirts, and solid but flexible shoes.'

There was much excitement generated amongst the hangar crew when they gathered in the hanger office on Monday morning to await the arrival of Des Herd. They set out the samples of their work that they had brought along. For Rosie, the recent developments of Lycra made her choice of clothing easy. Lycra was regarded as the modern fabric for use in active wear. She had had an early introduction to it with gymnastic costumes and swimwear. She brought a pair of Lycra tights and a tight-fitting shirt that could not only be produced in bright colours that would be easily seen, but the items would allow increased mobility and a range of movement that could be both flexible and comfortable. The men all had evidence of their research including strap and fabric samples plus diagrams and plans.

Des received a warm welcome and they all sat down to hear the response of the Air Transport Bureau. Chas's earlier comments on the importance of ideas in relation to new developments were discussed at some length and to the surprise and satisfaction of the group, a tentative agreement was delivered for the project to go ahead. The major issue was safety, and as Chas had presented in his report, they would only undertake fabrication and processes that were already proved worldwide for their safety aspects. Des had considered the arguments and said the Bureau had agreed that they could continue in an experimental mode but be closely monitored by the associated safety officers.

Since he had planned to stay in Gunnedah for the afternoon, Des accepted Chas's offer to go for a flight in the Tiger. Phil explained in detail the plans already made for the aircraft, including the location of the platform. They also planned to use a dummy, the same weight and dimensions as Rosie, to establish the correct weight balance and location of the harness. Des was satisfied with the day's proceedings and when the group invited him to dinner for the evening, he knew that it was a means of 'thanks' rather than any need for bribery. Rosie's toast to the group was well received.

'To you Des, my friends and workmates, and my dear partner, Chas, I thank you all. You are experts who have been so understanding. It seems my dream of walking in the clouds and sunshine, just might come true one day.'

As they clinked glasses there were smiles and words of encouragement all round.

After the past weeks of report writing and planning for Chas, Barry guessed he was going to have a little more time to himself. The run-of-the-mill construction of the platform and harness was to be in Steve's hands, following Barry's carefully laid out diagrams and plans. Steve was a very keen tradie and quite absorbed by the process ahead.

Barry planned in his free time to check out a couple of banks and a mortgage company to see how much money he could consider in John's property negotiations. He had several thousand dollars tucked away, an inheritance from his father. It had not been all that easy, but he had managed to add to his savings at a fairly slow rate. Once he knew how much money he could borrow and the rate of payment he would have to cover, he could then again go back to John and begin a serious discussion. He also realised that he would have to find a lawyer in town, preferably one that would not have any family preferences.

Chas had mentioned that there could be a remunerative advantage for all those concerned in the wing-walking project. He had suggested that a carefully promoted advertising opportunity, or even an investment style of business operation, could help all parties financially. Rosie's response to that was that if the Lycra company was approached, they might be able to see some lucrative response to the promotion of Lycra fabric in high winds. Chas agreed and said that he would approach someone he knew for on-going business advice.

It now seemed that word of the project could be let loose. Chas did feel somewhat anxious about making an announcement, but following his train of thought, he considered it an essential step. He did, however, suggest they keep it within the Parachute Club for the near future. Wing walking was still only a possibility because lots of hurdles had to be cleared, but Chas knew there could be strong support from an interested public. It would be obvious to workers in the hangar that something new was going on and Barry also suggested that a public announcement at the Parachute Club may down-play any perceived secrecy.

On Saturday evening at the club gathering, Chas, Rosie, Phil and Steve were all present, and Barry had taken the initiative to invite all the hangar staff for the evening. Standing up in front of the bar with Chas, he called everyone together to make an announcement explaining the wing-walking project. His opening remarks praised Chas and Rosie for taking steps to 'achieve the mighty goal of wing walking'. His acknowledgement of the fact that the stunt was still considered illegal received a few claps and boos. He then explained that the agreement with the Air Transport Bureau was only provisional for the time being and that many issues, in particular, safety measures, were being worked through. With a successful conclusion, Barry explained, the development of aviation in Gunnedah, and in general across Australia, would get a great boost. After Barry's praise of Chas's work, and that of the other members of the project team, the group applauded boisterously and gathered around the participants to offer words of encouragement and their good wishes.

The party atmosphere continued for some time, and everyone wanted to ask questions. Carly approached Rosie and whispered, 'Rosie, I knew you had some little secret tucked away. I did think it was all about Chas but apparently not. How much fun that must be for you two to have such a wonderful goal to share, and you couldn't put your trust in a barter pilot, hey?'

'Yes, it all really happened cos Chas and Barry wanted me to parachute, but I had already heard all about wing walking. When I suggested that I'd like to try, they told me to go off and do some research. I think they thought that by finding out that it would not be an easy activity to get going in Australia, that I would get over it. However, Chas was my stalwart and we decided we'd try and get things happening. It was then that Barry and the others supported our plans and here we are. Nothing is definite yet. Lots of things have to be worked on but it is fun, and the anticipation is so motivating.'

Carly nodded, and as they continued talking, she indicated her support, including helping out at the Gym Club. They were so engrossed in their heart-to-heart chat that Rosie did not notice Lisa approaching Chas. It was not until they were driving home that Chas mentioned his chat with the flighty nurse. 'I guess I had to expect it, but you know Lisa, she came up and wanted to talk tonight.'

Because he was driving, Chas couldn't see the scathing look on Rosie's face. 'Really? I guess she couldn't help herself. What did she say?'

'Oh it was all gooey, like what a wonderful idea I had and how she would really like to have a go at wing walking herself.'

'Oh Chas, you are kidding me? She can't even do a jump without having a person-on-person lecture about confidence, and Barry or Jeff convincing her that she can do it!'

'Yeh, I did say to her that you have to be very committed to be prepared to work on such a stunt, and then she asked me why I chose you to do it.'

'Is that right? What did you tell her?'

'Just the truth. I told her that the whole project was your idea and that each of us guys had said that we wanted to be involved and help you out. I don't think she liked that comment very much cos she just replied that she thought that you were very self-centred and did not think of the pressures that you'd put on us guys. I really had to laugh, and I then fobbed her off. I don't think she liked that either. Before she said goodbye, she went on about my state of health, insisting that I should be taking things easy and how she was concerned that I might be working too hard, even all this time after the accident.'

'Oh Chas, she is still trying to capture your attention.'

'There's no chance of that Sweetie. I love you.'

'Oooh, I love you too.'

CHAPTER 21

The weeks were slipping by and Rosie was making headway with the wing walking. One Monday, after an exhausting day at work, Rosie's attention was captured as she opened Chas's front door. She heard the introductory melody from a track on the *Jonathan Livingston Seagull* LP. She loved the song Be and sang the first lines along with Neil Diamond as she walked into the living room.

Lost, on a painted sky
Where the clouds are hung, for the poet's eye....

'Oh ho, Rosie, that is just beautiful. Where were you when they were recording that?'

'Hi Chasie. Oh boy, I do love that song. The words came to me as I was drifting down on my second jump. I knew exactly how Jonathan, the seagull, would have felt.'

Checking out Chas's hunky, athletic body stretched over the lounge, she could not help but ask, 'Just how long have you been home? You look like you've been here all day.'

'Well, I finished early doing a spray job and I wasn't required at the servo, so I thought I'd take some R and R.'I wish, I wish. we could spend more time together.' Rosie replied with a sigh,

'Yep, I wish that too.'

' Anyway, here you are.' Chas held out his arms and Rosie climbed on top of him to respond with a warm embrace. After a little chuckle, Chas continued, 'This week will really see things happening. I've had a chat to Barry and the dummy run is planned for next Sunday. We'll strap you on to the platform and taxi out to the runway but then we'll replace you with the dummy and I'll do a practice flight.'

'That sounds great. I can get my Lycra gear on and test it out clambering up onto the wing and doing a few stretches. On Monday morning I'm going to have that strong cup of coffee like I do before a gym or diving comp.'

'Ya reckon that'll be safe?'

'Of course! I've had doctor's checks and recommendations so it's not an issue. A lot of athletes have a bit of a boost with a cup of coffee. It just helps me with better co-ordination and concentration, and since the exercise is rather intense, it will help with endurance.'

'Wow, that's something to look forward to.'

The conversation continued until Chas decided to prepare dinner and Rosie started her prep for the next day.

Barry was on top of his responsibilities and had outlined the tasks for Steve, which meant he had a bit of free time over the week. He had several appointments lined up to check out the banks and see a lawyer because there was a realisation that

CHAPTER 21

he needed to know the legalities and an idea of costs before he made any major decisions. He had spent the last Sunday evening with Carly. She appeared delighted to have been invited out to dinner and then they went back to his place. It was a very low key and relaxing evening with most of the conversation hovering around parachuting. However, without mentioning names or locations, Barry did mention his yearning for some land in the region so that he could build a house. He kept the details out of the way but did say that he wanted to settle in a rural area.

Carly could not help asking the question, 'So do you want to start up a farm, Barry?'

'Oh no, no, not at all, I just like country settings and country life. I'm quite happy with aeroplanes and parachuting.'

'That's good. I'd hate to think you had no time for jumping days. I'm really keen to keep it up. Wasn't that fantastic news about the wing-walking report from the Bureau?'

'That's for sure. Chas and Rosie have been on about it for a while now and both Steve and I are so caught up in it too. It's going to take a bit of time, but I reckon it will all work out.'

'Barry, you are very supportive of them, and I do hope your wishes come true too. Do keep me in the loop.'

'Will do.'

The evening was enjoyed by both parties and when Barry hesitantly suggested they do it again, Carly was most enthusiastic.

By the end of the week, Barry had several options that he could consider regarding the financial issues at stake. He felt confident, so he phoned John and made an arrangement to meet on the farm during the following week to check out the block areas that John had in mind.

For the jump session on Saturday, it was a sunny afternoon, with only a gentle breeze drifting across the airfield. The promise of excellent jumping conditions had encouraged an enthusiastic group of twelve jumpers. Barry could see Lisa and Carly having an amiable chat and John was there along with Jim and Steve.

Barry greeted John with a quick, but jovial, pat on the back, wanting to avoid any casual discussion about the land until their meeting. Rosie was hanging around the Cessna while Chas did his pre-flight check. As Barry approached, she said, 'Hi Barry, I'll see you tomorrow. Have a good day,' and she moved off to the carpark.

The first jump group were getting into the aircraft when, as she was leaving, Rosie spotted John waiting for his turn. She called to him, 'Hi, g'bye, John.'

'Hey, Rosie, it's good to see you. Come over here and have a chat. Haven't seen you for a while. It'll be good to catch up.'

'I know, I guess you've been pretty busy too and I've had a load on my plate.'

A bit of talk followed about the wing-walking project and what had been happening.

'Yeh, it's great to know how well things are going for you at the moment. How long before you'll be doing the wing walking?'

'Oh, maybe in three or four weeks' time. We've gotta get the Air Transport guy back for the safety checks before I can do anything.'

CHAPTER 21

'Yes, Barry is caught up in all that too, isn't he?'

'Yes, he has been fantastic and so helpful in seeing things get underway.'

'You know he's pretty busy getting his finances arranged too.'

'What d'ya mean John? What finances?'

'He's told you about the possibility of purchasing a building block on *Ted's Place*, hasn't he?'

With her jaw dropping and her eyes wide open, John guessed the news was something of a surprise to Rosie.

'Yep Rosie, he's found out that he can legally buy a building block on the property. Sally and I are quite happy about that. It's a pretty big place so we don't have to be neighbours and I'll give him a bit of a choice that suits us.'

Shaking her head, all Rosie could say was, 'John, what? That sounds crazy.'

'Yeh, he'll have to pay a good price for anything, and it will have to suit us. He does seem very enthusiastic.'

'I'm sure he does, but you don't want to have an arrangement like that, surely?'

'Why not? It's all legal.'

'Legal it may be, but personal and familial intrusions would not be acceptable, John. Down the track he could start an activity of any sort that could not only be an imposition on your entitlements or privacy but a reduction in the value of the property.'

'What d'ya mean?'

'Exactly what I just said. *Ted's Place* has a legal connection with Dad's property and with skulduggery, dishonesty, and ownership affirmation, he could start the ball rolling on all sorts of claims.'

John was rather taken aback. 'Rosie, he's an honest guy whose grandfather owned the property. He just wants to touch on history.'

'Yeh, of course he does. That's now. His sense of history. I can understand that. However, think about what could be possible if down the track he marries, has children, loses interest or ability to continue the work he's doing or even if he gets passionate about what he thinks is his. You must think about the possible repercussions, John. You have to keep the property safe. Wally Hammond willed it to Grandad. It's our family's unless you want to sell him the whole thing. Of course, you don't want to do that. He has checked the legal issues, but have you checked them from the Franklin's perspective?'

John took a deep breath.

At that moment there was a loud call from Barry, the aircraft had returned. Barry was calling for next load of jumpers. Rosie couldn't believe that she and John had been chatting for half an hour. John seemed quite anxious. She now felt somewhat at fault for making him distraught before his jump. John waved to Barry and yelled out, 'Gotta go Barry, catch you later.'

Barry was surprised to see John get up and leave the hangar before his jump. He did think that some family issue had perhaps required him to return home.

That evening, Rosie discussed the situation with Chas. 'I hope I haven't disturbed a can of worms, but you do see my point, Chas?'

'For sure, but I don't think Barry has an ulterior motive. John should just make sure all issues are covered legally.'

'Yes, but sometimes people can be canny enough to find their way over what they see as hurdles and find an outcome that no one anticipated.'

'True. However, it's really a situation that is the responsibility of John and your dad. I'm sure they'll work it out.'

The conversation over breakfast did not go in any direction other than the day's plans for the first wing-walking venture. Des Herd was to meet them at the hangar at 1 pm. Undertaking a work project on a Sunday was being done out of respect for the difficulty to get all parties together on a regular weekday. Once all concerned had arrived, Des greeted them and outlined the safety check procedure. The dummy was double checked for weight and balance and Barry then put it in the back of his car to take it to the end of the runway where it was to be transferred to the top wing before take-off. The men pushed the Tiger out of the hangar and Chas then stood by to watch. All decked out in her Lycra, Rosie was most agile in climbing with some eagerness to the top wing of the aircraft. Once she was there, Steve, watched carefully by Des, made sure her feet were in the correct position on the platform before he manipulated the harness and fastened the cables around her. Even though she was not going to be airborne this time, Rosie felt the fervour of the situation and tried to absorb the sensation of what it would be like, one day soon.

Chas climbed into the cockpit, Phil swung the propeller to start the engine and, with the wheel chocks removed, the Tiger slowly began to roll down the runway. He gradually increased speed to see if there was any obvious interference of the airflow on the elevators or rudder. Rosie was to respond by stretching, relaxing, or turning in a limited manner to test how she could manage the strong current of air for the first time. Rosie was tuned in on her radio and there was a limited exchange of information with Chas. Before she had time to truly appreciate what was happening, the aircraft slowed. Chas taxied back to the end of the runway, stopped, turned, and then Barry climbed up to release Rosie's cables.

'Hope you enjoyed that?' Barry asked her.

As Rosie was quickly released from the harness and able to climb down, the dummy was strapped into position and Chas returned to the cockpit. He was well prepared for the trial flight and Des was watching intently as the plane took off. Barry and Rosie returned to the hangar.

'Wow, that was fun and easy. I could handle that blast of air, but I don't think it will be quite as simple when I am up there with the clouds and sunshine,' said Rosie as she pointed to the sky above. She had felt the thrill as the plane had moved along the runway, and her kicks and stretches had gone reasonably well. However, the blast of air had been quite mild compared with the currents that swirled around her head when she was sitting in the front seat during a flight.

'Good onya Rosie. The best is yet to come, hey?'

Chas was confident as he lined up for the take off. He did not anticipate any problems, but was prepared.

Chas opened the throttle. The aircraft quickly accelerated

and climbed straight ahead at 60 knots to 3,000 feet above the ground. No need to take risks so he avoided turning. Chas levelled out and let the aircraft accelerate in a slight dive to 90 knots. No problems. He did a complete turn to the left followed by one to the right. No differences in performance except for a slight humming sound and a little buffet on the elevators. Now to check for any abnormalities at slow speed. He had to slow down to land but he thought, *better to know of any problems at altitude than a nasty surprise on landing.* He turned and made sure there was no other traffic below him. As he levelled the wings for straight flight, he reduced the power to idle and raised the nose a little to simulate the attitude for landing. A few knots above the stall, the controls still operated normally. He lowered the nose and increased power. A complete stall was unnecessary. Chas had proven to his satisfaction, that he could fly the aircraft with Rosie on the wing. After about fifteen minutes, Chas landed and taxied up to the hangar where they were all there to welcome him. While he was still in the cockpit, Barry called out, 'C'mon, have a cider Chas and tell us all about it.'

A few minutes later, they settled down around the community table while Chas told of his experience.

'Well that really was amazing.'

'Oh, tell us Chas, did the Tiger handle differently?'

'The extra drag on top of the wing meant I had to apply more forward trim than normal, otherwise everything went well at normal operating speeds, under power. I did a steady climb to 3,000 feet to make sure I had time to make corrections if something wasn't right, and then a gentle dive. I picked up speed to make some turns then slowed to almost a stall. All the time I was expecting some effect on the aircraft's performance but there was none. Generally, it all seemed quite normal, and we won't be climbing to anything like 3,000 feet for the stunt.'

Des was still to have his private talk with Chas, but it seemed the first day of action had gone well. As they chatted between themselves everyone was pleased their efforts had been rewarded.

CHAPTER 22

On Monday afternoon, just as Chas was about to leave the hangar to go home, he was called to the telephone in the office. He was rather surprised to hear the familiar, strong voice of Jeff Dane.

'Hi Chas, it's Jeff, the schoolie jumper.'

'G'day Jeff. Now I wonder why you'd want to call me. It can't be a geography question, like 'What's the difference between latitude and longitude', can it?'

'Ha ha, no, but I would like to know when would be a good time to call in and see you? I don't finish here until about four thirty.'

'Oh listen Jeff, why don't you call around home? It's a bit easier to get to than out here. You know where I live. I'm generally there any time after five thirty.'

'Okay, that'd be great. What if I come around about six o'clock tonight then?'

'Sure Jeff, just in time for a beer before dinner.'

'Right-e-o see you then, thanks.'

Chas was curious as to why Jeff would want to see him. When he got home and told Rosie that he was calling in about six o'clock, he said, 'I guess he wants to talk parachuting. He's a very keen jumper and progressing well.'

'Okay Chas, I'll get the beer and put some cheese and bikkies out on the patio table. You can have boys' talk out there.'

On the dot of six the doorbell rang. Chas called out, 'I'll get it Rosie, that'll be Jeff.'

As he opened the door and began his welcome to Jeff, 'G'day, mate...' he stopped mid-sentence and stared at the other person standing beside him. It was obvious to Jeff that Chas was in a manner of shock, and he cut in on the broken sentence, 'Oh Chas, you know Lisa, she's out there jumping from time to time?'

'I do, I...do.' Chas was faltering in his speech. 'Well, hello Lisa, I didn't realise you were bringing anyone else Jeff.' Chas's mind was racing. *What was Rosie's reaction going to be?*

Lisa then replied softly, 'Hi Chas, we thought you'd be the person we have to talk to.'

Jeff quickly continued, 'Chas, she's a keen little butterfly and really interested in getting up in the sky. We figured we'd have a chat with you and see what's happening.'

'Come in. We're going out on the patio for our beer, Jeff. Lisa, would you like a drink?'

'Thanks Chas, just a lemonade will do me.'

As Rosie came inside from the patio to the living room to greet Jeff, an uneasy atmosphere spread through the room.

The confrontation was awkward. For Jeff it was an easy 'hello'

CHAPTER 22

and Chas then responded by explaining to Rosie that Lisa was interested in talking about parachuting too and that they would go and sit outside to talk so as not to bore Rosie with their chatter.

Chas took them to the patio and as they sat at the table, he excused himself and said that he would get Lisa's lemonade. As he entered the kitchen, Rosie looked horrified. 'What is she doing here, the cheeky flirt?'

'Rosie, it seems they want to talk jumping. All will be well. Just please yourself what you want to do, and I'll turf them out in half an hour or so, okay?'

'Just watch her. She will have an ulterior motive, that's for sure!'

Chas poured the lemonade and went back outside. Jeff had not been aware of the strained relationship between Lisa and Rosie.

'I hope we didn't interrupt any plans you had for the evening, Chas. Lisa and I can come back another time.'

'All's well, Rosie's got stuff to do for school tomorrow, so she's busy.'

Lisa had obviously been surprised to see Rosie in the kitchen. 'Is Rosie still staying here Chas?'

'Yep, we've made it a permanent arrangement. We have a lot on our plate at the moment and it's an ideal lifestyle to be close so that we can have meaningful discussions.'

Jeff became enthused. 'Yep Chas, that's right. Lisa and I have been following the development of your plans and that is actually what we came to talk about.'

'Really? I thought you wanted to know a bit about jumping.'

As Chas sipped his beer, Jeff continued in a most animated voice, 'No, no, we are really excited about all this wing-walking talk. I know there are a few guys helping you out, and Steve, Lisa's brother, is absolutely over the moon about the possibility of it all happening. He's explained to us how thrilling it will be. I reckon there will be so many wanting to be in the queue to have a go that Lisa and I thought we'd get our names down real quick so we could be at the top of the list. Gee, to be dancing around on the top wing of the Tiger would be just the greatest!'

Lisa then had to get a word in. 'Chas it'd be such an adventure. I trust you as a pilot so much that you could strap me on and do a roll and I'd be screaming with pleasure.'

Chas took a gulp of beer before he replied, 'Listen guys, the whole exercise is still wishful thinking. Steve would have told you that wing walking is actually illegal in Australia at this point in time. I have put forward suggestions and arguments for that to change, but nothing has changed yet. We have some support from the Air Transport Bureau but there are some big hurdles to get over.'

'Sure Chas, but we just want to make sure we're on the list, right up the top.'

'There is no list Jeff, and there won't be. It was Rosie's idea months ago and we are all supporting it.'

With a loud gasp, Lisa continued, 'But Chas, this is an opportunity for us all. It's something lots of the club members would love to have a go at. You can't just make it for one person.'

'Lisa, the whole process costs money. Those currently involved are personally taking care of that. The fact that Rosie is not only the instigator, but very competent and physically fit, is the reason she is the person up on the wing. Wing walking is illegal at the moment and there are enormous barriers that must be overcome. Checks and double checks through the Air Transport Bureau have to be done constantly and through the same personnel. It is not a simple process. If you and Jeff want to do it, then start your own process.'

'Hey Chas, I am quite as capable and physically fit as Rosie. How come she can just put her hand up and get picked? That is being so biased and prejudiced on your part, Chas.'

'She's the initiator, Lisa, don't you get that? It was her idea, and it has been developed with her encouragement. I think you should leave now. I'm sorry I can't be of any help.'

As Chas stood up and turned to walk down the garden path, Jeff showed far more empathy. 'I understand, Chas. It is obviously a win or no-win situation and there has to be a lot of effort associated with a successful outcome. I wish you all the best and will look forward to following the progress.'

Jeff stood up and pulled back Lisa's chair. 'C'mon Lisa, let's go.'

Lisa's comments came as they walked down the path. 'You are a wuss, Jeff. Fancy letting them just take off with the idea.'

Chas watched silently as the couple made their way to the side gate.

'Thanks for your time and the beer, Chas. Good luck.' Jeff opened the gate for Lisa and gave a 'thumbs up' as he turned to close it. Chas's heavy sigh indicated that he was so glad Rosie had not been part of the conversation. When he faced Rosie, she knew there was a drama.

He didn't want to talk about it, but with one question from her he replied, 'Yep Rosie. It was all about her. She wants to be the wing walker. What a laugh. Actually, Jeff is interested too but he accepted reality and the realisation that it wasn't something that could be achieved by just anyone, for just anyone. He's a good guy and I believe he's genuinely interested in our progress. The little madam, however, wants to be the star of the show.'

'That's right, and she wants you Chas, anyway, anyhow.'

Over the next few weeks, the wing-walking group were down to just a casual meeting during the week. Phil no longer considered his attendance necessary, and Chas and Barry swapped information from time to time. The Saturday jump session was progressing well and occasionally Rosie and Lisa crossed paths. It surprised Rosie that the flirty nurse seemed a lot more interested in prepping for her jump than she had been over the past months. She paid no attention to Chas at all but was keeping company with Jeff Dane, and they seemed preoccupied with each other. Occasionally, Lisa greeted Rosie with a smile but no words.

Although she was now able to attend most out-of-school gym sessions, Rosie was happy to be able to hand over much of the responsibility to Carly, who was becoming very adept at programming and student support. When the gym session finished on Wednesday afternoon and Rosie was packing her bag, she called out, 'Hey Carly, let's get a quick coffee?'

CHAPTER 22

'For sure, that'd be great.'

Minutes later they met up at the favoured meeting place and found a table for two outside.

'I've gotta say thanks again for all your help, Carly. It's certainly made things easier for me over the past weeks.'

'Oh, no problem Rosie. You know I'm getting lots more enjoyment from the sessions than I believed I would.'

'And how's things with Barry? Some of the staff are saying you're dating.'

'Well yes, I guess we are. We get on really well together and he's quite smitten with Gunnedah. He's meeting your brother this week, on Friday, to check out the property. You know he's interested in getting a block on the farm, don't you?'

'Yes, I do. I guess we'll just have to see how that works out. It will be an expensive exercise, I believe.'

'Oh, he's considered all that and is confident about the finances, however he does realise it is quite a step for John and Sally.'

'That's true Carly, but their farm and my father's property have a close association so, although there may be a legal confirmation of some arrangement, the legitimacy of the process could be questionable.' Rosie realised the chat was becoming a little too involved. 'Anyway, I wanted to tell you that the floor routine you've got those two students working on is superb. That's the one you'll use in the upcoming regional competition, hey?'

The focus of the conversation then switched, and the two women spent a good half hour talking through the requirements for the upcoming competition.

All through the week, Barry had been looking forward

to Friday. He had contacted John and had been invited for afternoon tea before they set off around the property to check out some sites. His confirmation of financial support from the bank had given him confidence; however, there were still legal issues that had to be worked through. When he arrived at *Ted's Place*, John and Sally welcomed him warmly as they walked to the veranda for a cup of coffee.

'Thanks for the invite and I must say how lovely and restful it is out here after a busy week in the hangar. I was sorry you had to leave before your jump last Saturday, John.'

With some hesitation, John held back on the details of that moment with Rosie. 'Yep, I had to shoot through, but I'll certainly be out there again, although the winter wet is making itself felt these days. I guess jump plans will be a bit unreliable.'

The conversation continued in a friendly fashion until, with John's suggestion, they moved off to the car to check out the land spots he wanted to show Barry.

It was a convivial exercise and Barry was shown several possible locations. There was one located near a creek. It was rather attractive but enormous in size, close to 500 acres and some distance from the main road. The other site, again rather large, and because of its location in bush land would require considerable clearance. After some easy chit-chat and numerous questions from Barry, a few of which baffled John and related to costings, they headed back to the farmhouse. It was during the drive that John seemed to get rather serious and began talking about the implications for building on rural land. Barry was surprised that there were inferences to the neighbouring

Franklin property. It seemed there was an undertone to John's comments whereby he was implying some negativity associated with any dealings that would relate to both Franklin properties. Upon reaching the house, Barry politely expressed his thanks for the couple's hospitality, and as he hopped into his car called out, 'See ya John for the jump tomorrow.'

Barry allowed the afternoon's discourse to reverberate through his mind on the way home. It did seem to him that, for all John's support over the past weeks, he had lost some enthusiasm about the division and sale of the parcel of land. Something seemed to undermine the fervour that had trickled through past discussions. He could not understand why the Franklin property had to be acknowledged. For sure *'Ted's Place'* had been willed to the Franklin's, but it was still a separate and independent property. An issue that had not concerned John and Sally in previous discussions.

As he got closer to home, Barry began thinking about the Parachute Club activities for the next day. Although John had mentioned that he would be jumping, he had not shown his usual eagerness. Something then clicked in Barry's mind. *Rosie? Had she said something to John before the jump last week? It was after that conversation that John had decided not to spend the afternoon with the club.*

Barry knew Rosie was not all that keen about a subdivision on the property and had shown a cynical response to the idea in the past. *Maybe she had put the germ of negativity into John's mind. Maybe she was the one that didn't want him to settle in the area.* He hoped the evening dinner date with Carly would lift his spirits.

Barry drove into Carly's driveway and walked up to the front door. He was dubious as to whether she would be her usual enchanting self. She and Rosie were good friends, so they would likely share their stories with each other. Tentatively, he pressed the doorbell. Within a moment or two the door opened and there she was, dressed enticingly in a silky grey tunic top with trendy flared trousers, and a charming smile to greet him.

'Hi Barry, it's great to see you.'

'Well, don't you look just gorgeous, dear lady. Aren't I the lucky man?' Then eagerly they set off for the Indian Restaurant. The couple spent a delightful evening sharing stories from their past and ambitions for the future. It was inevitable that Barry's aspiration to get settled in Gunnedah would become part of the conversation.

'I'm a little concerned that it may not happen, Carly.'

'I can imagine that there will be a few hoops to jump through, cos it's not all that common for farmers to divvy up their property, but don't give up Barry.'

'I don't want to get involved in your friendship with Rosie, but would you mind telling me if she has ever said anything to you about me buying land from John?'

'Not really, only that it was what you wanted to do.'

'I feel that she might be trying to dissuade John from having anything to do with me and my ideas.'

'I guess she's interested because there's a very close association between John and his father. Apparently, the management of the property has been focussed on family aspirations for years and years. Rosie has said that they tend to operate as one big property so she may see some legal connection between what happens on John's farm that could affect her father's property. I reckon if you go all out to get a good lawyer and cover the legal aspects, that will keep everyone happy.'

Leaving it at that, Barry went on to change the conversation and bask in the ambience of what had started out as a pleasant evening.

There would be no date for wing walking until Des Herd informed Chas when it suited him to witness a proving flight before the changeable winter weather set in. Rosie's school holidays, in a couple of weeks, had been suggested as an appropriate time. She kept focused by keeping up an acrobatic routine as a daily commitment, and strength exercises to keep her agility at a peak; however, she realised there was no reason to perform a routine. While on the wing she would be limited by the environment and could only execute movements that felt appropriate.

CHAPTER 23

Over the next week or two, Barry tried to follow up on his contact with John. It seemed that he was very occupied with farm commitments and, although he answered the phone a couple of times, John was always too busy to have a conversation. Barry felt rather disconsolate. Eventually, John phoned. 'Hi ya Barry. I really have been full at it for a while.'

'G'day John, good to hear from you. How's things?'

'Well Barry, I'm sorry to say, but at the moment we'll have to put all the block business on hold. I've had some chats with my dad, and it seems he, and the rest of the family, are a bit concerned about issues that can be difficult to cover legally. We've not given up, but we do have to work things through at our end.'

'That's a bit of a shock, John. I thought you had got all that stuff covered?'

'Sorry Barry, but not yet. You do understand that there is a connection between both properties, and we have to be sure that the family is covered for all events.'

CHAPTER 23

'Yeh, yeh, sure. It's not what I wanted to hear though.'

'Anyway, it should all work out. Cheers and I'll see ya around.'

'Okay, I look forward to hearing from you.' Barry couldn't believe it. *What was going on? John and Sally had been so supportive and encouraging.* He then remembered that Rosie had been avoiding him since John had turned down the jump a few Saturdays earlier.

Towards the end of April, Chas was pleased to get a notification from Des regarding the safety checks prior to Rosie's first wing-walk exercise. The school holidays were approaching and Des had suggested the first Monday in May, which would suit all parties. The weather was beginning to become a little less reliable but the weekend before the planned event was calm and settled.

On Saturday afternoon, Chas and Rosie arrived at the hangar for the jump session and Chas went to prepare the Cessna. Rosie looked around for any early arrivals and realised that she'd been seen first. Walking towards her with a sprightly stride was Lisa. They had exchanged casual greetings over the past couple of weeks, but Rosie was certainly surprised with the cheery comment from the young woman she regarded as her nemesis. 'Hi Rosie, are you jumping or watching today?'

'Neither actually, I just brought Chas out and I'm heading off to do other things.'

'Rosie don't get cranky with me, please. I'm sorry things turned out the way they did when I called around with Jeff, a while back. We had no idea that you and Chas were in a permanent relationship. I'm sorry if I offended you.'

Rosie was quite taken aback with the apology. 'Okay, I understand Lisa. I hope you enjoy your jump today.'

'Thanks, yes, it's a perfect day for it. Steve tells me that Monday will be the real thing for you. Your first venture in the harness. I hope the weather will be just as fine for you.'

'That's the forecast, so all should be okay.'

'I'd love to come and see all the preparation. Steve said I could just come and watch. Do you mind? I'm not on roster Monday morning.'

Rosie, thinking that the young woman was trying to make amends, replied, 'You can come if you want. It's quite a procedure and could be a bit boring for you. I've been told there will be a few people out here so there will be some regulations.' Rosie walked off to the car park. *That was certainly a surprising development. Lisa was relatively civil and polite, somewhat unusual for her. Maybe she was still looking after her own interests for further down the track.*

For Chas and Rosie, Sunday afternoon was a flutter of excitement in anticipation of her first experimental wing-walking stunt, and they talked of their history in getting things underway. Rosie got decked out in her Lycra and Chas watched on as she went through the range of movements that she planned to attempt while in the harness on the top wing of the Tiger. There were stretches with her arms overhead, moving to a position straight back from her shoulders, so that her head could also go back as far as possible to give her body a gracious curve. She imagined that movement would certainly be assisted by the force of the wind. For most of the stretches she would go with the wind and achieve a better performance with its strength. Using her body for bending and stretching would be more challenging, and she wanted to make her leg movements look clear and bold for the observers. Chas offered comments, but he certainly did not offer criticism, as Rosie had researched and practised her performance unrelentingly. Tomorrow was to be the big day. Des Herd and a couple of other Air Transport officers were expected to arrive at about 10 am and begin their rigid safety examination of the aircraft, the harness and cables, and Rosie's attire. Take-off would occur immediately after all that was complete and approved.

As she left the table after an early dinner, Rosie turned on the TV news and went to sit on the lounge.

'Hey Sweetie, have you seen the sunset? Go take a look.'

As she went to the front door and saw the coloured sky, it took her breath away.

'Oh Chasie, what a sight. The colours are just glorious.'

'C'mon, quick, in the car.'

'Whaddya mean? Why?'

'We're going up to the lookout.'

'Why?'

'It's so beautiful and we'll be able to get a photo.'

'Oh, okay then. Let's go.' Rosie was taken by surprise, but she guessed the view from Porky's Lookout would be outstanding. On arrival, they couldn't get out of the car quickly enough, and after Chas grasped a blanket from the back seat and pulled Rosie's hand, they scampered to a secluded spot. It was a soft grassy mound with a clear view to the west. Chas threw the blanket across the grass.

'Here, we'll sit here.' Chas dropped to the ground and gently pulled his love down with him so that the couple ended up in a tight embrace. As she relaxed from the passion, Rosie looked lovingly into Chas's eyes and said, 'Well, will we have time to see the sun before it sets?'

'You tell me. There's something else that needs attention.'

'Whaddya mean, Chasie love?'

'I've got something that you need to look at and will need to respond to, immediately.'

The quizzical expression that crossed Rosie's face made Chas chuckle as he held out a small velvety box for her. There was no cause for doubt as to what the box held.

'Oh, my darling Chasie, really?'

'Really Rosie. I love you to the moon and back, please marry me.'

She opened the box and held the beautiful diamond ring in her trembling fingers. Chas then took it from her and put it on her finger. 'I want us to be together forever.'

Loving words and a tender embrace enhanced the passion of the moment as they moved closer together. The blanket was soft and easy on their bare skin and their entwined bodies captured the depth of feeling that was an unspoken promise of the diamond on Rosie's finger. Chas's hands moved in a tantalising way over Rosie's bare skin as she succumbed to the overwhelming desire that enveloped the couple. The cool autumn breeze broke their reverie, and the sun had set before they pulled on their jeans and shirts, and made their decision to go home. As they drove into their driveway, Rosie said

CHAPTER 23

mournfully, 'Chasie, you didn't get a photo.' A woeful look crossed the happy man's face.

Next morning, when they woke up, Chas took Rosie's hand and smiled at the ring. Without any words being spoken, they embraced warmly. At 9 am, after an easy breakfast, Chas wanted to get moving. 'Wow, that was a great day yesterday. C'mon Sweetie, no school, so let's get going.'

'Oh boy, I thought yesterday was the day, but today's *the* day, hey? I'm so glad the sun's shining, but there is a little tightening in my gut.'

'Ha ha, you know what that is. It's just all your extremely fit muscles saying, 'it's time, let's do it'.'

'Okay, let's go.'

Barry, Phil and Steve were the early birds. Lisa had come along with her brother, but she was not easily seen where she was sitting at the far end of the hangar with her head in the newspaper, sipping on a coffee. When the men spotted Chas and Rosie walking into the hangar, they let loose with applause. There was an obvious thread of excitement between the couple. No words were necessary, but anyone could tell there was an invisible bond pulling them together. Chas pulled out the procedural safety list and gave everyone a copy. They had all used this throughout the preparation period but today they would only put ticks in the prescribed places as the safety officers had advised.

Rosie excused herself and decided to take some quiet time until Des and an expected additional safety officer arrived. To ease her mind, she picked up a couple of magazines on the wall bench and found herself a comfy chair. She knew which magazines had the occasional international wing-walking story and almost knew each of them by heart. The fact that they were real stories, and not some words of fiction, allowed her to get totally engrossed in the situations described. All were positive and most inspiring.

The guys had started sharing information and were walking over to the Tiger. Chas was eager to get everything started, 'Okay guys, let's push her out onto the tarmac.' The red and white aircraft looked neat and clean, ready for the day's adventure. 'Ya'll be there Barry to swing the propellor for us?'

'For sure Chas, a little bit of elbow grease from me can be my contribution for today.'

They returned to the hangar and before long heard a car drive in at about 9.45 am. Chas went to the open hangar door. 'Hi there, Des. It's great to see you.'

'Yes, back again with a workmate this time, Chas. This is Brian Ferly. We do a lot of this sort of stuff together but of course not quite like this.' Brian shook Chas's hand and replied, as he responded to the other welcoming gestures, 'Yes, we've been on a bit of a learning curve too. Wing walking, unreal Chas, an exciting venture for you all.'

Rosie then noticed Lisa standing with Steve.

'Hello Lisa, so you did decide to come today.'

'Yes, Steve has told me to keep clear, but it will be great to see it all happen.'

After Chas suggested a quick cup of coffee before they all got down to business, Lisa continued, 'Okay guys, if you tell me how you like your coffee, I'll get them for you.'

Rosie followed Lisa to the coffee machine. 'Oh Rosie, I know you just like a touch of milk and one sugar so, don't worry, you go do the talking and I've got a tray here, so I'll bring the cups over to the table.' Lisa had noticed the engagement ring on Rosie's finger but declined to make any reference to it.

'Oh okay, sure, just make mine two spoons, please,' and Rosie returned to the group.

The coffees arrived at the table with a plate of Arnott's biscuits and a brisk conversation continued around the table until Chas and Phil went over to the Tiger to do the pre-flight check with Des and Brian. Barry had left and Steve remained to ask Rosie, 'What have you got on your finger Rosie?'

There was a little giggle before she answered, 'So, you noticed, Steve?'

'Well, yes, it is a bit glary on the eyes.'

'It all happened last night.'

'I guess it was on the cards, but let me congratulate you and wish you all the best. You have my very best wishes for today. A great effort Rosie.'

'Thanks. I really haven't had a lot of time to think about it at all today.'

'So, are you feeling a little nervous?'

'Mm, maybe, but I reckon it's excitement for more reasons than one. I'll feel good when the straps are tight around me, I'm sure. Sorry, I'll have to shoot off and get my flight gear on, Steve. So, I'll see you at the Tiger in about five minutes.'

Rosie grabbed her bag of gear and headed off briskly to the 'Ladies Room'. Within minutes, looking sensational in her Lycra gear, she was on her way to the aircraft parked on the tarmac. The bright blue and yellow shirt atop the blue leggings would stand out brilliantly against the red and white paintwork of the Tiger.

CHAPTER 24

History was in the making. The experimental event had only been promoted to the Parachute Club but there were a few others who had been invited to the exciting occasion. The group of onlookers at the fence were watching intently. Everyone from the hangar crowded around the aircraft. Rosie pulled on the leather helmet that only allowed her curls to escape around her neck and arranged the strongly banded goggles. The helmet was some decades old, but it was light and had air-to-air, battery-operated speakers that allowed on-going contact between Rosie on the wing, and Chas in the cockpit. Barry had given Steve the job of strapping her into the harness. Des and Brian watched very closely. Chas climbed into the cockpit and Rosie lent over so that Chas could give her a quick kiss. As they began to taxi down the runway, the cheering and applause broke out. Chas could see Rosie standing like a beacon on the top wing. The curls from underneath her helmet, were blowing in the wind, and as she passed the crowd, she waved her arms and sent kisses from her hand.

The beautiful sunny morning really fired up Rosie. Chas turned the aircraft and began moving at increasing speed down the runway, past the crowd again. Rosie stretched her arms, waved, and heard Chas say, 'Okay Rosie, ready for take-off.'

Her reply was short, 'Roger.'

With that, the Tiger was airborne and Rosie could feel her body strengthen against the wind as the aircraft climbed at a gentle rate. With the increasing height she could tell that her heartbeat was increasing. At first, she considered that to be a normal response, but then she began feeling a sense of nervousness like nothing she had ever experienced before. She just didn't feel right. After another turn and flying straight and level, the plan was for Rosie to begin her movements. Chas waited for her word that all was well. He could see her but there were no bends or stretches. This delay was not part of the plan.

'Rosie, begin now.' There was no reply and no planned movement, only erratic and inconsistent beating of her hands against the harness. He then heard a rather high-pitched shriek over the radio followed by a bawling sound, which tended to distort his name.

'Rosie. Rosie, confirm okay.'

There was still no radio reply. With rapid thinking, he decided to land, and turned the aircraft towards the runway. He then called ground base, 'Going to land, something wrong. Rosie not responding.'

He landed, and was very concerned as he taxied towards the hangar and stopped as soon as possible. The onlookers, further along the runway, were most subdued.

CHAPTER 24

The hangar crew raced along the runway and met up with the oncoming aircraft as Chas drew it to a halt. There were several calls of 'Rosie, Rosie!' and Chas scrambled out of the cockpit to stand on the front seat where he could thrust out his hand to touch her leg. 'Rosie, can you hear me?' He then clambered up onto the wing to be closer to her shaking, trembling body, and put his arms around her. Steve immediately jumped onto the wing and with great agility climbed around Chas to get access to the straps, which he quickly released.

She was hyperventilating, so Chas tried to get her to slow down her breathing. 'Sweetie, take a deep breathe, try to whistle, try to whistle.' Together, both men took the weight of her body and levered her down gently to the willing, helping hands below. As Barry and Phil attempted to carry her into the hanger, she held out against their strength, 'P-p-please, j-j-just walk.' They held her tightly. Des and Brian were close by watching, prepared to ask questions as soon as practicable.

Having led Rosie to the daybed in the hangar, Barry and Steve could not get her to lie down. Chas then persuaded her to sit next to him on the bed. 'C'mon Rosie, here, sit with me.'

Barry then suggested, 'Rosie, this is not like you, let's call a doctor.'

While Rosie repeated endlessly, 'I-I-I'm okay, I-I-I'm okay', Chas said, 'Rosie, it's not okay. What happened up there?'

'I-I-I have no idea, Chas.'

After a few minutes, Chas suggested someone could get her some warm milk. Lisa returned with a glass of milk and handed it to Rosie. 'Rosie, drink this, it will help you to relax a little.'

'Thanks Lisa.'

Lisa said quietly, 'I do hope it will make you feel better, we were all so scared for your safety.'

'Thanks. I was well strapped in so there was no chance of me falling off the wing.'

Everyone in the hangar group was most concerned and wanting to do something to help. Lisa, in nurse-like fashion, attempted to test for vital signs. In so doing, she again noticed the ring on Rosie's finger.

'Rosie, is your head aching? Do you feel dizzy?'

In an abstracted voice, Rosie's words slurred, 'Y-y-yes… y-y-yes, and I feel so ho-hot and s-s-sweaty.'

'Rosie, just breathe slowly, your heartbeat is slowing, and I do believe your trembling is reducing. I'm sure you will begin to feel more comfortable in a few minutes.' Lisa then turned to speak quietly to Chas. 'I think she has had a panic attack Chas, there is nothing on-going with her symptoms and she is now breathing well, and her heartbeat is almost normal. I'm sure she's fine but she must have a good rest.'

'Thanks Lisa, you really were here at the right moment.'

Chas then turned back to Rosie. 'Sweetie, let's make you comfy and why don't you just relax here for a bit while I go and check out the Tiger?'

Rosie answered simply, 'Sure, I'll just sleep.'

As she dozed off, Lisa said she would stay by her side until Chas returned. Lisa decided that she would not mention anything about the engagement ring. She considered that it would be better if she remained ignorant of the fact.

CHAPTER 24

Des and Brian were with the Barry and Steve, still standing around the aircraft. After Chas explained Rosie's response in the hangar, they were all relieved. Des said to them and the hangar crew, 'Your concern for safety, and the excellent preparation, obviously prevented any catastrophe today. However, we do need to understand how prepared Rosie was for any such incident.'

Chas answered quickly, 'Look, what happened up there was totally out of character for Rosie. She is not only physically capable but also mentally capable of the challenge to wing walk. I suggest we wait until she is feeling calm and collected before we chat to her. It can't possibly be the result of any mishandling of the aircraft, and I wonder if she may have some realisation of what may have caused her reaction.'

Des and Brian had spoken to the others, so Chas then had a few private words with the safety officers before they left. It was a foregone conclusion that there would have to be a written report of the incident.

Back in the hangar, Chas found Rosie still asleep and Lisa sitting quietly nearby with the newspaper. 'Okay, thanks Lisa, I'll take it from here. We'll see how Rosie feels when she wakes up, and if necessary, I will call by the hospital. You certainly helped us out.'

'Oh, that's fine Chas. Hopefully she will be okay. It was just a minor panic attack. They can get much worse than Rosie's reaction so I think she should be very wary of what happened.'

Steve then called out to Lisa, 'Are ya ready to head home little sis? See ya Chas.'

'Bye Chas.'

'G'bye, and thanks again Lisa.'

As Steve left, Barry found himself a beer in the office refrigerator and sat alone to consider the day's proceedings. He had not wanted to have any close association with Rosie during the exercise, but after the incident he was concerned with her well-being. At first, he thought that maybe she got what she deserved as a result of her selfish chat with John, but then he realised that was rather a bitter thought. When Chas spotted Barry, he called him inside and Chas found himself a beer. They kept busy talking about aeroplanes for about half an hour until Rosie began to stir. Chas and Barry both seemed relieved that Rosie now seemed close to her usual self.

Barry went over to hold her hand and said, 'Rosie, dear lady, I hope you have no problems getting back to good health and make sure you look after that engagement ring. Congrats to you both. I'm going to head off now, but we'll chat soon. See ya.'

There was a gentle, 'G'bye Barry,' from Rosie and, 'See ya later, mate,' from Chas, who then turned to Rosie, put his hand lovingly on her cheek and kissed her gently, 'Okay my dear, let's go home and make you comfy.'

When they arrived home, Chas set about making sandwiches as Rosie relaxed on the sofa. 'Would you like tea or coffee with your sandwich, Sweetie?'

'You know what Chas? I'd just like an orange juice, thanks.'

'Okay, it's on the way.' Chas had *Jonathan Livingston Seagull* on his record player, so after he gave Rosie her lunch, he pressed the button and they sat quietly side by side listening to the familiar melodies. As he took away the empty plates, Chas asked, 'Rosie do you feel you can talk about this morning?'

'Oh yes, for sure. I can honestly say Chasie, I did not feel like me, up there on the wing. The trembling and feeling of dizziness, just came over me like a sheet, isolating me from reality. I wanted to do my sequence, but it was like I was not allowed to and couldn't. It was scary. I've never been scared of an adventure. You know me.'

'Oh Rosie, that I do. Lisa reckoned it was a panic attack and I guess that's what your symptoms seemed to indicate.'

'I have no idea why something like that should suddenly hit me. I have never had any sense of fear with any of the challenges I've undertaken.'

'Do you think you should chat to a doctor about it?'

'No, I don't want to do that, but I will do a bit of research over the next day or two. Did Des and Brian say that we could continue with our flights?'

'Not yet, but we have to send them a detailed report and hopefully we will then be able to get you back on the wing real soon, if that's what you want.'

'Oh, yes, I do so want to get back up there.'

The next day, Chas began to write a report for the Air Transport Bureau and Rosie set about researching panic attacks. At the library she found the medical and health section and carefully chose a couple of relevant books that she took to home. There, she read the details of several accounts of panic attacks, and recognised the symptoms she had had, as very closely resembling those of a panic attack. The sense of fear and anxiety that had her trembling and hyperventilating was described exactly the way she had felt. However, as she pursued the research, she found that everything listed, from genetic causes to medical conditions and phobias had nothing at all to do with her attack. Which made her question, 'was it a panic attack?'

For her next line of inquiry, Rosie thought that maybe she had eaten or drunk something that may have caused the attack. There had been a lot in the news over the past few years about the likelihood of processed foods, refined cereals, and even coffee that could create anxiety, so she followed that line of research. It was also of interest for her that although caffeine occurred naturally in tea and coffee, it could be sourced and added to soda drinks to provide a stimulant. Rosie knew that she had not had any drinks, other than her usual coffee, and was somewhat sceptical that her cup of coffee caused the unpleasant incident. However, after reading of some of the side effects, she decided she would simply watch her diet. She then sat down with Chas and suggested that in his report he should mention how quickly she had recovered, and, from thorough research, she had now decided to watch her diet with careful awareness.

The report was submitted, and Des Herd replied, indicating that since all had gone so well with the flight programme, they would give a go-ahead to the team. Such good news allowed Chas to continue with his plans to do two or three practice attempts before they attended a public flying show. The next flight was organised for the last Friday of Rosie's holidays. It was to be conducted by the hangar crew, without any publicity

CHAPTER 24

and absolutely no one was to be invited to the airfield. Over the days before, Rosie took great care with her diet and cut out her cup of coffee prior to the event.

On the chosen day, Des and Brian turned up at the same time and everyone followed the same plan. It was a raging success. Rosie stood there on the wing like she was part of it. As Chas took the Tiger into the air, Rosie showed no sign of distress or anxiety, and her grace and movements absolutely captivated the onlookers. At the gathering in the hangar after the event, Des was also elated.

'I am so pleased to give a positive report to you all. You have achieved something that is certainly a historic aviation event for Australia at this time, and of course that means the Air Transport Bureau will have to be making some new regulations. Rosie, you looked spectacular, and we trust that your decision to pursue your dream of dancing up there with the clouds has now come true to your satisfaction. Chas, your planning and preparation, along with that of your crew, is highly commendable and we wish you some great flying events in the future. Just let us know where and when they will happen, please. Thankyou everyone for your co-operation. I'm sure we'll meet again.'

CHAPTER 25

With the extra work and excitement of the wing-walking exercise in abeyance, and parachuting days limited because of winter weather, Barry now had time to reconsider his future in Gunnedah. He had been so disappointed with John's last conversation a few weeks back when he had said that he had to check out some details with his father. It had constantly been on Barry's mind and when Carly told him back then that Rosie thought the close association of the two properties could allow things to get difficult in the future, he thought that maybe Rosie had put doubt in John's mind.

Barry certainly did not want to create issues that would bring angst to the Franklin family, but he did see Rosie as interfering in his life. Barry decided to make another visit to his lawyer in Tamworth. At the meeting, he disclosed the issues that were bothering him and appreciated the sincere concern that the lawyer held for his position. He did tell Barry that the conditions were dependent not only on the laws but upon the desires of the landowners. On the drive back home, he decided that he would meet with John again with confidence and a straightforward approach. After a phone call that night, he felt very much at ease because John had invited him to the farm for lunch the next Sunday.

The inclement weather hit Gunnedah with little respite. Flying, parachuting and wing walking were all going to be off the agenda for several days. Chas was rather pleased because, for the first time in quite a while, he could give his boss at the servo a bit of a break. Rosie had no intense training in the outdoors lined up, so she and Carly were able to concentrate on the potential champions they were coaching at the Gym Club. The evenings were warm and cosy around the open fire in the lounge room, and Chas and Rosie had conversations about their future. When she came home one afternoon, after spending a couple of hours with her parents, Rosie told Chas, 'You know what Chas? Mum and Dad want to have a family barbecue to celebrate our engagement and the wing-walking success.'

'Wow, really?'

'Yes, Anne and Greg are coming over from Tamworth. They are going to be here next week on June thirteenth for the Queen's Birthday long weekend.'

'That's great. So, they don't have any children, do they?'

'No, but John and Sally will be there with their kids.'

'Hey, that'll be quite a party. I'm looking forward to it.'

Barry arrived at John's on Sunday morning and was surprised by the welcome. The men sat down in front of the fire, each with a beer, and John began talking about the wing-walking stunt.

'I'm rather glad we weren't there to see Rosie collapse. That would have been frightful. I mean she has been so keen about it all. Who would have thought she'd have had such a reaction?'

'Yeh, it was horrible, but it seems that it was something she had eaten rather than a nervous response.'

'Could be, I guess, but then Rosie doesn't eat rubbish. She keeps to a pretty good diet.'

'That's right, but she does like her coffee and that can have a pretty strong effect sometimes.'

'Barry, she has drunk coffee for years and always just before a physical challenge of some sort. I don't think it has ever affected her before.'

'M-m-m, okay. Who knows? Anyway, on the second attempt she was amazing and did a great job.'

'So I heard. By the way, you should come to the barbeque Mum and Dad are having at their place on the Queen's Birthday weekend. It's at Sunday lunchtime and my sister Anne and her family will be here too. It's to celebrate Chas and Rosie's engagement and the successful wing walk. Bring Carly with you.'

'Oh thanks John, that'd be great.'

'Now let's go and find the block you have set your sights on, and we'll come back for lunch. Okay?' With that the two men set off for the paddocks.

During the drive to Barry's choice, the block by the creek, Barry mentioned that he had heard there was concern over the legalities associated with the purchase.

'How does your father feel about a division of the property?'

'Barry, yes, he is somewhat concerned about development and

CHAPTER 25

we've both checked out with the council. We're not able to sell a small block of land. You'd have to purchase at least 500 acres for it to be a legal arrangement according to the land subdivision laws, and of course, I'm not sure we could do that.'

'Oh gee, that really takes the wind out of my sails.'

As John drove up the track to the block by the creek, he tried to make Barry feel more optimistic.

'What we can do, is let you lease the spot here and we suggest that you just put up a very simple little cottage that won't cost you a pocket of dollars. It will be yours to use as you wish, permanently or temporarily. You have the responsibility of all costings, but should *Ted's Place* ever be sold, any commitments you have to the block and improvements, will be null and void. Sorry mate, that's the best we can do.'

As they walked through the grass to the little creek, Barry was obviously holding back the outrage. 'You're saying, if *Ted's Place* should ever be sold. Is that likely to happen?'

'I don't see it happening in my lifetime, but such contingencies have to be considered with related legalities.'

Barry then clenched his fists and shouted, 'It should have been my land,' and then emphasising the 'my', he continued, 'My land. This all belonged to my grandfather.'

'Listen mate, that's history. It can't be changed. If you were interested in farming and wanted to pay 500 dollars per acre for 500 acres, plus the costs of a farmhouse, then you'd probably be able to get a deal. But I don't think that is what you want.'

'All I want is a place to call my own. That should be my own. Let's get back to the house.'

There were no words spoken during the drive and when John parked his ute at the house, Barry jumped out and without a word, slammed the door and walked over to his car. His departure was quick and there was no further communication. As he drove savagely back to town, he realised he had to control his angry thoughts. The malaise he felt, centred around his association with Rosie. It was she who had aroused the dubious response from John and his father. He certainly wouldn't be celebrating her achievements at the barbecue.

The weather forecast promised a clear sunny weekend for the Queen's Birthday holiday. Parachute jumps were planned for the Saturday and the barbecue party was to be on the Sunday. Chas was gathering interest in doing another short wing-walking practice on the Monday, but it depended on the attendance of Des and Brian. He was delighted when he received the notification that they would attend, weather permitting.

Rosie spent her time on Saturday helping her parents prepare the barbecue for the next day, while Chas was busy flying the Cessna. Being such good weather, about a dozen enthusiastic jumpers turned up and Barry and Chas were kept very busy. It was about 4 pm when they had the final jump and the drop zone was cleared. Chas then suggested, 'Hey Barry, let's go for a beer at the Regal.'

'Thanks all the same Chas, but I'm heading home.'

'Okay, we'll see you and Carly at the barbecue tomorrow.'

'Oh yes, we were invited, but I'll have to say 'no' and also, I've checked Steve out for the wing walk on Monday. I won't be there. See ya.'

CHAPTER 25

'Hey Barry, whaddya mean?' Chas called out, but Barry had gone. Chas was quite perplexed at the quick departure of his wing-walking stalwart.

They thought they were arriving for the barbecue at the right time, but Rosie and Chas were obviously the last ones. The family was standing on the front veranda steps waving and cheering as the car pulled up in the driveway. There were kisses and hugs all round and comments of congratulations, tied in with exclamations of pride related to the wing-walking venture. Mary eventually broke up the gathering by announcing the barbecue was underway. Out on the back patio, the family celebrated the engagement and congratulated the couple with glasses of champagne. Chas was then pestered to give a speech on the progress of the wing-walking stunt. It was when he returned to his place at the table that Chas turned to ask John the question he'd been holding back.

'Listen mate, I thought you had invited Barry and Carly along today?'

'Yep Chas, I did. I don't know why he's not here. The usually breezy, high-spirited Barry was not someone whom you would expect to turn down a party invitation. I know he was a bit disheartened last weekend when he could foresee his plans to build on *Ted's Place* were not going to come to fruition.'

'Oh, is that right? I know Rosie told him at one stage that there were some issues that were troublesome. Anyway, who knows? He'll get over it I guess.'

On the way home, the happy couple continued talking excitedly about the afternoon. When Rosie said that she had been expecting Carly and Barry, Chas replied, 'I spoke to John about that. It seems he's given up on his plans to get a block on the farm. He must have been feeling dispirited.'

'Oh my, if that is so? It would really rub him up the wrong way. There'd be no way he would've wanted to be amongst the family today, then. I guess Carly will tell me all about it,'

'…and he's not coming out to the airfield tomorrow, either.'

'I'd say he's really on a downer then. Will we still have the practice flight?'

'Yep, for sure. No problem with that. Steve is going to do the strap in just as he has before.'

The pre-flight routine on Monday morning went ahead as planned. Nobody questioned the fact that Barry had not turned up. Steve did the job of strapping Rosie into the harness while Des and Brian double checked the safety issues. The flight repeated the success achieved by the forerunner. Rosie was ecstatic. On landing, she gave Steve a quick kiss on the cheek as he released the straps.

'Steve, I just felt so exuberated up there. I felt comfortable but thrilled … and you kept me safe.'

Des and Brian were most satisfied with the proceedings and Chas told them that there were still two more trial flights before the big AgQuip day in August, when the venture would be pre-announced state-wide.

On the way to the car park, Chas suggested, 'I think we'll have a romantic dinner out tonight. Where would you like to go, Sweetie?'

'Chas, anywhere with you will be romantic.'

CHAPTER 25

Because they hadn't been there, Chas chose Trelawneys in Conadilly Street. Rosie had heard of its reputation for fine dining so when she dressed, she matched the hearsay. She had recently bought a Princess-Diana-style, silky, puffy-sleeved pink blouse that she matched with a tight-fitting, deep-pink skirt, nipped in at the waist with a wide elastic black belt. She looked magnificent and when Chas saw her walk from the room his words brought a smile to her lips.

'I've changed my mind, Rosie. It's romantic here. I reckon we'll get takeaway and spend dinner time at home.'

'In that case Chasie, you'll probably be alone, cos I want to check out Trelawneys and its reputation for being warm and cosy. After all, we have to turn up for the booked table.'

When they arrived, they were shown to a small dining room set up with one table and two chairs. Rosy was amazed at its size and how snug it felt with soft music playing in the background. It also had an overwhelming romantic feel about it, induced by the décor and the early 1900s architecture. Chas explained that there were several dining rooms of different sizes. The menu offered a range of delectable dishes that made the choice for the evening exceedingly difficult. Eventually, with the help of the attentive waiter, they both ordered. Chas could not help but look adoringly across the table at his fiancée.

'Sweetie, let's set a date.'

'Can I believe that you're suggesting a date for our wedding?'

'You're right. Let's get married.'

'I'd like to do that. Maybe just before Christmas, then we can have a long honeymoon.'

After a delicious meal with a glass of wine, the couple praised the staff as they left and promised to return.

Rather tired after their busy day, they arrived home and slipped into bed within minutes.

'Oh Chasie luv, you really know how to treat a lady.' Rosie cuddled up to her hunky man as he held her close and allowed the overwhelming feelings to take over. The long, sensitive kiss was just the beginning of a play in bed that was always so satisfying. With the hardness of his body pressed against her, Rosie would succumb to Chas's teasing desires, so sleep could engulf her with dreams that made the night so satisfying.

CHAPTER 26

As Phil, along with Barry and Steve, were about to leave the hangar on Friday afternoon, Chas greeted them with some welcome news.

'I have just had a message from the AgQuip organisers to confirm a spot at the air show in August.'

Competing with hoots of delight from Steve, Chas continued, 'It'll be on Thursday the 25th, mid-afternoon, and we'll have half an hour to set up and do our stuff. We'll only be in the air for a maximum of ten minutes. We'll have one more practice run in early August.'

The men sat down and began exchanging information. In reply to a question about any further practice runs, Chas suggested, 'Yes, I think we could do a couple. Des has suggested one more, but I think one at the end of July and maybe one early in August.' His remark was met with agreement from all.

Chas was concerned that Barry had not contributed very much to the chat. Over the past couple of weeks, he seemed to have been definitely out of humour and had taken on a rather disgruntled demeanour, reflected by his standoffish manner when Rosie was around. As Chas saw Barry, round-shouldered with a slumping gait, make his way out the door, Chas followed.

'Hey Barry, ya gotta minute?'

'What's up?'

'Awe, I just wanted a few words. C'mon over to the bench.'

'If you insist.'

'Hardly insisting, but we may as well just sit down. Listen, I don't know what's bothering you, but you've obviously lost some enthusiasm.'

'Yeh, no worries Chas. I'll be right.'

'C'mon, what's biting you?

'Look I'm sure I'll sort it out, but I've had a bit of disappointment from John Franklin regarding the block purchase. I've gotta think about it, mate. I just don't want to talk about it.'

'Okay, but don't let it suck away your zeal from the project. You're an important contributor, you know.'

With Barry tapping his fingers restlessly on the bench, it was clear that he wanted to get going. 'Okay mate, seeing there'll be no jumps this weekend, I'll see you next week.

All Barry wanted to do was get home and veg out. The only positive in his life, as he saw it, was his relationship with Carly. He was meeting her for dinner, so he definitely didn't want to show up with an obvious chip on his shoulder. When he walked in the door at home, he put on a Jimmy Barnes record, turned up the sound as loud as he dared, and headed for the bathroom.

CHAPTER 26

Carly had invited him to her place for the evening, so he was determined to cheer up and face the challenge of discussing the situation with her.

Carly heard the doorbell ring and zipped down the hallway to open the door. 'G'day Bazza, you're right on time.'

She accepted the bunch of roses she was offered with a big smile and gave the man a quick kiss. 'So pleased there weren't any hold ups after work.'

'No, all good. A quiet weekend will be nice for a change.'

The evening went well. Barry enjoyed the chipolata sausages in tomato, onion and spinach sauce that Carly had cooked to perfection. He was never ambitious in the kitchen when he cooked for himself, so she hit the spot with one of his favoured dishes, chipolata sausages. Initially, the conversation at the table was very casual with chatter about the weather and work. Carly had known of his impending visit to John's a couple of weeks back, but on the few occasions they had met since, Barry had never opened up a discussion about it. She guessed that something was bothering him, so she decided to ask a question.

'Did you eventually get to John and Sally's?'

'Oh yes.'

With such a short answer and no further information, Carly went further. 'So, did you see the block? Are you able to get things moving?'

Barry was starting to feel uncomfortable, but knew he should provide an explanation. 'Carly, I loved the block, and I loved the location, but there is not going to be a sale.' Barry went on to describe the entire situation, becoming increasingly distressed as the story unfolded. His last words left him breathless and Carly, with wide eyes and a gaping mouth. 'Bloody Rosie had more to do with it than anybody knows.'

The silence that followed was most uncomfortable. Eventually, Carly composed herself and asked, 'Okay Barry, how about I get us a coffee?' Carly left Barry at the table, and when the coffee was ready, she put it on the coffee table in front of the sofa. 'Let's sit here, it's more comfortable.' A few more words were shared but when Barry finished drinking, he turned and gave Carly a quick hug before he excused himself.

'Thanks Carly, it was a delicious meal and I hope we can do it again. I really must be off. I'm sorry, all this is something I have to come to terms with.' Barry's rapid departure certainly left Carly most upset.

During the week, Chas contacted Des for a date that was mutually compatible for the next practice. It seemed the last Sunday in July would suit everyone. Chas put the word around and everyone settled down for a couple of weeks. Steve's responsibilities had increased over the months because Barry considered it was all part of his apprenticeship training, even though Barry did still check and double check his work, whether it was related to regular hanger jobs or wing walking. However, it did give Steve greater confidence and enthusiasm for any aircraft work and although he loved the wing-walking project, he had never had any desire to get out on the wing himself. He was telling Lisa one day, 'When I strap Rosie into the harness it's like I'm the one having the thrill.'

'Ha ha,' said Lisa with a giggle. 'C'mon Steve, the thrill is up there chasing the clouds.'

CHAPTER 26

'You know, sis? You're a bit like Rosie. She doesn't want to jump so much as just stand up there on the wing.'

'Yes, I really think I could do that a lot more easily than jumping out of an aircraft that is flying perfectly.'

'Okay, if you're serious, then you should get your act together.'

'What do ya mean, Steve? We've already run the idea past Chas and he's just not willing to take me on board.'

'Right, but I reckon we should take it further and maybe, cos the project has gone so well, Des Herd, the safety officer, might be willing to provide opportunities for other willing parties.'

'Interesting. So how will you do that?'

'Leave it with me. I'll give it some thought.'

Steve figured that if the stunt became a crowd-pleaser attraction, there would be money in it. The people to give the approval would be at the Air Transport Bureau, not Chas Anderson. He knew Jeff Danes was also interested so he gave him a call and put the proposition to him that if the Bureau gave permission, would he be interested, and Jeff's answer was a strong 'Yes'. Steve then set about making an appointment with Des Herd.

The outcome of the meeting with Des Herd turned out to be relatively positive. He explained to Steve and Jeff that if there was a business plan, and people were prepared to cover costs and requirements, it was possible for the stunt to be available to others. There would not be any changes in the regulations, but if there were applicants who presented with suitable physical attributes and attitudes then consideration could be given. After the meeting, Steve and Jeff met up with Lisa.

'Oooh really? That's exciting news.' Lisa was overjoyed. 'That means I should get started on an application, hey?'

Jeff agreed with her. 'I don't think anything will be happening soon, but we could be thinking of a bit of prep work.'

Steve was also encouraging. 'Yeh, for sure. You've both done parachute jumps, so you're part of the way there. I reckon you'd have a load of fun Lisa, and although Rosie is pretty good, I reckon you could match her.'

'Thanks for the confidence, Steve, you're a great bro.'

Rosie was pleased that there would be two more practice flights before the AgQuip show. Her experience from the last flight led her to believe that she should make more use of the wind. Even with some careful positioning, she could use the wind to accentuate sideways bending and arching. The movements definitely had to be held for a brief period so they could be appreciated by the onlooking crowd.

Since the supposed panic attack, she had adapted her diet and even given up coffee entirely. Her preparation for any gymnastic routines also now included a brief ten minutes of meditation. Since her research suggested relaxing and stretching the muscles, along with breathing exercises, Rosie recalled the yoga lessons from her student days in Sydney. Now they were really blissful sessions.

On a trip back home to the farm, she managed to find her yoga floor mat tucked away in her wardrobe and, as she pulled it out, the memories of the mindful practice came racing back. In a quiet environment, she knew that the yin technique, with its long slow stretches and deep controlled breathing, could increase circulation in the joints and improve flexibility. She found also that it could increase the sense of control to remain calm and mindful of the event ahead. It had certainly helped her to focus throughout her gymnastic routines in her student days, and also to develop confidence and assertiveness. She explained it all to Chas so that he could understand and support the changes in her lifestyle.

There was also the suggestion that she had made to Chas, that there could be someone describing the movements on the ground. 'Do you have anybody in mind, Sweetie?'

'Well, yes, what do you think if I ask Carly? I could prime her up, but she already knows how to describe the physical movements. She can use the right words, like flexibility, arabesque, a layout, and there are others.'

'Yes, Carly would be an excellent choice. Get her to come to the next practice session. She can record her presentation and then you can discuss it with her afterwards.'

'Okay, will do.' When Rosie approached Carly, she agreed to come to the practice flight but was not as enthusiastic as Rosie imagined her to be.

'You do really want to help out Carly?'

'Yep, that's fine. Maybe you could give me a list of the movements you are planning in some sort of rough order. I guess a lot depends on the strength of the wind and whether the aircraft is straight and level or climbing or diving?'

'That's for sure, you're spot on Carly.'

Later, Rosie had a chat to Chas.

'You know Chas, what Carly is going to do is what I do for

you when you are doing an air show.'

'That's right. So when you are planning the script be sure she understands the aircraft movement terms, so when we are 'climbing', we're not 'taking off'. Okay?'

'I've been thinking. Chas, if I put some ribbons around my wrists, as the wind blows them back that would accentuate the arm movements. What do you reckon?'

'Yes, an innovative idea, but they mustn't be too long to get in my eyes, in the cockpit. If they were short, wide and silvery they could show up really well.'

'Okay. I'll see what I can find.'

The next practice flight was arranged for the last Sunday in July. The crew had plenty of time to make the preparations and eagerly awaited the day.

CHAPTER 27

'Hey Rosie, are you fit and feisty for today?' As Rosie sat up, Chas gently laid the breakfast tray across her lap and then sat on the end of the bed.

'For sure, what time do we have to be at the airport?'

'Pretty well nine o'clock. Des and Brian will be there at about ten o'clock and we'll try to get onto everything immediately so we can be back on the ground again by ten-thirty.'

'Well, I've been through everything with Carly, but I told her nine-thirty. That should be okay. You're planning the timing to fit in with the requirements of AgQuip on the Show Day, aren't you? It seems like it will be rather tight, but I guess as long as we get our ten minutes in the air, all should be fine.'

Rosie felt a little disappointed as she looked out of the window. 'Gee, there're a few clouds around.'

'Yep, that won't worry us. We'll be well under them today.'

Rosie packed her Lycra gear and the ginger tea that she had prepared. She liked the idea of ginger as an alternative to coffee because it helped boost energy without caffeine. The recipe she found during her research explained how to prepare a ginger root for strong tea and then to add lemon and honey to taste. The cold prepared drink was something she looked forward to most mornings because she could take it to the staff room in a bottle for morning tea.

They made it to the airport easily by 9 o'clock. Chas had a list of things he wanted to cover with Barry before Des arrived. Rosie went off to the lost corner in the hangar to get into her Lycra tights and shirt and do her yin yoga for meditation before Carly arrived. After fifteen minutes, she leisurely walked back into the hangar and spotted Carly sitting at the table. 'Great to see you here well before time, Carly.'

'Yes, no problems for me. I'm an early bird. A bit facetious to say that to you when you're the bird, hey Rosie?'

'No, no, that's okay, good for a little laugh. Let's see what words you're going to use today.' The two young ladies poured over Carly's piece of paper until the hangar crew arrived with Lisa in tow. Des and Brian arrived a few minutes later.

Chas welcomed everybody and then said, 'Well, we are all bright and early, with a few minutes to spare, so let's have a quick coffee before the fun starts.'

'I'll do the coffee for you,' said Lisa, 'while you guys have a meaningful moment.' As Lisa made her way to the coffee machine with Steve, who was carrying a plate of biscuits, Rosie called out, 'Don't worry about me Lisa, I've got my bottle of tea here.'

Barry also slipped up behind Lisa and was seen to have a few quick words before he returned to the table. He then glanced

CHAPTER 27

across at Rosie and raised his eyebrows as a swift smile crossed his face. Rosie thought, *that's the nicest acknowledgement I've had from him for a while.*

Barry asked her, 'So you can put more coffee in a bottle, hey?'

'No Barry, it's ginger tea. I'm off coffee altogether.'

When they were all sitting down, Steve handed around the biscuits until there was just one left, but Rosie was not interested. 'No thanks, Steve.'

'Awe c'mon Rosie, I made them just for you. You'd better have the last one.'

'Just to please you, Steve. They do look like healthy ones.'

'Yep, they're chocolate cookies with nuts.'

'Well in that case I'll have just one, thank you.'

The excitement of the day was quite subdued, but there was an eagerness to get everything underway. As the coffee cups were emptied and put on the table, Des and Brian handed out their check sheets to those concerned.

'Okay.' Chas was on his feet, an indication that things were going to get moving. 'Carly, you've got your recorder set up, haven't you?'

'Yes Chas, all good.'

'And Rosie, you've had your pep-up tea?'

With a smile on her face, Rosie repeated Carly's words, 'Yes Chas, all good.'

As each individual left the hangar and made for the Tiger, they offered their 'stay safe' and 'good luck' lines. Barry actually said, 'Have fun Rosie. We're all watching.'

Everything was going according to plan. Within a few

minutes, Rosie was strapped in and talking animatedly of the challenge ahead. To the cheering of the hangar crew, Chas turned the Tiger onto the runway and started his take-off run. There was a quick exchange on the radio and then a smooth lift into the air as Rosie began some strong, vigorous movements. The aircraft turned to fly straight and level over the airfield and the onlookers could hear Carly delivering her commentary. Without warning, Carly screamed as she pointed wildly to Rosie's slumped figure. Chas was in emergency mode as he had just tried to communicate with Rosie when he witnessed her total collapse in the harness. He could not get any response from her and turned immediately to land.

As he pulled up at the hangar he called out, 'Rosie, Rosie, what the hell is going on?' There were other exclamations of absolute terror. The scramble to get Rosie out of the harness was repeated, but this time Chas yelled, 'Get an ambulance! We need an ambulance now!'

Once she was carried to the hangar bed, Chas tried to get Rosie to respond while Lisa checked her heart rate.

'Chas, her heart is absolutely pounding, and her heartbeat is so erratic. We must get her to the hospital.'

Chas was holding Rosie gently, but he could feel her arms and legs jerking, and as he could not hear her trying to say anything, he assumed she was unconscious. The crew were hanging around closely but there was nothing they could do until the ambulance arrived, and then they helped the paramedics access the hangar to get the medical trolly through to the bed. Moving the unresponsive Rosie to the ambulance was done efficiently and quickly. The paramedics were at her side helping her breathe, so Chas ran to his car to follow the vehicle to the hospital. Lisa ran after him, 'Chas, can I come with you?'

'Yeh, okay, get in quick.' Chas obviously didn't want to talk as he drove so Lisa just said, 'Chas, I don't think it's a panic attack.'

At the hospital, they had to sit in the waiting room. Lisa was off duty, so she had no access to the emergency cubicle where Rosie had been taken. Time passed slowly. All Chas could do was close his eyes and allow thoughts of the morning's proceedings muddle his mind. Lisa sat close by and watched the TV that was always turned on. It was 12.30 pm before the doctor came to talk to them.

'Hello there Chas, you know me, Fred Johnson, from your hospital days. So your friend Rosie's been wing walking? The paramedics just filled me in. Oh, and hello Lisa. Let me tell you that Rosie will be okay, but she was a lucky lady.'

Taken aback at the flippancy of the comment. Before Chas questioned the doctor, he asked Lisa to leave the waiting room him so he could speak with Dr Johnson alone. Reluctantly, but without argument, Lisa left.

'What do you mean 'lucky'? She is in a terrible state.'

'Chas, she has signs of panic disorder that are very disabling. The symptoms she displayed, a fever, profuse sweating, breathing difficulty, visual disturbance, and erratic heartbeat. Are all consistent with an excessive level of a stimulant in her body, possibly caffeine and it—'

Butting into the explanation, Chas said, 'Well that is wrong

Doctor Johnson. She's had no caffeine for weeks. Tell me what is going on.'

'Chas, let me finish. We have taken blood samples which are now on their way to the Tamworth laboratory. The results will be back later this afternoon. This will confirm whether it is caffeine or another stimulant.'

'There's no way she could have overdosed on caffeine?'

'That might be something she can tell us when she is able to respond lucidly.'

'And when will that be?'

'Because we are not sure what she has had, how much she has had, or how long ago, we will need to keep her in hospital and monitor her vital signs for at least two or three days. There have been cases where excessive caffeine has proved to be fatal.'

'Doctor, there is no way Rosie would have taken any caffeine by choice. It was suggested that when she had similar symptoms, but far less severe, during a wing-walking flight about six weeks ago that she'd had a panic attack. Once she got over it, she did some intensive research about her symptoms and there was an inference that coffee could have made her feel that way, even though she'd had only one cup before the event.'

The doctor continued to listen intently. 'That prompted her to give up caffeine totally. She'd used a cup of coffee for years as a driver of energy before her gymnastic competitions. So, she decided to switch to meditation and ginger tea to provide focus and an energy boost in preparation for the wing-walking stunt.'

'Chas, if what you are telling me is the truth, and Rosie tells me the same thing when she can, then there is something suspicious about all this. She may not be all that coherent yet, but come with me and we'll see if we can talk to her.'

Chas shook his head and put his hand over his mouth as he followed the doctor down the corridor.

Rosie was lying on her back with her eyes closed. It was just over two hours since she had collapsed on the aircraft. Dr Johnson moved to her side and spoke her name slowly and clearly. 'Rosie, Rosie, can you hear me? Would you like to talk? Chas is here.'

Rosie opened her eyes slowly and moved her head very sluggishly as she gazed around until her eyes met Chas's.

She put out her hand and called his name in a whispery tone, 'Chas.'

He took her hand, put it to his lips, and then replied in a tender voice, 'Rosie, sweetie, we're with you. I love you. I love you so much.'

Rosie looked intently into his eyes and repeated his words in husky low tone, 'I-I-I love you.'

The doctor then posed the question, 'Rosie, do you want to talk about what happened this morning?'

'Oh, I-I was w-w-wing walking. W-w-what…. what happened?'

The doctor looked at Chas with raised eyebrows to indicate that he could continue the conversation.

'Rosie, how did you feel? Did you feel the same way that you did a few weeks ago when you collapsed on the wing?'

With her eyes closed, Rosie continued, 'I-I collapsed?'

'Do you recall how you felt when that happened?' The doctor was listening.

'I-I was nervous. Sh-shaking.'

'Those people with you thought it was a panic attack due to drinking coffee. Did you have coffee today? Did Lisa bring you a coffee at the table?'

'No... no coffee.' Rosie coughed as she slowly shook her head. The doctor was aware that Rosie was not comfortable speaking with them.

'What did you drink before take-off?'

'G-g-ginger tea.'

Dr Johnson took Chas to the side and whispered, 'Leave it at that, Chas. Say goodbye.'

'Rosie love, you must rest. I'll be in to see you tomorrow. Have a good night. Love you lots.'

'L-l-love you, Chasie.'

They left and the doctor turned to Chas as they walked back down the corridor. 'Well my boy, you're correct. She has not knowingly taken any caffeine. I think we need to get in touch with the local police. If she has been given something surreptitiously, they need to know, because what Rosie went through could have been far more serious, and even been the death of her. I will contact them now, as such a situation is more official coming from me.'

When Dr Johnson contacted the police station and explained the situation, he suggested that they send an officer around to the hospital. He expected Rosie to be more articulate in an hour or so. Since the blood samples had been sent off to Tamworth during the morning, it was possible they could have a result by mid-to-late afternoon by telephone. The doctor then suggested

CHAPTER 27

that Chas should come by the hospital early in the morning as he would probably have the blood sample test results by then.

The police turned up at the hospital at 2.30 pm just before Chas left. Detective Sergeant Holt and Constable Gardner sat with Dr Johnson in his office while he explained all that he knew of the circumstances that morning. As Chas was about to leave, Dr Johnson introduced him and referred to his role in the incident. The sergeant then requested meeting with Chas in a few minutes, following their time with Dr Johnson. Chas stepped out of the office and walked to the waiting room. Lisa was not there. She had left.

Sergeant Holt was particularly interested in the process used to gather and transport Rosie's blood sample, and the doctor's assumption that the symptoms were caused by an overdose of a stimulant, possibly caffeine. The sergeant was concerned in regard to the safe transfer of forensic evidence.

'So, Doctor, you believe the woman's blood samples will show an excessive amount of some stimulant?'

'Yes Sergeant Holt, that's right. When she was admitted, she was unconscious for a brief period.'

Dr Johnson described the symptoms Rosie had shown. 'I can now say that the impact of the stimulant has decreased and with rest for two or three days, she'll be discharged. Had the symptoms been slightly stronger, the impact would have brought about a very intense adverse response that could have led to her death.'

They were then shown to Rosie's room. Dr Johnson and a nurse stood at the head of the bed. Sergeant Holt sat at

Rosie's bedside. She was considerate of the young patient in front of her, and although the questions were short and precise, and she asked them in a gentle and empathetic manner, she realised the interview would have to be very concise. Constable Gardner was taking notes. Sergeant Holt wanted to know what the situation that morning had been about; what Rosie had been doing and why; were there other people involved, and could she explain why she had excess caffeine in her body. Most of the time Rosie only needed to respond with short answers until she had to explain why she no longer drank coffee, and with what had she replaced her regular cup of coffee. Because of the length of her answer, the talking proved to be rather onerous for the patient. Sergeant Holt finished her questioning prematurely. She and her partner then left the room but waited in the corridor for the doctor. The sergeant had a couple more questions.

'Let's take this a little further, Doctor Johnson. Who called the paramedics?'

'The paramedics were called by a member of the hangar staff at the airport. I believe the aerial stunt which Rosie was performing was progressing well until she collapsed in the safety harness, and it was suspected that she'd had a second panic attack. Chas Anderson was the pilot and is the person to speak to for precise information. He will know all about it. Phil Jennings, the leading aircraft engineer and manager of the hangar will tell you where to find the others who were involved.'

'Thanks Dr Johnson, you have been very helpful. We may

have to be in touch with you again. You certainly did the right thing calling us in and we'll be looking closely for any suspicious circumstances.'

CHAPTER 28

Doctor Johnson had suggested the police officers continue their chat with Chas Anderson in his office as he was required to be elsewhere. Constable Gardner checked the waiting room and asked Chas to join them.

Sergeant Holt began, 'Mr Anderson, we are aware that you, along with Dr Johnson, believe there are suspicious circumstances related to the unfortunate mishap that took place at the airport this morning. If you could just answer a couple of questions now, in regard to your role in the wing-walking project, we would then request you to come to the station tomorrow morning to make a full statement.'

'For sure, that's okay.'

Chas willingly provided the information regarding the development of the project. He gave details of how Rosie had become so enthusiastic in regard to wing walking, and of her past history of using coffee to give her an energy boost before any physical challenge. He then went on to describe the panic attack

CHAPTER 28

on the second trial flight and how Rosie then put a complete stop to her intake of coffee, replacing it with ginger tea and meditation. He also mentioned that it was Lisa Jennings, a nurse, who suggested that Rosie had had a panic attack on that day.

He added, 'However, on the way to the hospital yesterday morning Lisa said to me, very definitely, 'It's not a panic attack, Chas', and I believe she knew Rosie had given up coffee.'

'Dr Johnson took us to see Rosie and she did confirm all that you have said. It appears at this stage, someone who obviously knows that coffee can give the symptoms of a panic attack, has surreptitiously given her an excessive amount. We now must ask the questions, 'Who could have done that?' and 'Why would someone want to do it?' and 'How was it done?' Do you know of any person with whom Rosie has, or has had, a relationship with recently and who would possibly have an underlying disagreement or grievance with her?'

It was the first time that Chas had actually considered Lisa as the perpetrator so his reply was rather circumspect. 'The nurse, Lisa Jennings, and Rosie have shown animosity towards each other from time to time, but I can't believe Lisa would be involved. When I was hospitalised after my accident, months ago, Lisa was full-on about taking care of me and really resented Rosie being my carer when I was discharged. Barry Moyle, who is an aircraft engineer in the hangar, also has had grievances with Rosie, I think because of her connection to a Franklin family property with which he is involved. Barry and Steve Jennings, our hangar apprentice, have worked together on the fabrication issues for the wing-walking stunt, but I don't believe Steve and Rosie have any problems. They work really well together.

'Oh, and Jeff Danes, he's a teacher at the high school who was trying to get a go at wing-walking, along with Lisa. They talked more with me than with Rosie but were rather put out by the fact that she was the one doing the stunt. I explained to them that it was not possible for them to be involved at this stage because of the safety issues, and our agreement with the Air Transport Bureau. However, he and Lisa did not want to accept my explanation. There is also Carly Kent. She's Rosie's good friend and teaching colleague who recently became part of the team. She is to be the announcer when the wing-walking event goes public. I would not believe that she has any hard feelings towards Rosie. But again, it does not seem likely that any of them would be so outraged to threaten her safety in such a way.'

'Well, that is for us to decide, Chas, but thank you for your assistance and we would like you to come to the station tomorrow, Monday, at 2 pm. I am sure we will have more questions for you by then.'

As they were about to leave, Sergeant Holt asked Chas if he had contact details for Barry Moyle, Lisa and Steve Jennings, Jeff Danes and Carly Kent.

'It is possible that Phil Jennings will be able to help you with that. He is sure to be at the airport in the hangar this afternoon.' Chas decided to leave the hospital and return for visiting time at 6.30 pm.

The next checkpoint for Sergeant Holt was the hangar. Her partner, Constable Gardener, was always in position by her side,

CHAPTER 28

taking notes, and they worked together in a very professional manner. From their discussion with the doctor, it was obvious that they needed the full story and the circumstances that led to Rosie's hospitalisation, so they headed off for the airport. The police car pulled up outside the hangar, and the two officers hopped out to make their way through the open door.

Phil was somewhat surprised to see the police officers walking towards his office. He met them at the door and extended his hand. 'I'm Phil Jennings, how can I help you?'

The officers introduced themselves and Sergeant Holt said, 'Mr Jennings, you are aware of the unfortunate incident that occurred here at the airport this morning?'

'Oh, certainly. Rosie Franklin has been admitted to hospital.'

'Yes, and we believe she was participating in an aerial manoeuvre of some sort.'

'Yes, that's correct. I really think you would get more information by speaking with Chas Anderson. He is the pilot and is the organiser for that activity.'

'Yes, we have spoken with Chas. I believe you have been the overseer of the aerial activity.'

'Initially yes, but more recently the Air Transport Bureau has been involved.'

Sergeant Holt continued, 'Well Mr Jennings, what do you know about this morning?'

Phil proceeded to explain the wing-walking project. In the conversation that followed, he mentioned the length of time that Chas and Rosie had been working on it and the involvement of the Air Transport Bureau along with the attendance of safety officers, who had always been satisfied with the preparation and safety measures undertaken. Phil also covered the details of Rosie's similar panic attack incident that had occurred on a previous trial flight.

Sergeant Holt expressed her thanks and asked, 'Can you tell us of any other people who were around this morning?'

'Oh yes.' As he rose and went to the door, Phil pointed to the end of the hangar. 'If you go to the aircraft at the end of the wall, down there, you'll see two guys working on it, Barry Moyle and Steve, my son. They're just doing a bit of a Sunday check-up. They have both assisted in the stunt project.'

When both the engineers lifted their heads from under the engine cover to acknowledge a greeting, they were obviously surprised to see the uniformed police officers.

'Hi, I'm Barry Moyle. How can we help you?'

'G'day sir. We believe you and Steve Jennings were both present in the hangar this morning preparing for the wing-walk flight.'

'Yes, that's right.'

'We request that you come to the police station tomorrow, Monday morning, Barry, to make a statement about your involvement with the wing-walking project.'

'Er, well, why would I need to do that?'

'Sir, it is being considered as a suspicious situation, and at this stage we need as much information as possible. We are asking all people who were present here at the time, and others who are associated with Rosie Franklin, to be available for an interview. Mr Jennings, we request that you come along as well.'

CHAPTER 28

Barry and Steve looked at each other with quizzical expressions. Barry said, 'Yes, okay.'

Steve asked, 'Why me?'

'Sir, everyone who was there this morning will have to be questioned.' As Constable Gardner made notes with each name, he also suggested they give him a time when they could attend the station. The police officers then made their way to the car park.

Although Barry understood that anyone who had been at the hangar at the time of the incident was to be questioned by the sergeant, he was rather sceptical as to why. It seemed pretty obvious to him that Rosie was blaming the project crew for some coffee indulgence that she had used to prepare herself for the presentation on the Tiger wing. He had come to regard her, over the past weeks, as a rather selfish, egocentric young woman.

He decided to call Carly to see if they could catch up for a Sunday night dinner. Barry suggested that she come over to his place for an easy meal. She was okay with the idea. and although his cooking skills were limited, when he said that he would put together a spaghetti bolognaise with garlic bread, she could not decline his offer.

Carly was pleased to think Barry was carrying on as usual. On Sunday evening, she dressed in her casual flared trousers, matched to a smart T-shirt, and arrived with a bottle of blue Curaçao in her hand. As he opened the door, she handed him the bottle. 'Let's make it an interesting evening, Barry.'

With a loud laugh, Barry replied, 'Hello dear lady, you're welcome anytime, for sure.'

He felt cheered immediately and followed her down the hallway of his flat. The evening began with a very slow reference to the incident that morning, but when the meal was finished, and they sat on the sofa with their after-dinner liqueur, the bleakness of the day permeated the living room.

Carly was sensitive to the increasing melancholy that was enveloping Barry, so, with a confident manner, she suggested, 'Barry, what happened today had nothing to do with you, and Rosie certainly did not set herself up for such a disaster. Someone has covertly arranged a situation whereby she will be considered responsible for the collapse of the project. I don't know who it could be, but a lot of people have been part of the project.'

'Sure, but why would anyone want to cause such a disaster?'

'You know, even Chas might have been trying to find a way to discourage her from continuing the adventure. Barry, you have worked so hard to make it all a success. Rosie knows that. She has often told me how fantastic you have been in getting everything right for her.'

With a snicker, Barry replied, 'I'm not so sure about that. You know I've got an interview with the police tomorrow?'

'Barry, so have I, and so has everybody else who was at the hangar this morning. They'll ask questions and we just tell them what we know. Listen, you're angry with Rosie because you think she has been involved with the collapse of your purchase of the block from the Franklin's property.'

'But she has Carly.'

'Not to specifically deter you though. She's talked to me

CHAPTER 28

about it several times and even from my point of view I can understand why she suggested that John should double check everything. She is quite happy for you to be involved but insists there must be very tight regulations. You know, there could be circumstances down the track that could influence the property ownership, if not by you but other people, and even people using the Franklin situation to undermine ownership on other properties.'

'And you have really talked to Rosie about it all?'

'Yes Barry, there is nothing personal in her determination to turn you off the opportunity, she only considers that there should be a very specific contract to safeguard the Franklin properties. She thinks you are a great guy.'

'Oh-oh, so I'd better tell her I've assumed a bit too much.'

'Yes, but I wouldn't do anything like that until the police inquiry is over.'

When Chas arrived for the evening visiting hour at the hospital, right on time, there was a short queue in the waiting room before he could be directed to Rosie's room. As he walked through her doorway, he was pleased to see his dear love, resting comfortably with a couple of pillows under her shoulders. 'Oh wow, you look a bit sparky, Sweetie.'

With a little chuckle from Rosie, she replied, 'Oh Chasie, it's so good to see you.'

'Rosie, your voice seems a little better too. Any symptoms still?'

'Oh, a bit of this and a bit of that, you know, feverish and aching arms and legs, but getting better.'

Chas wanted to avoid any more talk of the day, so he told her about his quick chat with her parents, who had arrived at the hospital as he left after his morning talk to the police.

'Yes Chasie, they had wanted to see me earlier but because of the police they came back a little later this afternoon. Do the police know anything yet? I don't remember very much from when they were here. I really was out of it. Even you Chasie. I feel this morning was all a dream.'

The conversation continued for a short while in a low key and loving banter. Seeing her look tired and rather exhausted, he kept the visit short, and with his strong arms gently entwined around her, he gave his sweetheart a cuddle and a soft kiss as he said goodnight.

CHAPTER 29

Chas was the first one at the hospital reception desk the next morning and he enquired if Dr Johnson had any information for him in regard to Rosie Franklin. He was told to wait a moment. Dr Johnson was notified, and Chas was asked to go to his office.

'Good morning, Chas. I guess you're up here to see Rosie?'

'Of course, Doctor. Have you had any news about the blood test?'

'Certainly have. It came through late yesterday and they tell me it shows an overdose. Now, a single cup of coffee contains approximately one hundred milligrams of caffeine, which increases caffeine in the blood to about five milligrams. It seems Rosie's blood level showed about one hundred milligrams of caffeine, and that means the equivalent of twenty cups of coffee. People who have died of a caffeine overdose, as a form of suicide, average one hundred and eighty milligrams in their blood. Anyone researching the data Chas, would possibly understand that, and have used caffeine powder or pills to increase the dosage, without wanting to make it lethal. Of course, the ultimate response is dependent upon underlying health issues or side effects. Sergeant Holt now has the information, and the inquiry is in the hands of the police.'

'So possibly, it has been a deliberate attempt to put Rosie out of the event by creating what seems to be a panic attack?'

'Could be Chas, but the police are onto it now.'

'Yes, they came and saw me yesterday and I'm off to the formal interview at 2 pm today.'

Chas was relieved that he could visit Rosie's bedside at such an early hour. She looked comfortable, with her eyes closed, and was lying easily in the bed. One hand was uncovered at her side, so he took it in his and kissed it gently. Slowly Rosie opened her eyes and gazed adoringly into his. 'I love you so much Sweetie. Just think, we will be Mr and Mrs Anderson in five months.'

'So how will that be different from now?'

'Well, you will have a different name and another ring on your finger. Maybe I'll have one on mine.'

'Would you like one Chasie?'

'Of course, ours is going to be a marriage of equal opportunity, just like the way we share the dominant position in bed,' he chortled. 'If you've got a ring, then I can have one too.'

With a few chuckles to follow, the couple ended up in a warm embrace. Rosie continued, 'That policewoman who came to see me was very considerate and asked me a few questions, but why do you think they came along to see me, Chasie?'

Chas explained what he and Dr Johnson had considered

suspicious circumstances in regard to the reaction she had had on two occasions.

'How do you think you could have been given a load of caffeine, Sweetie?'

'Oh, I have no idea. It was only ginger tea that I had in the morning. I don't miss my cup of coffee one bit, even though I do like the taste.'

'Could someone have had access to your bottle of tea, do you think?'

'Impossible, after I had made it and left home, it was with me the entire time. It was even within my sight while I got into the Lycra gear.'

'Anyway, the police are on to it. Someone has tried to mess things up for you and make your wing-walking venture very dangerous. I'm so glad Des and Brian were there to witness everything cos at least the incident has nothing to do with safety checks. You were held safe even though you had no control. So do you know where you left your bottle after you had drunk the ginger tea?'

'Well, yes, I'm pretty sure it would be in my gear bag. I took it back to the car before we prepped for take-off.'

'Good, I'll take it to my interview this afternoon. Do you remember anything at all about the wing walk?'

'I can tell you, as I told Dr Johnson, I was fired up to get going and take-off. Once the plane had left the ground and started to climb, I remember a very strong sense of – well, like fear. I felt positive and so excited, but then I started breathing very fast and everything went blank.'

'Would you ever consider trying again?'

'Of course, of course Chasie. You went through more than I did at the time. I don't remember enough to stop me from getting into the harness again. Do you think Des and Brian will give us another go?'

'I reckon as long as we find out who did this, because it's a personal attack, the safety checks remain intact, but I'm sure the Bureau will be right onto the police investigation.'

'Oh good, I'm keen and willing. Dr Johnson said that if I continue my rate of improvement, it's possible I'll be out of here on Wednesday morning. Would you mind calling Carly and telling her it will be a few days before I get back to school?'

'For sure, my sweetie. Now, you have a good rest today, and we'll catch up tonight.'

With a tender kiss, Chas waved goodbye as he left the room. Before he left the hospital, he left his phone number and a message for Dr Johnson to contact him.

After having been able to set up contact details for those they wanted to interview, Sergeant Holt and Constable Gardner followed up on the addresses that Chas had given them. With ease, they were able to arrange a time during the afternoon for Lisa Jennings, Jeff Danes and Carly Kent. It was going to be a very busy week ahead. The sergeant had taken the day's notes home with her on Sunday evening to spend some time getting the order of events clear in her mind, as well as an awareness of the people involved in the incident. At one point she considered that she should also speak with the Air Transport Bureau officers.

CHAPTER 29

Barry was the first to arrive for his appointment at the police station on Monday morning. Constable Gardner had a typewriter set up at the end of the table, and as Sergeant Holt directed Barry to be seated, her affable manner tended to put him at ease.

'Good morning, Mr Moyle. Thank you for arriving right on time. Constable Gardner will be with us taking notes.'

Barry nodded to both officers. 'Yes, G'morning Sergeant Holt, Constable Gardener.'

The sergeant began by asking Barry his full name, date of birth, address, and occupation. 'Barry, how long have you known Rosie and how did you come to be involved with the wing-walking stunt?'

'Well, although I have known her for about eighteen months, we only really started working together on the aerial stunt about five months ago when approval was granted by the Air Transport Board.'

Sergeant Holt followed this up with questions related to the specific work for which Barry was responsible. The working relationship unfolded as an amiable exercise that did not indicate any developing tensions.

'Have you ever had any reason to feel irate towards Rosie?'

Barry now began to feel uncomfortable but he knew he had to tell the truth because so many others knew of his disappointment and the degree of anger he had felt towards Rosie in regard to the Franklin property discussions. His answer encompassed the fury he felt when he thought that she had been responsible for the decision made by her brother John, in diverting his enthusiasm away from the negotiations. He then explained that when he thought about it, he realised had that he had been unreasonable in jumping to conclusions in regard to the outcome of the discussions.

The sergeant's questions changed tack. 'Have there been occasions when you and Rosie shared a coffee time?'

'Oh yes, quite often. Whenever we were working on the project, we'd all break off for a while and have a chat over coffee.'

'Did you ever hear Rosie talk about her need for a coffee before attempting challenging physical activities?'

'No, not really a need. I only ever heard her say that coffee actually helped her confidence and concentration.'

'Have you ever made a cup of coffee for Rosie?'

'No never, but she's made them for me.'

'Did you see her have a cup of coffee on Sunday morning?'

'No. She was drinking from a bottle. She's been doing that for a while. When Lisa went to make the coffee, Rosie said that she had her own bottle of tea. I asked her what it was, and she explained that she had made her own ginger tea.'

'Did you see her eat or drink anything else in the period before she was strapped into the harness?'

'We weren't there to eat but, like always, there was a plate of chocolate biscuits on the table that we all finished off. I think she probably had one, although I didn't see her eating it.'

'Okay, well thank you Barry. We'll be in touch if we need to clarify anything else.'

Barry then left, somewhat satisfied that he had answered all the questions satisfactorily. Barry's interview had been convincing, even though Sergeant Holt had detected his discomfort at some stages.

Steve Jennings was already waiting in the reception area. After he was ushered into the meeting room, his interview began with the same regulatory questions Sergeant Holt had asked Barry, and the answers were as expected. When he was asked the question that was related to any feelings of anger towards Rosie, Steve did have plenty to say.

'Well, I'm not really angry with her, but she has certainly upset my sister.'

'What do you mean by that, Steve?'

'I've never had any issues with Rosie at all. We've worked well together on the project and often had a few laughs, but she has upset Lisa quite often.'

'In what way?'

'Oh, I know Rosie didn't like the way Lisa flirted with Chas and then when Lisa approached Chas about doing some wing walking, Chas was totally on Rosie's side and didn't even consider Lisa's aspirations at all. When Rosie found out that Lisa had wanted to wing walk too, Lisa said she just became so rude that she found it very hard to be friends with her.'

'Did Lisa ever sit around and have coffee with you all in the hangar?'

'No, she was usually on duty at the hospital.'

'But she was there last Sunday morning?'

'Yes, she wasn't at the table, but she made coffee for us all and Rosie just drank her ginger tea.'

'Thanks Steve, for your time and answering all our questions.

We may have to talk again.'

Steve left the room in a jovial manner. 'No problem.'

It was to be a brief and early lunch for the police officers. Sergeant Holt sat down to discuss the morning with the constable.

After a few minutes, she checked her watch. 'I believe Lisa will be here in about ten minutes. I'm looking forward to hearing what she has to say.'

'Well, she seems to be the one with the biggest grudge, at this point anyway.'

When Lisa arrived, she was met by Constable Gardner as she hesitantly opened the door to the reception room.

'Good afternoon, Miss Jennings, I'll show you to the meeting room.'

After greeting the Constable rather coyly, Lisa followed him along the corridor. Sergeant Holt was waiting at the table.

'Well Lisa, after such a disturbing weekend, I hope you are feeling better today.'

'Thank you. Yes, Sergeant I am.'

Sergeant Holt asked the regulatory questions following the same pattern. However, when it was suggested to Lisa that she had had some disagreements with Rosie from time-to-time, Lisa became agitated and somewhat critical of Rosie's behaviour towards her. Sergeant Holt detected an indication of jealousy related to the relationship Rosie shared with Chas, just as Steve, her brother, had suggested.

'So, you felt Rosie was trying to create a conflict between you and Chas?'

CHAPTER 29

'Sort of. I would ask Chas a question and she would either change the subject or make some excuse for them to leave me. Chas is a nice guy, but she really made him do stuff that pleased her, and she was so over the top after his accident.'

'Did you want to help Chas after his accident?'

'Of course. I was the nurse. What did she know? I just tried to offer him advice and help him, but she told me to leave him alone.'

'Did you ever feel that you would like to do wing walking?'

'Yes, I did.'

'Your brother told us that you did ask Chas if you could do it too.'

'Yes, Jeff Danes, a guy I parachute with, and I both wanted to go wing walking, but Chas would not even consider us. He just spoke of it all being Rosie's project.'

It was not until the sergeant questioned Lisa about offering advice to Chas at the time of Rosie's first panic attack incident, that Lisa appeared even more uneasy trying to find an answer. 'Um, well, she was finding it difficult to breathe and seemed to be having spasms.'

'Once she was lying on the bed you, in your medical capacity as a nurse, considered there was no need for a doctor. Is that right?'

'Well, I did say she looked more relaxed.'

'Did you know that Rosie always had a cup of coffee before a physical event?'

'Yes, she told me once that she used to have a cup of coffee before gymnastic competitions because it was most stimulating.'

'Lisa, can I suggest that maybe you thought that if Rosie couldn't handle the stunt, then Chas may ask you to do it in place of her? I think you knew that Rosie wasn't in a serious condition after her first so-called panic attack because you made her coffee that day, and you made it stronger, so that she would have a bad reaction up in the air. Is that right?'

There was a period of silence while Lisa put her fingers to her lips and was deep in thought before she answered.

'I will tell you the truth. Yes, I am a nurse, and I know all about the effects of caffeine on the body. I have read medical reports on the use of caffeine, and how soda companies are now producing decaffeinated drinks because of the effects of excessive use of products containing extra caffeine. Rosie was a fine example of how you could use coffee safely, just a cup, to increase energy and motivation. Research suggests that caffeine can be boosted by a pill. I popped a couple of two-hundred-milligram pills in Rosie's coffee that day, which would have made her cup a little over the equivalent of five cups of coffee, and yes, I expected it to have an effect equivalent to a mild panic attack. Which it did have. I knew she was strapped in safely, but I wanted her to feel that she would not be able to do the stunt again.'

'Lisa, you realise you have admitted to a felony that could have taken someone's life.'

'I have not committed a felony. I simply gave her an extra couple of coffee pills thinking she would not feel well in the air with maybe nausea and a bit of dizziness. She was quite safe with the extra quantity of coffee. I made sure of that because I didn't want her to come to any real harm.'

CHAPTER 29

Sergeant Holt took a deep breath before her next question. 'Lisa, that may have been on that occasion, but what about Sunday?'

'Sunday? Sunday had nothing to do with me. I did not give Rosie anything. She had her own bottle of ginger tea, and a chocolate biscuit, like the rest of us. I had no intention of doing that all over again.'

'So, you are not aware of how Rosie could have got an excess of caffeine in her body?'

'No way.' Lisa then slapped her hand on to the table before continuing fervently, 'I did not do it.'

Sergeant Holt and Constable Gardner exchanged glances before Lisa was told, 'Okay Lisa, you can leave now, and I thank you for your honesty. However, you will be charged for the felony and we will be speaking again.'

Lisa glared across the table at the officers as she left the table and stomped towards the door.

Constable Gardner closed the door behind her and then turned to say, 'Well, that's a move in the right direction. What do you think?'

'I must say I do believe she is being truthful. What she said about a mild dose of caffeine creating a questionable response seems quite reasonable, and her input as a nurse was somewhat rational. However, what did happen on Sunday?'

Gardner's next statement made Sergeant Holt turn quickly, 'You know, we haven't considered the bottle? After all, Rosie made that tea herself. Did it really have ginger tea in it?'

With her mouth open and finger in the air, like something

had raced through her mind, the sergeant was silent for a few seconds before she replied, 'Wow, Constable, that is something we must check out. I wonder where the bottle is now. We must follow up on the ginger tea bottle ASAP. Let's get on with the interviews and get Jeff Danes in here. Chas is due in at 2 pm.'

It had proved to be quite a long session and Jeff Danes was waiting patiently at reception. Jeff was taken to the meeting room and thrown the same introductory questions. Apart from his visit to Chas with Lisa, asking about the opportunity to have a go at wing walking, there was nothing that could be developed that was related to the incident. Jeff's association with Rosie was as a work colleague, and he spoke highly of her as a competent and friendly associate.

The interview with Carly Kent followed. It also was concise and to the point. Carly's close friendship with Rosie confirmed that Rosie's passion for motivating and challenging exploits was an important part of her life. Coffee was not a big deal, except for a little stimulation before a demanding event. Carly mentioned the rift that had occurred between Barry and Rosie, and although Sergeant Holt kept that in mind, she now assumed it probably had nothing to do with the incident.

It had been a busy day. As they sipped a quick coffee and Constable Gardner checked his notes, the sergeant mentioned the possibility of further interviews with Steve and Lisa. The constable also again raised the question of the bottle of ginger tea. 'I think we should go and have a chat to Rosie. I'd say we need that as evidence.'

CHAPTER 29

'A good idea. We'll make an appointment with her at the hospital for this afternoon.'

Constable Gardner was quick off the mark. 'It's almost 2 o'clock, so I'll call now and set up a time.'

Chas was due for his appointment at the police station at 2 pm, so after his morning of work at the servo, he slipped back home to pick up the ginger tea bottle to take it to the interview, just as he and Rosie had discussed the day before. He handled it with gloves on and wrapped it carefully. He arrived at the police station just in time to meet Constable Gardner as he stepped into the reception area.

'Good afternoon, Mr Anderson.'

'Hi there, Constable, you can call me Chas, we have met a few times now.'

With a chuckle, Gardner led Chas to the meeting room where he sat quietly while the preparations were made. After she got through the initial questions, Sergeant Holt began questioning Chas's on-going relationship with Rosie and his apparent focus on her participation in the aerial stunt. The constable then asked, 'Chas, did you notice anything different in Rosie's demeanour as she was strapped in for the flight?'

'No, not at all, she was totally focussed on Barry and Steve as they strapped her in and checked the safety factors.'

His answers were very succinct and easy to follow. Due to the apparent support and expectations of the Air Transport Bureau, the officers understood Chas's rejection of the request made by Lisa and Jeff to be part of the project. When the question was asked about the gathering around the table before the flight on Sunday morning, and Rosie's participation, Chas excused himself as he bent down to pull Rosie's drinking bottle from his bag.

'Rosie and I were trying to work out how she could have got the extra caffeine and we wondered if her ginger tea had been tampered with somehow. I found the bottle in her gear bag in her car after my visit to the hospital yesterday. Here it is.'

Chas handed the wrapped bottle over the table to the sergeant. 'I have avoided touching it, so if you test it for prints it should only show Rosie's. As far as she is concerned no one else could have had access to it.'

Sergeant Holt, with a quick glance at the constable, replied, 'Well, thank you for that Chas. It is something we definitely want to view.'

The bottle was very quickly transferred to the laboratory at Tamworth.

CHAPTER 30

Rosie's ginger tea bottle was transferred to the laboratory at Tamworth on Monday afternoon and the police officers awaited the results before they left the station on Tuesday morning. A quick phone call confirmed that only Rosie's fingerprints were on the bottle, and it had contained nothing but ginger tea. Sergeant Holt and Constable Gardner left for the hospital. Doctor Johnson required Rosie to stay another day and possibly be discharged on Wednesday. The officers believed it was to be an enlightening day, and as they were led into her room, Rosie was sitting up in bed, bright-eyed and cheerful as she welcomed them.

'Please, do sit down. The staff have been very kind arranging a couple of comfy chairs for you.'

Sergeant Holt was pleased to note that Rosie now seemed like the affable young lady who had been described in several of the interviews.

'Thanks, Rosie. We are very pleased to see you looking so well after the past few days.'

Rosie smiled again and gave them a 'thumbs up'.

'Yes, the experience has made me realise that I was very lucky to have so many people looking out for me and helping me come to terms with what happened.'

Constable Gardner was eager to ask, 'Rosie, do you feel confident and willing to hop into that harness on the aeroplane, again?'

'Oh, yes, very much so. Actually, I've had the after-effects to deal with, but I don't remember anything while I was on the wing after the take-off and the negative experience up in the air.'

Sergeant Holt explained that they had been busy following up with interviews in the hope that there would be some clues as to how, and why, excessive caffeine had shown up in her blood sample.

'Rosie, you are adamant that you did not have any caffeine intake on the morning of the incident, so do you have any idea how the excess that showed in your blood sample, could have come about?'

'Sergeant Holt, I have given up coffee. My pre-activity, meditation sessions, and my own home brew of ginger tea have proved to be very satisfactory. I honestly don't need coffee any longer.'

'Did you have anything related to caffeine for breakfast that day?'

'No. Not at all.'

CHAPTER 30

'And what did you have for morning tea at 10 am on the day of the flight?'

'My ginger tea and a chocolate biscuit. Everyone else had a biscuit and they were okay, so I guess it couldn't have been the problem.'

This was where Sergeant Holt began to show increased interest and she asked the next question. 'Rosie, who gave you the biscuit?'

Without any sense of dismay, Rosie replied, 'Oh, Steve Jennings. He's a nice guy, he has helped me so much. We have both been on a learning curve, and his enthusiasm, along with his support, has really motivated me. I didn't really want anything to eat on Sunday morning. When he handed the plate around, the biscuits disappeared like hot cakes. There was one left and he offered it to me saying that he'd made the biscuits just for me – chocolate biscuits with nuts.'

'Oh, that he'd made them for you. Did it taste okay?'

'Oh yes, for sure. It was crunchy, with lots of chocolate and – like a … cinnamony type of taste, but so yummy.'

'So Steve actually said that he'd made them for you?'

'Yes. That's right. I felt obliged to have one cos he does look after me on flying days.'

Sergeant Holt continued, 'So, how long after morning tea would you say that you began to feel some effect or, different from the way you usually feel at take-off time?'

'Um…' Rosie put her hand to her cheek and closed her eyes. 'I reckon, considering the strapping in and the take-off, probably about fifteen to twenty minutes. I remember the take-off and

Chas had just begun to climb when I can honestly say I can't remember anything else.'

'So, it was all pretty quick.'

'Yes, yes.'

'Okay Rosie, we'll leave you now to have a good day resting and I'm sure we'll see you again.'

'Thank you so much for all the effort you are making. I can't see how the episode can be anything but a mistake or accident somehow. All those people associated with the project have always been kind and helpful. Er, except maybe Lisa at times.'

Constable Gardner raised his eyebrows with the last comment and said, 'Thanks Rosie, see ya later.'

Sergeant Holt said her 'goodbye' and both the officers left.

As they strolled down the corridor, the officers looked at each other dubiously. They were both considering the same question. They hopped into the car and with a glance at one another, the same words came out of their mouths, 'The biscuits?'

The constable followed up with a snarl in his voice, 'So, some caffeine was added to the biscuits?'

Sergeant Holt replied quickly, 'Well, not all of them, but maybe the instigator had kept a specific one for Rosie. One that was prepared just for her.'

'Well, I guess that is possible.'

Holt continued, 'Lisa used two pills when she made Rosie's coffee, so three or four crushed pills could create a strong adverse effect that would depend on an individual's sensitivity to caffeine. We assume we know who made the cookies. Rosie told us that Steve had said that he made them for her and even

CHAPTER 30

after she had declined the offer, he insisted she have the last one on the plate.'

It was then decided that they needed to call in on Steve Jennings again.

Steve agreed to meet the officers late in the afternoon. It was 3.30 pm when he arrived at the police station. There was a cordial exchange of greetings at reception and Steve was taken to the interview room where he asked the first question, 'How can I help you?'

Sergeant Holt immediately put Steve on tender hooks, 'Steve, you like cooking?'

'Er, well, not really. What do you mean?'

'Steve, you made some chocolate biscuits for morning tea in the hangar last Sunday morning. Rosie didn't really want one but was delighted when you said you'd made them for her. They were popular and so you saved one for her.'

'Er, yes, she had the last one.'

'Let me suggest that that was a special one for Rosie because it had a load of caffeine tucked away in the ingredients.'

'How could that have been? Everyone had a biscuit and no one else had any after-effects.'

'Steve, no matter what happened as you handed around the plate of biscuits, you would have had that particular one in such a position that it would have been offered to Rosie when she was ready. Whatever you did, you manipulated the process so that she would have that particular biscuit. Am I right?'

'Oh, how could I have possibly done that? Anyway, why would I want to create such an incident for Rosie?'

'You did do that Steve, because Rosie ate a particular biscuit that gave her an excessive amount of caffeine, and you are telling us that you made the biscuits. Now, why would you do that?'

'Awe, c'mon.'

'Steve, tell us your side of the story now or we will simply arrest and charge you on the evidence to date.'

With a heavy sigh, Steve put his head in his hands and shook it slowly. 'It was not supposed to be like that. I didn't want to hurt her. I just wanted to make her frightened.'

'Steve, why did you do it?'

'I wanted her to give Lisa, my little sister, a chance. Lisa has been hanging out to go wing walking and the only way she would have got the opportunity was if Rosie couldn't handle it. Lisa had popped a couple of caffeine pills in her coffee cup before one of the earlier experimental flights and that gave Rosie a panic attack and I just thought if it was a bit stronger, she'd be convinced that she wasn't able to do the stunt.'

Sergeant Holt needed more information, 'So, Steve, how did you know about the caffeine pills?'

'After Rosie's first panic attack, Lisa told me that she had spiked Rosie's coffee with a couple of caffeine pills. I did think that I understood why, because over the weeks Lisa had become so stressed, I believed she was becoming sort of depressed. I guessed it was because she would have liked to have had the chance to do the wing walking. I thought, if I just up the dosage and hopefully created a sort of anxiety in Rosie, she would willingly hand over the opportunity to wing walk to Lisa, so I checked out the pharmacy and found some pills.'

CHAPTER 30

'So, even though you admired Rosie's skill and called her your friend, you were prepared to undermine her efforts for the sake of your sister.'

'Well, yes, I guess so. Lisa has had a rough time since Rosie arrived back home at the beginning of last year. Dad moved here in 1978, after Mum died and Lisa and I had a pretty tough time getting by without our mother. Lisa then started her nursing qualifications and didn't have any close friends to talk to. When I started my apprenticeship out at the hangar, she used to eye off Chas Anderson when he was working out there, and she'd talk to me about how hunky she thought he was. They'd never met or anything but when Rosie came to teach here, she and Chas apparently resumed a relationship they'd had since school days. Lisa was most upset about seeing the two of them together cos, as she told me, she wouldn't get a look in. Rosie then began getting all the attention with wing walking and Lisa got really depressed. I was just trying to help her.'

'Steve, you could have caused Rosie's death. When she finds out about your involvement in the incident it will be most disheartening for her. Fortunately, she has survived, and her spirit I believe is unconquerable. You will now be charged with the offence of spiking the food of the victim, Rosie Franklin. You must be aware that it is an offence to put a drug in, or 'spike', a person's food or drink without their knowledge. You have the right to remain silent and speak to a lawyer. We are now going to take you to the charge room, where you will be formally charged and bailed.'

'P'raps I'd better call my father. He has no idea of what I've done. It's going to knock his socks off.'

The sergeant agreed to Steve's request but before he could make the call, there was an official procedure that had to be followed. The constable came forward and officially arrested him with the words, 'Steve Jennings, I am arresting you.'

Sergeant Holt continued, acknowledging Steve's rights. 'Steve, do you wish to say anything in regard to the accusation? Are you guilty or not guilty of the stated crime? You are entitled to wait for the presence of your lawyer or speak now.'

'I'm guilty.'

'Are you sure that's what you want to say?'

'Yes, I'm guilty. I never meant any serious harm. I didn't want to hurt Rosie so badly.'

'Okay Steve, I think it is best that you speak with your father and arrange for a lawyer.' The sergeant then agreed that Steve could make one phone call.

Steve dialled his father's number at the hangar. When he heard his father answer the call with, 'Good afternoon, Phil Jennings,' Steve replied, 'Dad, it's me, Steve. I've got something I have to tell you. It will shock you. I'm sorry.'

'What is it, son? I knew you weren't at work this afternoon.'

'Dad, I've just been arrested for giving Rosie an overdose of caffeine.'

The yelp of distress from the other end of the line was more than Steve could handle. He dropped the receiver, slumped in the chair, and buried his head in his hands, sobbing.

Steve's arrest, and his admission, was a great shock to

CHAPTER 30

his friends, work colleagues, and the people of Gunnedah. When he first arrived in the well-known country town with his distraught father and grieving sister, there were times when he bucked the system, or resisted friendship, to his own detriment. By nature, he was a bright, jovial young man, but the move to a new social environment had enforced a feeling of loss on many counts. He acknowledged the warmth and affection his father offered, but over the past couple of years he had felt a remoteness develop between him and the fun-loving sister of his childhood years.

Lisa was more than just angry. Steve knew she had accepted the challenge of her first years in nursing rather well, but she could still not come to terms with the loss of their mother. All he wanted to do was make her happy again. He wanted to see her playing with all that child-like nonsense that she used to portray. Instead, she seemed to have developed an inconsiderate and selfish approach to her wellbeing. Her passion for parachuting was limited by her inability to have the attention of Chas Anderson. and her focus on the jealousy she felt for Rosie. Franklin. There were other young men in her sight, but even though Steve had introduced her and encouraged her to meet up at parties and have fun, she only seemed to want Chas. That was why Steve had tried to set up a situation whereby Lisa could slowly wheedle her way into Chas's life.

When Phil visited Steve, he learned of the relationship between the circumstances of Rosie Franklin's wing-walking project and Lisa's passion for Chas Anderson. Steve's admission of guilt could not be taken back, but Phil and Lisa both felt responsible for all that had happened. Phil procured an excellent lawyer, who was remarkable in the way that he understood the situation. He set up a complex inquiry that was presented to the magistrate. It showed Steve as being the young man he really was. His health, the background issues that he faced as a result of his mother's death, and his love for his sister were presented as the precursor of his actions.

When the lawyer suggested to Steve that if he maintained his guilty plea, and thus limited his court appearance to that of a magistrate, it was possible that he would have a very limited jail time or conceivably, even a good behaviour bond

CHAPTER 31

Rosie was discharged from the hospital by Dr Johnson at 11 am on Wednesday and Chas had made sure that he had no commitments so he could be at the hospital waiting for her. The greeting was an embrace of some length with words of endearment that had not been used for at least five days. There were smiles and chuckles all the way home until Chas lifted Rosie from the car to carry her inside.

'This is not the last time I'll carry you over the threshold, hey Sweetie?'

At last together, in each other's arms, the couple relaxed on the sofa. Rosie relished the closeness of his body and Chas could not resist the touch of her soft, sweetly scented skin as he let his hands wander over her, as if in a discovery mode rather than one of sweet memories. After a prolonged and ardent kiss, Chas's enthusiasm to pursue his desires had to be diverted. Rosie heaved a sigh and murmured, 'Oh Chasie, at home at last. I want you too but I'm not sure the passion will sit well with me at the moment.'

Chas's mind returned to reality. 'I've missed you so much Rosie love. My life is not complete unless you're with me. You know, Mick at the servo has given me the afternoon off and there's no flying jobs, so I'm all yours. It's certainly going to be an R and R afternoon.'

After lunch, and a chit chat about future wing-walking exploits, Rosie was expected to rest, so Chas set about getting a message to the Air Transport Bureau. Des Herd had requested that he keep them up-to-date in regard to the ongoing inquiry. However, as Chas was not aware of how Steve was involved, he had little to tell Des, other than that Rosie had come through it all very well and was enthusiastic about continuing with the project. Just as his writing was coming to an end, the phone rang. It was a call from Carly, and when Chas explained that Rosie was resting, she just said she'd call back later in the afternoon. He no sooner had hung up than the phone rang again.

'Hi, Chas here.'

'G'day mate, Barry. I'm just calling to check out on how Rosie is coming through her ordeal.'

'Good on ya Barry. Yeh, she's doing real well. I picked her up from the hospital this morning and apart from having to take things pretty easy for a few days, she's just fine.'

'I believe the inquiry is continuing. I guess you'll be pleased when that's all settled.'

'Oh for sure.'

'Listen mate, I really have a few things to say to Rosie. I got off track for a while and I think she deserves an explanation. Do you reckon she'd be up to having a chat?'

CHAPTER 31

Chas had an inkling of what had been going on over the Franklin property dispute and knew that it had upset Rosie. He was rather hesitant with an answer as Barry continued, 'Yeh, I'd like to smooth things over and certainly don't want to irritate her.'

'Okay. She's sleeping at the moment, so I'll let her know you called, and she will phone you back, I'm sure...'

'Thanks, yes Chas, please do that. I look forward to hearing from her.'

Rosie wandered out to the living room about a half an hour later and walked up to Chas who was sitting at the table looking over some papers. With her hand moving over his head and around to his chin, she whispered, 'Oooh boy, I'm feeling so much better. So glad everything is getting back to normal.'

'Well, you're right there, Sweetie. There were two phone calls for you. Carly rang. I think she must have just finished school, so she'll call you back a bit later, and Barry rang.'

With wide eyes and obviously surprised, Rosie sat down next to Chas. 'Barry rang? My gosh what did he want?'

'Well, apart from checking up on your wellness, he wanted to come and have a chat.'

Rosie answered with a rather quizzical tone to her voice, 'Really? That's interesting.'

'Shall I make a time for him to come around?'

'Yes, for sure.'

After making a phone call, Chas told Rosie that Barry would be around after work and have a pre-dinner drink with them. Just after they had finished lunch, Chas received another phone call. It was from Sergeant Holt to say that they wished to visit at 3 pm. After clearing away the dishes, Rosie and Chas sat waiting. They anticipated that the officers had some information in regard to the inquiry and discussed what it might be.

'Chas, I do think Lisa must be the instigator. I don't know what she did, or how she could have been so sneaky to get away with giving me extra caffeine, but she's the only one who had a strong enough reason to want me out of the stunt.'

'I sort of agree with you Rosie. I know Barry hasn't been very happy lately, but I don't think he'd jeopardise the exercise in any way.'

The doorbell rang. The officers were welcomed into the living room and when everyone was seated Sergeant Holt began her explanation. 'It is good to see you looking really well, Rosie. From what Dr Johnson told us you could have suffered far more serious complications. However, we now know the circumstances and can tell you that the instigator was Steve Jennings.'

Chas and Rosie looked at each other with shock and surprise. In a high-pitched voice, Rosie spoke first, 'Steve? You are saying Steve overdosed me? How could that have been possible? Steve is the friendliest and most helpful guy.'

Sergeant Holt continued, 'Rosie, we arrested Steve this morning. He has admitted that he was trying to deter you from performing the wing-walking stunt. He does think highly of you. Unfortunately, he developed a strong resentment against you because of his sister, Lisa, who was antagonistic in regard to your opportunity to do the stunt and possibly jealous because of your close relationship with Chas. It seems he did not wish to cause you any permanent injury but none-the-less, because of the chance that, there could have been more adverse circumstances, he will have to go to court and possibly do jail time.'

Chas was curious as to how it happened. 'How did Steve do it?'

'Chas, it was the biscuits.'

'The biscuits? No one else was overdosed.'

'That is so, but the situation was carefully managed so that the one biscuit that was for Rosie was manipulated by Steve to be available only for her. When she declined the first offer, Steve simply went back to her, with the apparent last biscuit on the plate and persuaded her to take it.'

Chas could not contain his disgust. 'That ruthless devil. He's just a heartless, cruel fiend.'

'Chas,' Rosie spoke his name gently, 'Chasie, Steve's motive was his sister's distress. She's the one who undermined his natural goodwill. She's the one who is responsible for him taking such action.'

Sergeant Holt then felt it necessary to intervene, 'I must say, we are all responsible for our actions. Sure, others can influence and be blamed for certain outcomes, but ultimately you have to be responsible for misdeeds that you have incurred upon others. Steve accepts this, and I believe his sister does accept her role in the incident. Now we must leave you to come to terms with the development. It is probable that you will both be required to appear before the magistrate when the time comes.'

Constable Gardner gathered his notes. 'Rosie, you have been through a pretty grim ordeal. It hasn't broken your spirit, so can

I say, we wish you well in following your ambition and hope to see you walking up high in the sunshine in the not-too-distant future.'

Sergeant Holt echoed his words, 'I think you will have some fun times ahead Rosie, and we wish you well for future plans. Take care, both of you.'

The sergeant and constable left, and Chas and Rosie sat quietly to ponder the outcome. With a cup of coffee for Chas, and a cup of herbal tea for Rosie, the couple began chatting to consider the next step in the wing-walking exercise.

'You know, Sweetie, it's just great that Des and Brian have upheld both their side of the project and all the work behind our efforts. They've chatted with the police and there is no hesitation in regard to our procedures.'

'Yes.' Rosie was obviously concerned. 'They've been fantastic, but it is disconcerting and disappointing that we've had that underlying dissension in the group all because Lisa couldn't grow up and show a bit of maturity.'

Chas nodded his head as he replied, 'I agree, and she has affected more than our lives. I do feel for Phil, having lost his wife and now seeing how his kids go haywire.' A quick look at his watch and Chas got up. 'Hey, I'd better get the beer out. What would you like to drink when Barry gets here, Sweetie?'

'Oh, a gin and tonic for me thanks.'

Within a few minutes, Chas went to the door and greeted Barry, who had come armed with a bottle of beer. As Barry walked towards Rosie sitting on the sofa, she put out her hand. Barry took it gently, and with an uncertain smile, kissed it as

CHAPTER 31

he handed her a box of chocolates.

'G'day Barry.'

'Hi Rosie. It is so good to see you. You look really well and chirpy.'

'That I am, for sure.'

'Let's open the beer Barry, and here's your G and T, Rosie.'

Chas handed around the drinks and then excused himself, saying, 'Well, I think you guys have something to talk about, so I'll just get a few of my commitments out of the way and then I'll be back to help you finish off the bottle, Barry.'

Chas left and there was a quiet moment in the room until Barry broke it.

'Rosie, I had to come and say how sorry I am that I got so upset over the property discussions.'

Rosie looked openly at Barry and replied in her straightforward manner, 'Barry, you did all that you wanted to do and what you had to do. Your grandfather and mine were great mates. They helped each other over the years. There was never a moment that I didn't want to help you, but I felt that there was more to the situation than a block of land and a cosy house.'

Barry smiled and was about to say something, but Rosie continued, 'Let me explain. I've talked to John, and he says that it would be great to have you as a neighbour, however, we both agree that there must be documentation that covers all sorts of contingencies that could affect not only the ownership of your property but that of the Franklin's. Let's get stuck into the legalities and make it happen to satisfy us all.'

Rosie's spiel took Barry rather by surprise. He had thought

that he would abandon his desire for a block of his own, if only to keep peace with the Franklins, but now it seemed that things could still happen.

'Rosie, to be honest, I came to apologise for creating a bit of turmoil in your family. Of course, Wally's property now belongs to your family. It all happened due to the circumstances of the time and who knows how it could have turned out with other options. I will follow your suggestion and hopefully John and I can work together to make things happen that suit us all.'

Barry and Rosie then clinked glasses and settled into an easy conversation about the wing-walking project.

After ten minutes or so, Chas returned to the room. 'I'd say it's getting close to dinnertime, and I've been rather remiss in organising something for tonight. How about we eat out?'

With a unanimous cheer of agreement, the threesome took only a few minutes before they headed off to the Regal.

CHAPTER 32

Phil Jennings was struggling. He had managed the hangar as the leading engineer for four years. As a widower, he had moved to Gunnedah, and the welfare of his children had become his priority. He had had a great deal to contend with because he was the only family member to whom his son and daughter could turn to for advice and support at a crucial time in their lives. The pleasure and pride he felt when Steve became entrenched in the aircraft environment of the hangar was most satisfying. After leaving school, Steve had had an unpredictable couple of years, and eventually with his father's support, decided to begin his aeronautical engineering apprenticeship. Lisa obviously mourned for her mother, but it seemed she had solace in her relationship with her older brother. Her choice of nursing as a career had been made while she was still at school and over the period of her mother's illness. Phil had had no idea of the development of Lisa's disillusionment that she had so carefully withheld from him. Apparently, it had been Steve's shoulder that she had chosen to lean on.

When Phil heard the news of his son's arrest, he was stunned – Steve, a kind young man who, although he had lost regard for himself in his earlier teenage years, had always accepted his responsibilities and showed respect for those around him. Phil was yet to hear the full story of Steve's involvement, but he already had a sense of remorse that he had not been there for his children in their time of need.

After Rosie's recovery, the follow-up talks with Des Herd towards the end of July went as well as was expected. The overdose incident had no effect on the safety issues associated with the stunt, and the aircraft, along with Chas's piloting ability, were unquestionably satisfactory. Plans were set for one more experimental flight before the AgQuip event. Chas had again approached the mayor of the Gunnedah Shire. His support of initiative and development within the shire had helped Chas in the past. If all went well and the Air Transport Board was totally on-side, Chas felt confident the mayor would promote the flight along with AgQuip events. The show was to take place towards the end of August so they had nearly four weeks, but the wing-walking event would not be added to the final programme until there had been another successful final practice flight.

Rosie was back at work but had no trouble finding time to get her agility back. She would do a workout after the Gym Club had finished and Carly was there to offer advice and support. She was as strong and supple as she had ever been but was very much fixated on maintaining her alertness. She had not changed

CHAPTER 32

the pattern of her movements, but she did put greater effort into the use of her arms to create the ribbons on her wrists as a focus. When she had been about to use the yellow and silver ribbons on the previous flight, she had lost consciousness so she was never aware of their position and patterns. The ribbons were to bring attention to the extensive movement of her body.

Chas, Rosie and Carly spent considerable time going through the flight pattern and Rosie's routine. Carly had no problem explaining the relationship between the aircraft's position and Rosie's movements. It was hoped that Carly's commentary would spark up the interest. The next step was to get the hangar crew together and tighten up the preparation procedure.

The practice flight was set for the week of August. All the crew turned up on the pre-arranged Sunday morning, along with Des and Brian from the Air Transport Bureau. Rosie was approached by the safety officers as she walked into the hangar. In his very sober but empathetic manner, Des put his hands on her shoulders, and while looking into her eyes said, 'We are so proud of you Rosie. The strength and resilience you have shown has helped to convince us that Chas's philosophical approach to the wing-walking project can be considered a model for young people seeking confidence to develop their own endeavours. When observed by other people, whether they are involved in the exercise or are onlookers, the overcoming of obstacles that appear in the path of someone else's ambition, can give people strength to meet their own challenges. Well done young lady. We are eagerly awaiting today's flight.'

Rosie took heed of Des Herd's words. They made sense to

her and had stimulated her understanding of Chas's ambition. She absorbed the sense of what had been said and tucked it away to embolden her movements in the course of the oncoming activity. She had asked Chas to get to the airport with enough spare time to allow her to have fifteen minutes for meditation to predict her wing-walking movements. For the hangar crew, there was no Lisa to prepare the coffee, so Chas stepped in for that responsibility and, while the crew were taking their break, Rosie, carrying her bottle of ginger tea, found the bed in the quiet spot of the hangar and let her mind take over.

At the end of her fifteen minutes meditation, Rosie pulled on her Lycra tights and shirt, and attached the coloured ribbons to her wrists. She packed up her gear bag and made her way to the Tiger.

She reappeared as the members of the project were moving on to take care of their responsibilities. Carly gave her a quick hug and a few encouraging words and then she found Barry, ready and waiting for her. Phil had to step into Barry's role, and Barry took over Steve's job of strapping Rosie into the harness and doing the final safety checks. With the deftness for which Barry was renowned, Rosie was strapped in with the correct angles allowing freedom of movement. As she stood in the harness on the stable wing, she proceeded to work through the routine, as she had during meditation, with a consciousness that she could change things when airborne. Chas climbed into the cockpit and stood on the seat to stretch up and touch her hand. She leaned over with just enough leeway for them to exchange a soft brief kiss. It was take-off time.

CHAPTER 32

It was a beautiful day with a few high fluffy clouds. The anticipation of the associated crew was felt as vibes around the group. Goodbyes and good luck were thrown at the aircraft. After Barry swung the propellor, Chas headed off for the runway. He took off into a gentle climb and Rosie could be seen beginning her movements. The blue and yellow of her Lycra stood out, and the yellow and silver ribbons appeared as short electrifying threads as they flashed in the wind. When flying straight and level, Rosie's movements could be easily observed. The performance was astounding, and Carly added to the appreciation of the spectators with her encompassing commentary.

It was a successful ten minutes of flight time for Rosie and Chas but there was a sense of 'more', 'more' from the hangar crowd. The aircraft made a perfect landing and Rosie felt the thrill of having achieved something to her own satisfaction. Barry was the first to jump up on the wing as the aircraft came to a standstill. 'Oh, perfect. That was just perfect.'

The others standing around, clapped and cheered as Rosie slithered off the wing, and Chas called out as he climbed from the cockpit. 'Hey, that went okay, don't you reckon?'

There were yells of agreement and then Des and Brian moved over next to Rosie and Chas. Des spoke clearly to everyone, 'I'd like to say congratulations to this hardworking couple. When Chas first approached the Bureau with what we considered a hairbrained idea, we were not confident of a successful outcome of the aspiration that this couple shared. However, with firm conviction and a focussed ambition, they have achieved something that we can record at the Bureau as the operation of a well-managed risk activity. An activity that was once considered illegal but now, with the correct planning, preparation and management, may be undertaken by others with the strictest of supervision by the Air Transport Bureau. Well done Chas Anderson and Rosie Franklin.'

Within minutes, someone suggested a celebratory lunch. Before too long, they all headed to the Regal. Chas had made a booking on the understanding that there would be a lunch to mark the hard work and support of those connected to the wing-walking hangar crew. Everyone was elated by the success of the morning's flight. There were cheery conversations, and everyone wanted to have a few words with Rosie and Chas.

Carly and Barry joined Rosie and Chas at the same end of the dinner table and the conversation had many twists and turns. Initially, there were stories shared of the thrills of parachuting that drew in Rosie's tales of wing walking. It also revealed that now she had achieved her goal, and she loved the exhilaration of wing walking, Rosie was merely interested in promoting the skills for others. Chas, however, was quick to step aside on that idea, suggesting the costs involved, including the exorbitant price of having Air Transport Bureau officers on duty at weekends, certainly would discourage many would-be wing walkers. However, the general consensus was that the development and promotion of the art of wing walking was worth a great deal to the overall marketing of Gunnedah as an aviation enthusiast's ideal setting.

Carly, whose general interest and teaching skills revolved around art teaching and gymnastics, made a comment that made them all look at her with raised eyebrows. Referring to

CHAPTER 32

Chas and Rosie, she began, 'If you two put a course together that covered the skills and fitness level required for wing walking and sought out venues and competitions both nationally and internationally, you might be able to establish a financially independent training venue that could have tentacles reaching out to interested parties both here, interstate and overseas.'

The proposition was kept under cover but both Barry and Chas could see that it did have potential.

As people left the table to go home, the strands of conversation in their farewells showed their enthusiasm for the next event, the AgQuip Show. The hangar crew already knew that on the last day of the show, Thursday August 25th, two or three aerial performances associated with agriculture would take place at the airport. When the mayor had the report back from Air Transport, the wing-walking stunt would have the go-ahead to be part of that aerial show.

The four friends were the only people left at the table and it was then that Rosie picked up on the earlier discussion and suggested that the promotion of wing walking could be done, along with parachuting.

'You know, there is an effort underway to promote the town as a tourist destination. There are many ideas out there for development associated with sporting activities and competitions like cycling and running, and some learning workshops have been suggested like ecotourism and photography. Maybe aerial activities could also provide a tourist boost. Wing walking and parachuting could get people interested. Whaddya think?'

'Rosie, don't get too carried away.' Chas was obviously

reluctant to take the conversation further. 'Maybe down the track we can see what could happen, but right now we have enough on our plate. See you later Barry and Carly, and thanks to you both for making it such a great day.'

They all made their quick goodbyes and then Barry escorted Carly back to his car. On the way home, he discussed with her how he wanted to get his block purchase sorted out. She was very encouraging and suggested he set himself up with the best lawyer in town and then re-establish a good rapport with John and Sally. Barry was grateful for Carly's support but knew that he had a load of work to cover in regard to the assets he had to access that would help with lawyer's fees and the final settlement.

The following Friday, Chas received the eagerly expected phone call from Des Herd. 'Chas, g'day.'

'Oh Des, great to hear from you.'

'Yep, just calling Chas, to say the paperwork is in the post. You've got all the necessary approvals and I'd say the 25th of this month will be an ideal wing-walking day.'

'Des, thanks, we all appreciate your support so much. Look forward to seeing you soon and I will be in touch before then. Bye.'

CHAPTER 33

It was Monday, the 23rd of August and the crowds were flocking to Gunnedah.

'Gee Rosie, the farmers love their field days.'

Chas and Rosie were sitting on the front patio on a beautiful balmy pre-spring evening, and they could see the incoming traffic slowly moving along Kamilaroi Highway at the end of their street. 'But Chasie, they also want a bit of time for sightseeing, and with the school term ending on Friday, some families can make it part of the school holiday.'

'Your holiday starts on Friday.'

'Yes, but remember I am getting a couple of hours off on Thursday afternoon. What about you?'

With a chuckle, Chas responded, 'Yes, that's right, me too.'

'Oh Chas, it is all so exciting. Our dream is coming true.'

'Rosie, the wing-walking stunt has never been a dream, it has been an essential core for our lives over the past eighteen months. However, there is a dream.'

'Okay, what's that?'

'When you say, 'I do' in the church, Sweetie, I will know for sure that reality has overtaken the dream.'

'Well, we have already decided that it will be at the end of third term, in December, so let's set a date and get it secured by the pastor.'

'Oh for sure, let's do that.'

'Yep, I think term three ends on December 16th, so our wedding day will have to be on the Saturday, which will be just one week before Christmas Eve. We'll see the pastor next Monday which will be the first day of second term holidays, then I can spend the next three months thinking about my wedding dress, cos I'll need a lot of time for that.'

'Wow, you've got it all worked out already.'

'Yes, I like to be organised Chasie.'

Over the next two days, the pressure related to the aerial event on Thursday increased to the point where both Chas and Rosie could not talk about anything else. Even during morning tea in the staff room, Rosie would keep Carly's attention, with discussions about the ribbons, or a particular leg stretch movement or even her waves and aerial kisses to the spectators. Chas, on the other hand, talked to Barry, who was working closely with John and Sally in regard to the purchase of the block on the Franklin property. Although it was seemingly good news, Chas suggested they keep any information for Rosie until after the event on Thursday.

The only situation that produced some concern for Chas was

CHAPTER 33

on Wednesday afternoon after a crop-dusting job. At the hangar chatting with Barry, he saw Lisa Jennings sheepishly step into the hangar.

'Excuse me Barry, I reckon I should take care of this,' and with that, Chas stepped out briskly to meet the young lady. It was the first time he had seen Lisa since Steve had been arrested. He knew that he had to approach the situation in a calm and rational manner, but was wondering if that was going to be too difficult. In a rather subdued tone, Lisa was the first one to speak, 'Chas, hello. I was hoping you'd be here.'

'Well, hello Lisa.'

'I know you are sure to be dubious about my appearance here, but it is because I feel so repentant and wish to apologise for the difficult times I caused and for which I must accept responsibility.'

Chas was taken aback and he simply nodded his head, although there were no smiles.

Lisa continued, 'I have undermined the lives of so many. The dreadful punishment that my dear loving brother is experiencing is because I was selfish and because I did not think of how the impact my egocentric behaviour can influence the lives of others.' Lisa stopped and drew a deep breath as a tear drifted down her cheek.

'Lisa, regrets can be positive and make us better people.'

'Thank you, Chas. I kept a childish infatuation for you that disrupted your life and that of the person you love. I am truly remorseful and wish you well. I must go.'

As Lisa wiped away the tears and turned towards the door,

Chas put his hand on her shoulder, and without their eyes meeting, he said, 'Your life is yours, Lisa. Your decisions will make it what you want. Take care.'

With that, Lisa walked quickly to the door and farewelled him with a soft, 'Thank you, Chas.'

There was no way he was going to tell Rosie about Lisa's visit, not yet. It was certainly an important step in the right direction for them all. The acknowledgment by Lisa could be taken as a possible path to reconciliation for all those involved in the wayward circumstances of the past months. For the moment, however, the participants in the wing-walking project had to be concentrate on the matters at hand.

Rosie woke on Thursday to a clear blue sky. Although she was always happy to have light clouds around her when she was high above the earth, the weather at this time of the year could not be guaranteed to provide the setting she preferred. However, the clouds were part of the environment to which she had to adapt. Today it was beautiful. No heavy grey cumulous clouds on the horizon they were just puffy like fairy floss..

She was off to school, her head was clear, and her thoughts were directed towards the afternoon's proceedings. The staff at work knew what she would be doing later in the day and were offering good wishes that included a sunny afternoon and happy spectators. After the lunch break, she and Carly made their way to the airport, hoping they would be early enough to avoid the extra traffic that would be wending its way in the direction of the airport for the start of the flying show at 2 o'clock.

At the hangar, there was a flurry of excitement. Rosie and

CHAPTER 33

Carly were greeted by other participants in the afternoon's aerial show. All were very busy carrying out their specific preparations, and amidst the hectic movements and sounds, they found Chas chatting with Phil and Barry. Although Steve was permitted to continue working while on bail and had been operating in the hangar for the past couple of weeks, his decision not to attend on the AgQuip Flying Show Day was sensible. He was to face the magistrate on Monday morning. The known witnesses, along with Steve's reputation around the town and in the workplace, seemed to indicate a very strong assumption that he would be given a good behaviour bond.

When Des and Brian from Air Transport arrived to join the discussion, the hangar crew were altogether. Chas suggested that after the big AgQuip party that had been arranged for Saturday night, they should all get together on Sunday at the Regal for a casual lunch. He thought a more personal celebration of their achievements would be very satisfying.

Their enthusiasm was escalating, and some humorous comments were made, like, 'Ya want a parachute, Rosie?' and 'There'll be a queue from town to the airport with the number that are going to want a ticket to wing walk!' Because minds were on other things, the response was generally a chuckle rather than hearty laughter. Barry soon moved off to prepare some cups of coffee, and they all settled down to enjoy a break. Rosie began to sip from her ginger tea bottle and then excused herself to find her quiet spot, to change into her Lycra and for her fifteen minutes of meditation.

The wing-walking flight was to take-off at 2.45 pm. Rosie

had timed herself well, and with ten minutes to spare, she made her way to the Tiger parked in its usual spot, a short way from the hangar. The prep procedure was followed carefully with all checks and details considered in precise order. Then came Rosie's time to be strapped into the harness. Everyone was aware of Steve's absence, but no one spoke about it.

Barry was there to do the job and his precise manipulating of the straps was accompanied by a philosophical comment, 'Rosie, the clouds have left. The sky is blue. Look for the sunshine and your dreams will find you.'

On the other side of the runway, she could see the spectators. The last aerial performance had just finished and the crowds were waiting eagerly for the wing-walking event to begin.

They were set to go. The afternoon was perfect with a few fluffy bunches of cloud high in the sky and a slight breeze wafted over the crowd. Chas climbed into the cockpit and cheekily reached up to touch Rosie's hand. She was waiting and leant down for the quick kiss. Barry came over to swing the propellor and the engine started. It was obvious they were now the centre of attention. Carly's commentary began and then there was waving and cheering as the Tiger set off along the runway. Rosie threw out her aerial kisses and waved in return.

Carly's commentary came across as a clear and robust description for the start of the event. 'Rosie is ready to go, and in the care of Chas, our well-known local pilot.'

She then referred to the crowd, 'Your enthusiasm and waving are the sparks that will set off this amazing stunt. Chas is concentrating on the aircraft's performance and Rosie is

CHAPTER 33

confronting the wind and gravity. If you can imagine putting your hand outside the car window when it is travelling at 100 kilometres per hour, you will have only a smidgeon of an idea of what Rosie is experiencing. As she feels the pressure and vibration, she knows what she can do, and she wants to show you.'

After take-off, Chas and Rosie exchanged a go-ahead with the term 'Roger'. Then there was a gentle climb before Chas turned the aircraft just high enough, and far enough, above the other side of the runway, for people to get a clear view of Rosie. The red and white colours of the Tiger and the deep blue and yellow of Rosie's Lycra caused her shapely body to stand out well. The vision of her figure performing amazing stretches and movements with the wind, were enhanced by the flashing yellow and silver ribbons tied to her wrists and ankles. Rosie's mind was out of the clouds and basking in the intoxicating sunlight. Along with Carly's commentary, the performance was stunning. The crowd loved it.

Rosie could sense the cheering and clapping from the spectators way down below and felt that all was good. The clouds were scattered and pretty, but way up high, the ideal aerial canopy. The sun was warm, and although the wind over the Tiger Moth was powerful and strong, it was steady, like the current in a smooth-flowing river. Rosie's movements appeared robust and were manipulated with grace. She planned the strongest body movements for when the plane was more distant. Closer to the crowd, she used her arms to stretch back and sideways and then she bent forwards as she moved her legs high up behind her. With wind assistance, those actions proved to be most dramatic. As Chas turned the aircraft for landing,

Rosie felt that her performance had been the absolute best she could have done.

After landing, the shouting, applauding and waving of the excited spectators was noticeable as she acknowledged them from the wing. Chas connected with her on the radio and his yells of delight indicated his joy as well. When they pulled up at the hangar, the Tiger was met by overwhelming excitement and there was great eagerness in getting both of them out of the aircraft and onto the ground.

The press pack thronged around the aircraft. Rosie and Chas were asked for pictures, videos, and to say a few words by the several reporters, photographers, and television camera operators, all scrambling for close-up shots. There was pride in the fact that it was a local, national and international event for aviation enthusiasts. It was a personal, colleague, town and country achievement that would be recognised as a positive tick for Gunnedah.

The excitement related to the three days of the AgQuip Show, continued over Friday and on to the weekend. The Saturday night celebration and the decision by the hangar crew to have a Sunday lunch together were both eagerly awaited.

On Friday afternoon while doing a crop-duster check for the week ahead, Phil approached Chas in the hangar. 'Can we have a quiet chat, Chas?'

'Hi mate, for sure. You wanna toss down a coke while we talk?'

'No thanks, not for me, but you go ahead.'

Chas grabbed a can from the fridge and both fellows sat down at the table. 'Good onya Chas. I'm sure you realise that

CHAPTER 33

the past few weeks have been pretty intolerable for me. Steve needs a great deal of support at the moment and Lisa is in dire straits as well.'

'Phil, I doubt there's a single soul around here who is not aware of what you are going through. There's little we can do or say that would make things easier for you, but just know that your hangar mates are here for you. We support you.'

'Thanks Chas, it's tough but I can hang in there. I won't be making it to the celebration tomorrow night, however I will be along on Sunday. The thing is Chas, and I'm sure you're aware of Lisa's mindset these days, I was wondering of it would be acceptable to the group if I brought her along?'

Chas hesitated but replied convincingly, 'Phil, I would see an invitation for Lisa as a possible rejuvenation of friendship, but do you mind leaving it with me for the time being? I'll get back to you tomorrow morning.'

That evening over dinner, Chas very carefully approached the subject with Rosie. He first explained his meeting with Lisa on the Wednesday before the Gunnedah Airshow. He told her how he had considered Lisa's approach to be mature and very much non-threatening, and also in no way flirtatious.

'She said she realised how her part in the whole incident was, to use her words, 'egocentric behaviour', and that she regretted the torment that she had put us through. She didn't try to be persuasive or coy, in fact she was genuinely upset and, after her words, just wanted to leave.'

'You really think it was a genuine approach, Chas? She wasn't just trying to back out of everything?'

'Definitely not! She was owning up to something and not asking for anything in return, not even forgiveness. She is truly sorry, I'm sure, and expressed how horrible her actions had been towards us and our relationship.'

Chas paused before continuing in a rather tentative manner, 'This afternoon, Rosie, Phil approached me. He is very disturbed over Steve's arrest. He is not going to attend tomorrow night and he does have considerable concern for Lisa as well at the moment. I did not tell him that she had come to me with an apology for her actions over the past months. However, he then asked me if the group would consider it acceptable if he brought her along to the lunch on Sunday.'

'O-O-Oh my, I'm not sure about that.'

'It's up to you, Sweetie.'

Rosie wavered with her reply, seemingly trying to overcome her feelings of antipathy, 'I've heard a few whispers about Phil, and I do understand how the police inquiry has impacted upon him. Of course, it would be difficult for him to be amongst the AgQuip crowd tomorrow night. That man must be going through hell with his family undergoing a breakdown. Look, I'm not saying that I'm forgiving her for what she put us through, but I will be the tolerant one, also in consideration of Phil. I'd say we'll let her come to lunch and see what happens. This is my last ounce of pity for her.'

'Okay. I'll contact Phil in the morning.'

A celebration for recognition of the contributors and the aerial performances was held on Saturday night. Rosie and Chas, along with their families and the hangar crew, including

CHAPTER 33

Des and Brian, were invited by the mayor, AgQuip personnel, and a number of other influential people from around town, to a party at the Town Hall. There were so many speeches and congratulatory messages related to the numerous events and productivity of the AgQuip Show during the evening, that not everyone had a chance to speak. Chas was chosen by the hangar crew to deliver a few words and towards the end of his delivery, he handed the microphone to Rosie. After her words of gratitude for the community's support and that of the project team, Rosie finished her short narrative of drawbacks and success, with the words, 'The clouds will only hold back your joy if you let them block out the sunshine.'

The gathering exploded with much cheering and whooping.

Chas held out his hand for the microphone and unbeknown to Rosie made an announcement, 'Our joy tonight is encompassed by our impending marriage. Rosie and I have set our wedding date for December 17th.'

The applause was most enthusiastic, followed by more cheers and the sounds of clinking glasses.

The next day, the hangar crew, Chas and Rosie, Barry and Carly, Phil and Lisa, along with Des and Brian and their respective partners, met at the Regal, where the alfresco dining was very pleasant. Des and Brian were very popular guests and were given affirmation that they held a great deal of responsibility for the success of the project. When Phil arrived with Lisa, there were a few quizzical expressions but polite conversation over lunch. Phil Jennings had not attended the celebratory dinner the night before. His absence was noted and of course most people who attended were aware of his son's recent arrest and bail. Being outdoors, once the meal was finished, it was possible for the guests to get up and move around with ease. It seemed there was a desire for individuals to have quiet, one-on-one conversations with their associates. Before long, Lisa was quietly engaged in conversation with each of the guests and she approached Rosie with words of respect, 'Rosie, you have achieved so much. You are tremendously strong. I so admire you.'

'Lisa, thank you. I do appreciate your comment. There have been hard times for you, as there have been for me. Maybe we'll have understanding for each other over the time ahead.'

Carly was wanting to share some news with Rosie, so as soon as she could see an opportunity, she moved towards her. 'What a wonderful weekend it has been.'

'Oh yes Carly, for sure, and you certainly were the sugar on the cake with your fantastic commentary.'

'You know Barry spent a few days with John last week, and apparently they actually confirmed an area that Barry could purchase. You should have a chat to him.'

Taking her at her word, Rosie turned, spotted a lull in Barry's chat with Chas, and intervened, 'Hi Barry, it seems it's been a great day for us all and you apparently have some good news of your own. Carly mentioned that you'd met up with John again.'

'Well, yes Rosie, and it is good news.'

With that, Carly moved towards Chas and they both listened to Barry's account. 'Just to put you in the picture, John has been generous enough to give me access to an area of land that is

CHAPTER 33

not particularly productive for him. It's an acreage, rather than just a building block, so I just may find something I can use it for along the way. The costs have set me back a bit, both for the lawyer and the bank. It seems that the bank is really going to help out, and after all, I guess that's what aspiring young workers do at some stage in their early life. Legally, John and I are both better off.'

With a cheerful smile, Rosy replied, 'Barry, I'm sure that's the best move. If you have a good lawyer and both of you feel satisfied then that's a great start. So you will have the connection with your grandfather after all, and just think, you don't even have to be a farmer.'

'You've got that right. Carly's pretty happy about that too.'

Rosie looked at Barry. She smiled and gave him a quizzical glance. 'What do you mean? Is Carly involved? Are you not telling us something?'

By this time, the other members standing around were all listening in.

'Carly?' Barry looked inquisitively across at Carly.

She smiled and nodded her head.

'Rosie, you and Chas are getting married, and Carly and I are getting engaged.'

Chas put both his hands in the air with thumbs up. 'We're going to have some pretty good parties ahead, I think.'

Everyone clinked glasses with smiles, and good wishes were bandied forth around the group.

www.ingramcontent.com/pod-product-compliance
Lightning Source LLC
Chambersburg PA
CBHW031408290426
44110CB00011B/301